THE
National ‹SABR› Pastime

The Future According to Baseball

Edited by Marty Resnick
and Cecilia M. Tan

‹SABR› Published by The Society for American Baseball Research

THE NATIONAL PASTIME — 2021 EDITION

Copyright © 2021 The Society for American Baseball Research

Editor: Marty Resnick and Cecilia M. Tan
Design and Production: Lisa Hochstein
Cover Art: Kyla Erin
Fact Checker: Clifford Blau
Proofreader: Norman L. Macht

ISBN 978-1-970159-37-0 (print edition)
ISBN 978-1-970159-36-3 (ebook edition)

Society for American Baseball Research, Inc.
Cronkite School at ASU
555 N. Central Ave. #416
Phoenix, AZ 85004

Web: www.sabr.org
Phone: (602) 496–1460

Contents

Introduction: The Future According to Baseball

At the 2003 SABR national convention, SABR launched a survey about the future of baseball.[1] SABR members as well as members of the general public were invited to respond. The instructions given to the respondents read as follows: "Answer the questions in light of what you believe will be true in 2020, not what you wish would be true, except where noted." The questions were mostly focused on Major League Baseball and included topics like new franchises, Hall of Fame inductees, and who would still be playing in 2020. (As a Dodgers fan, I am proud to say Pujols was identified correctly.) Inspired by the survey, for this year's issue of *The National Pastime*, we decided to run a similar survey and ask SABR members once again to look two decades into the future.

The Future According to Baseball survey invited respondents to answer 16 questions about baseball 20 years in the future, framed by the following understanding: "[T]hat just as baseball, and its history, is a reflection on culture and society in the past and present, it could also be an input, context, and/or predictor for predicting plausible futures of the United States and other countries." The goal became to predict what the world might be like in 2040, and how that will be reflected in the game we love.

Table 1 displays the questions and the top choice answer from each question.

Table 1.

Question	Top Answer	% of Respondents
How likely will Major League Baseball still be around in 20 years?	10, on scale of 1–10	77%
What emerging technologies will have the most impact on Major League Baseball by 2040?	Advances in Medical Technology	63%
Will Major League Baseball allow a person that has been "augmented" to play the game by 2040?	No	74%
What position will the first woman to play in Major League Baseball most likely play?	Relief Pitcher	41%
Will Major League Baseball lose its Antitrust Exemption by 2040?	Split Yes and No	50% each
In addition to the US and Canada, what countries will most likely have a Major League Baseball franchise by 2040?	Mexico	79%
What will be the most significant issues impacting Major League Baseball by 2040?	Climate Change	34%
What is the likelihood an openly transgender individual will be drafted by a Major League Baseball team by 2040?	10, on scale of 1–10	20%
What is the likelihood of the Minor Leagues (or at least its direct relationship with MLB) being decimated by 2040?	8, on scale of 1–10	24%
In light of the changes and advancements you anticipate, how fast will a pitcher be able to throw a ball by 2040?	106–110MPH	80%
What will be the fastest exit velocity of a baseball in Major League Baseball by 2040?	122–125MPH	37%
By 2040, how likely will it be the distance to the outfield walls will be increased?	5, on scale of 1–10	21%
By 2040, how likely will it be the distance of the pitching mound to home plate will be increased?	1, on scale of 1–10	30%
By 2040, how likely will it be that Umpires are no longer needed?	8, on scale of 1–10	14%
By 2040, how likely will it be that Major League Baseball will allow non-human players (i.e. robots)?	1, on scale of 1–10	80%

Some issues, which seemed far in the future when the survey was taken in 2020, have already become reality by the summer of 2021: the minor leagues have been contracted by fiat, and experiments with using a greater distance from the mound to the plate are taking place this season in the Atlantic League. The future sometimes arrives faster than expected.

EMERGING TECHNOLOGIES

What would a discussion of the future be like without exploring emerging technologies? To take a deep dive into the question of emerging technologies on the survey, we asked respondents to choose all the emerging technologies they felt would have impact on baseball. We provided respondents with the following definitions:

Virtual Reality: Provides a computer-generated 3D environment (including both computer graphics and 360-degree video) that surrounds a user and responds to an individual's actions in a natural way, usually through immersive head-mounted displays. Gesture recognition or handheld controllers provide hand and body tracking, and haptic (or touch-sensitive) feedback may be incorporated. Room-based systems provide a 3D experience while moving around large areas, or they can be used with multiple participants.

Augmented Reality: The real-time use of information in the form of text, graphics, audio and other virtual enhancements integrated with real-world objects. It is this "real world" element that differentiates AR from virtual reality. AR integrates and adds value to the user's interaction with the real world, versus a simulation.

Exoskeleton: Exoskeletons are placed on the user's body and act as amplifiers that augment, reinforce, or restore human performance. The opposite would be a mechanical prosthetic, such as a robotic arm or leg that replaces the original body part.

Digital Twins: A digital twin not only mirrors a unique individual, but is a near-real-time synchronized, multipresence of the individual in both digital and physical spaces. This digital instantiation (or multiple instantiations) of a physical individual continuously intertwines, updates, mediates, influences, and represents the person in multiple scenarios, experiences, circumstances, and personas.

Synthetic Materials: Man-made and cannot be found in nature. Synthetic materials are things like plastic that can be created by combining different chemicals, or prepared compounds and substances, in a laboratory.

Figure 1 displays the percentage of respondents that thought each emerging technology would impact baseball by 2040.

Figure 1. Emerging technologies that will have the most impact on Major League Baseball by 2040

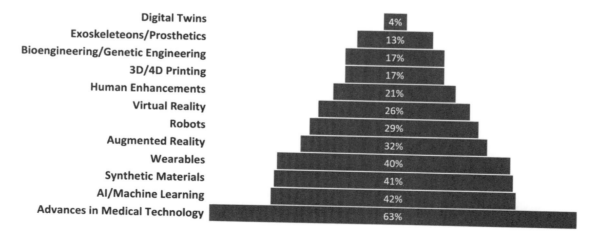

Technology	Percentage
Digital Twins	4%
Exoskeleteons/Prosthetics	13%
Bioengineering/Genetic Engineering	17%
3D/4D Printing	17%
Human Enhancements	21%
Virtual Reality	26%
Robots	29%
Augmented Reality	32%
Wearables	40%
Synthetic Materials	41%
AI/Machine Learning	42%
Advances in Medical Technology	63%

LOOKING AT 2040

These results, as well as the rest of the survey, have become the theme and roadmap for this edition of *The National Pastime*. The writers in this edition had one directive: create thought-provoking articles in a variety of disciplines, presenting the future through the lens of baseball. This edition includes research articles, flash fiction, short stories, and sci-fi prototypes in the form of press releases from the future, encompassing a wide variety of themes: Human Augmentation, The Metaverse: Virtual Reality and Augmented Reality, Climate and Globalization, Future Fan Experience, Rules Innovations, International Expansion, Women in Baseball, Future of Collectibles, and Emerging Technologies (Artificial Intelligence, Blockchain).

As we turn the clock ahead to 2040, baseball will continue to reflect what's happening in the world around it. We hope you enjoy this tour of the future and take comfort in knowing that through all the many disruptions that will come over the next 20 years, we project that the game we know and love will prevail.

— Marty Resnick
July 2021

Note

1. SABR treasurer F.X. Flinn presented the results of the 2003 survey as part of the 2020 SABR Virtual presentation series. To view the results of the 2003 survey, see https://www.youtube.com/watch?v=NjWdNhhnpOg&t=1973s beginning at the 32:53 mark.

Baseball Uniforms in the Future
What Might They Look Like Two Decades from Now?

Gary Sarnoff

Imagine you are sitting in a ballpark in the year 2040, and you are noting the uniforms of the two teams on the field. Can you imagine what baseball uniforms might look like twenty years from now?

For some perspective, let's turn the clock back to the late 1990s, when what baseball clothes might look like in the future became more than just an idea. Baseball uniforms of the future became a hot topic thanks to "Turn Ahead the Clock Night."[1] Originating with the Seattle Mariners in 1998 as a one-night promotion, "Turn Ahead the Clock" went national in 1999 as a promotional gimmick between MLB and real estate company Century 21. Twenty-two of the 30 major league teams took part in the promotion by wearing their version of futuristic uniforms for one game. "We don't know what 2021 will look like," admitted Joe Billetdeaux, the Pirates director of merchandise. "We took a stab at it."[2] The results were not widely praised. The attempts at a futuristic look included jerseys with colors described as "blinding,"[3] silver batting helmets, capped jersey sleeves, and jersey numbers and players' names crawling vertically down the back.

A decade and a half earlier, the Mizuno Corporation of Osaka, Japan, had introduced their style of a futuristic uniform that focused on a baseball player's needs. The one-piece uniforms were made from an all-weather polyurethane material—the same fabric used in ski outfits—and were designed to keep players warm on a chilly day or cool on a hot day. The major selling point of this uniform was the reinforced padding in areas where it was most needed. For example, an infielder's uniform would have extra padding in the knee and shin areas to protect them from being spiked by a baserunner. The Mizuno style uniforms appeared to make an impression when unveiled in February of 1983, but because equipment and uniform changes had to be approved by the rules committee, it was said that it would be a while before these uniform would be in the major leagues; however, a Mizuno Corporation representative said he hoped to test the new uniforms during the current college baseball season.[4] If the rules committee ever had their say or if

college teams tried out the futuristic uniforms was never recorded.

So, if the far-fetched uniforms designed by the Mizuno corporation and the out-of-this-world style worn for the Century 21 promotion are unlikely to be adopted by Major League Baseball, what could we see the two teams wearing at that game we attend in 2040? Anne Occi, who was hired to start the MLB Properties design department in 1990 and became "MLB's de-facto chief marketing officer,"[5] came to the job with ideas about what would influence baseball uniforms in the future. As part of her job, she subscribed to trend reports and color forecasts, paid attention to demographics, and listened closely when club management would tell her what kind of look they were looking for. "We know for a fact that the navies are starting to take over the popularity of black," Occi said of the mid-1990s trends, "and there's a switch from silver to gold metallic, and to less shiny metallic, such as bronze, and green is the color of the '90s."[6] Occi recently retired after thirty years at MLB, but her successors will likely continue trying to predict color trends.[7]

Other factors could play a role in the baseball uniforms of 2040. According to author Marc Okkonen, night baseball inspired shiny satin material on game uniforms. Games televised in living color led to the rise of uniforms with bright colors and multiple color schemes. The popularity of America's space program and putting men on the moon led to a fascination with the future and new trends in baseball uniforms in the Space Age. Some teams replaced traditional road grays with light blue, and button-down jerseys were replaced by pullovers. Teams like the Oakland A's went so far as to replace traditional black cleats with white cleats. But that only lasted until nostalgia itself became a trend. In the late 1980s and early 1990s, perhaps inspired by the movie *Field of Dreams*, love of nostalgia blossomed, and baseball teams began to go back to gray road uniforms, old logos, and a traditional uniform look.

Events and milestones can also play a role, such as when every player in the American and National Leagues wore a sleeve patch in 1939 to honor the

KANSAS CITY ROYALS

The Kansas City Royals had so much fun on Turn Ahead the Clock Night, they decided to bring the promotion back for its 20th anniversary in 2018. Pictured here are (L) Whit Merrifield in 2018 and (R) Johnny Damon in 1998.

invention of baseball, or in 1918, when World War I inspired patriotic fervor and an abundance of flags and red-white-and-blue shield patches appearing on uniforms. In 1942, World War II inspired teams to wear a patriotic patch with the word, "Health." Perhaps an event or milestone will inspire the jerseys you see at that game in 2040, or it could be something unimaginable for purists, like multiple patches. Perhaps individual uniforms will be spotted with patches like NASCAR drivers' uniforms. This might sound outrageous, but who would have ever predicted that the White Sox would wear Bermuda shorts for three games during the 1976 season?

The thought of baseball uniforms becoming billboards might make you laugh, but you may have noticed that in the 2021 season the Nike logo sits visible on the chest of every major league player. The topic of advertising on the uniform was in discussion back in 1999. According to *Chicago Tribune* writer Chip Scoggins, "Major League Baseball [*sic*] and the Players' Association are discussing a plan that would allow teams to sell 1-to-1½ inch square patches containing a company's logo."[8] The 1999 proposal was met with disdain from traditionalists—with pitcher Mike Mussina likening it to the Bad News Bears being sponsored by Chico's Bail Bonds—and it went nowhere. But "for a cool $1 billion"—about $3 million per team—MLB did add the Nike swoosh in 2020, and it will stay there through the 2029 season.[9] And the patch idea that was shelved in 1999? It was revived in 2019, with a tiny patch on the uniforms of the Yankees and Red Sox during their London Series, and is now being discussed between MLB and the players in advance of the next collective bargaining agreement.[10]

Seems likely that unless there is measurable backlash, MLB uniforms will be decorated with patches of sponsorship at that 2040 game you attend.

Fashion in 2040 also might be entirely different from anything we can predict. Factors such as COVID-19 influenced fashion in ways we couldn't have previously imagined: masks are now a new norm in people's wardrobes. The sleek form of smartphones and other tech devices may lead us back to the color schemes of metallic and black or navy, or perhaps baseball uniforms will be going through another nostalgia phase, with teams wearing throwback uniforms. Maybe it will be a fashion that is optimized for viewing technology that will allow you and the other spectators to see the uniforms in a form other than what they really are. For example, a ballplayer might be wearing the home white uniform, but when the onlookers have their VR headsets on or look through a lens, the uniform may appear to change color or even provide information to the viewer. Perhaps future uniforms will be marked with the dynamic strike zone, whether visible to the human eye or only to the "robo umps."

While it may be impossible to predict how baseball uniforms will look in the year 2040, one thing you can count on is that uniforms of the future will make every attempt at safety and comfort. While you are sitting in the stands at that game in 2040, you can bet that there will be more safety equipment worn by players than there is today, as the trend of increasing safety is unlikely to reverse any time soon. In recent years, even base coaches must wear helmets, and given the amount it costs a team to have a player go down with an injury, they are invested in keeping them unhurt. In 2014, Padres pitcher Alex Torres became the first pitcher to wear a protective over-sized padded cap in the field. By 2040, it could become mandatory for pitchers to wear protective caps in the field. And perhaps pitchers will wear masks, the kind you see in collegiate women's softball, to protect their faces and heads from the 120-plus mile per hour exit velocity comebackers that hitters produce.

But safety in the uniform could go so much further. By 2040, players will undoubtedly be wearing uniforms built around keeping them cooler. Increased cooling ability could be necessary to combat the effects of global warming on athletic performance. "Modern athletic wear can already regulate body temperature, reduce wind resistance and control muscle vibration," writes Joshua Hehe in an article titled "The Clothing of Tomorrow." "Just imagine what it will be capable of in the next few decades. Man-machine interface in the clothing industry will undoubtedly take everything to a whole new level in many ways."[11] A "smart" uniform might not look different, but it could be tracking a player's biometrics and alert the coaching staff to injury or changes in performance.

So, we can't predict exactly what the uniforms of 2040 will look like. So many different trends, events, requests, contracts, and other factors will inspire and influence the outlook of baseball uniforms in the future. The desires of the owners, the popularity of colors, the needs of ballplayers, safety, demographics, patriotic fever, tradition, the future, and other factors will lead to what we see the players wearing on the diamond. However, one thing is for sure. We will know when we are there, in the ballpark in the year 2040. ■

Source

Marc Okkenen, *Baseball Uniforms of the 20th Century: The Official Major League Baseball Guide*, Sterling Publishing Company, Inc. New York, NY., 1991.

Notes

1. Paul Lukas, "The Man Who Saw the Future," August 14, 2009, UniWatch.com, https://uni-watch.com/the-man-who-saw-the-future/; https://enwikipedia/wiki/turn_ahead_the_clock.
2. Christina Rouvelais, "Pirates play games in uniforms with a futuristic pitch," *Pittsburgh Post-Gazette*, August 18, 1999, E2.
3. Jayson Stark, "In the promotions department, Seattle goes out of this world," *Philadelphia Inquirer*, July 26, 1998, C6.
4. UPI, "Futuristic baseball garb made in Japan unveiled," *The Tribune*, Scranton, PA. February 17, 1983, 18.
5. Terry Lefton, "Anne Occi reflects on a grand career she designed at Major League Baseball," May 11, 2021, *Sports Business Journal*. https://www.bizjournals.com/losangeles/news/2021/05/11/anne-occi-reflects-on-grand-career-she-designed-at.html.
6. Patricia McLaughlin, "Marketing baseball's makeover," *The* (Madison, WI) *Capital Times*, March 21, 1994, D1.
7. Lefton, "Anne Occi reflects."
8. Chip Scoggins, "Is Nothing Sacred?," *Chicago Tribune*, April 2, 1999, Sect. 4, page 4. https://www.chicagotribune.com/news/ct-xpm-1999-04-02-9904020103-story.html.
9. Anthony Stitt, "For a Cool $1 Billion MLB Adds the Nike Swoosh to Uniforms," December 19, 2019, *Forbes*. https://www.forbes.com/sites/anthonystitt/2019/12/19/for-a-cool-3-billion-mlb-adds-nike-swoosh-to-uniforms.
10. Terry Lefton, "Patches in Progress for MLB," July 15, 2019, *Sports Business Journal*. https://www.sportsbusinessjournal.com/Journal/Issues/2019/07/15/Leagues-and-Governing-Bodies/MLB-patches.aspx.
11. Joshua Hehe, "Clothing of Tomorrow," *Predict Newsletter*, June 25, 2017. https://medium.com/predict/the-clothing-of-tomorrow-cd3f72c377ef.

Major League Baseball
280 Park Ave.
New York, NY 10017
Office of the Commissioner
Contact: David Krell / (212) 555-1876

FOR IMMEDIATE RELEASE
January 7, 2041

COMMISSIONER ANNOUNCES NEW ALIGNMENT AND
ADDRESSES MLB 2041 SEASON INITIATIVES

(NEW YORK, New York)—Major League Baseball Commissioner Roberta Clemente "R.C." Goldstein announced today the changes for the 2041 Major League Baseball season, via telestream. A transcript of her statements follows:

There has been much speculation about changes to Major League Baseball's structure for 2041. We have worked tirelessly with the owners, players, and fans to achieve our goals of entertaining the public with baseball of the highest caliber. Our goals of ongoing profitability, safe ballparks, and social consciousness remain priorities along with furthering the mental, emotional, financial, and physical health of our players and staff.

But the 2040s give us a unique opportunity to emphasize the history of Major League Baseball. There will also be highly significant changes to the schedule and a renewed effort to address social issues.

Honoring History

We're proud to honor the 100th anniversary of the extraordinary 1941 season. July 16th will be Joe DiMaggio Day. All players will wear Joe DiMaggio's uniform number 5 to mark the date of the 56th and final game of the Yankee Clipper's hitting streak. Even with the incredible capabilities of today's players, it's a record that stands today. Only two other players have broken the 50-game barrier. In 2029, Glenwood Redwood of the Hawaii Kings reached 53 consecutive games. Steve "Crocodile" Lyle's streak was 51 games with the Buffalo Bisons in 2033.

On September 28th, players will wear Ted Williams's uniform number 9. Williams played in a season-ending doubleheader and went six-for-eight to finish the 1941 season with a .406 average. He could have sat out the twin bill to protect his .400 average. Williams is the last player in the American or National Leagues to hit .400 or above.

These honors will be for the 2041 season only.

New Schedule

In 2035, the White Sox-Mets World Series did not end until November 12th because of the Halloween storm that dropped 14 inches of snow on the Chicago-Milwaukee region. Game Six had been scheduled for November 2nd and was postponed to November 10th. Chicago's 7–0 victory forced Game Seven, which the Mets won, 3–1. Commissioner Goldstein's remarks:

We are reducing the schedule to 153 games and eliminating interleague play. These are decisions that we do not take lightly. Even though a reduction of nine games will impact the bottom line, we can no longer risk having the World Series extend into November. It's simply too dangerous to risk having games in under 40-degree weather, which has happened several times in addition to 2035, and weather extremes are on the rise. In addition, an increase in doubleheaders will ensure that the World Series is finished by October 21st.

This 153-game schedule is balanced. Through the elimination of interleague play and with the expansions in 2026 and 2032 (to Las Vegas, Vancouver, Albuquerque, Honolulu, Nashville, and Buffalo), each team will play every other team nine times in their respective leagues. Historic rivalries will be heightened in this paradigm.

Women and Broadcasting

I'm proud to be the first female commissioner of Major League Baseball. MLB continues to strive to increase the participation of women and underrepresented minorities across the board—announcers, umpires, players, front-office staff, owners. We've accomplished a lot since the turn of the twenty-first century, but we certainly have a long way to go. So far, there are five female play-by-play TV announcers and four play-by-play radio announcers in Major League Baseball. We also have six women in the umpiring ranks.

I'm pleased to announce the creation of the Effa Manley Award, which will be given to a woman who has demonstrated excellence in an MLB team's front office. Please note that although it is named after an owner—Manley co-owned the Newark Eagles of the Negro Leagues with her husband, Abe—only non-owners will be considered for the award.

In 2006, Manley became the first woman inducted into the National Baseball Hall of Fame in Cooperstown. Joan Payson, the original Mets owner, was inducted in 2030. Helene Hathaway Robison Britton was the first woman to own an MLB team—the St. Louis Cardinals 1911–1917. The Hall of Fame inducted Britton in 2032.

Regarding players, the highest level for a woman player has been Triple-A. But I'm confident we'll see one in an MLB uniform before 2045.

Name Changes

We've had productive conversations about name changes for teams. Fans will recall the changes that occurred in the '20s, inspired by the social justice protests during the summer of 2020 and the move of the 2021 All-Star Game from Atlanta to Denver over Georgia's regressive voting laws. In 2022, Cleveland changed its team name from Indians to Commodores, in honor of Commodore Oliver Perry and the Battle of Lake Eire. A year later, Atlanta changed from Braves to Freedom, inspired by Martin Luther King, Jr.'s "I Have a Dream" speech, which emphasized that word and concept.

But we support the decisions of the Kansas City Royals, San Diego Padres, and Hawaii Kings to keep their names in the face of detractors who claim they foster imperialist attitudes. While there is continuing scholarship on the impact of settler colonialism to native populations, the Padres organization honors the missionaries who built San Diego. King Kamehameha unified the Hawaiian Islands as one entity. That unity remained when Hawaii became a US territory and then a state in 1959. And the Royals moniker simply reflects a benign regality.

In recent years, we've seen anti-alcohol organizations protest the Brewers and atheists protest the Angels. The Brewers moniker honors the working class of an industry that employs millions of people. MLB has doubled our budget for Public Service Announcements regarding alcohol consumption and alcoholism. The Angels label has no religious implications.

Health

The MLB community is dedicated to participating in the continuing destigmatization of mental health services. Beginning this season, every MLB team will be required to have at least two mental health professionals on staff. It's the latest part of our project first initiated in 2025: We're All on the Same Team. We've also had great success encouraging counseling for the public with announcements on the stadium screens, plus the PSAs on TV, radio, and podcasts. Ballplayers are taking their obligation as role models very seriously, so expect to see them engaging on this topic in personal appearances and media interviews.

Robots, Technology, and Artificial Intelligence

Robotic umpiring will be installed to call balls and strikes in 2041, but umpires will still be behind home plate and in the field to call plays.

Advancements in bionics have caused us to revisit the possibility of replacement body parts and limbs. There are no changes to the policy banning bionics at the present time.

The commissioner's office outlined the new alignment for teams:

AL East
Baltimore Orioles
Boston Red Sox
New York Yankees
Tampa Bay Rays
Toronto Blue Jays
Buffalo Bisons

AL Central
Chicago White Sox
Cleveland Commodores
Detroit Tigers
Kansas City Royals
Minnesota Twins
Texas Rangers

AL West
Los Angeles Angels
Oakland Athletics
Seattle Mariners
Albuquerque Roadrunners
Vancouver Loggers
Las Vegas Flamingos

NL East
Atlanta Freedom
Miami Marlins
New York Mets
Philadelphia Phillies
Washington Nationals
Nashville Sounds

NL Central
Chicago Cubs
Cincinnati Reds
Milwaukee Brewers
Pittsburgh Pirates
St. Louis Cardinals
Houston Astros

NL West
Arizona Diamondbacks
Colorado Rockies
Los Angeles Dodgers
San Diego Padres
San Francisco Giants
Hawaii Kings

- 30 -

The Future of Women in Baseball

An interview with Janet Marie Smith and Bianca Smith

Katie Krall

When does a moment become a movement? If you'd asked just two years ago what the future held for women in baseball, we might have said that the changes that have taken place over the past several years weren't coming until 2040. But since 2018, the world has watched trailblazing women break glass ceilings in baseball that many believed would never be shattered in their lifetimes. From Alyssa Nakken being hired by the San Francisco Giants as the first full-time female coach in MLB history to Kim Ng ascending to the top of the Miami Marlins front office as general manager in November 2020, progress has been made with significance that transcends the sport.

Against this backdrop, some might say that we are entering a golden age for women in the game—one that recognizes the value and importance of diversity on and off the field. To assess where the industry stands, I sat down with Janet Marie Smith, Executive Vice President of Planning and Development for the Los Angeles Dodgers, and Bianca Smith (no relation) a minor league coach for the Boston Red Sox. Janet Marie has constructed and renovated some of the most iconic stadiums in baseball including Camden Yards, Fenway Park, and Dodger Stadium. Bianca's hiring this off-season made her the first African American woman to serve as a professional baseball coach for an affiliated team. As a Baseball Operations Analyst for the

Cincinnati Reds and product of the inaugural class of MLB's Diversity Fellowship program, I wanted to share our perspectives on what the future of women in baseball will look like during this decade and beyond. The following conversation has been edited for clarity and length.

KK: Thank you both for being here! Janet Marie, how do you think the response to women in the game has changed during the course of your career?

JMS: It's obviously far more accepted today. To see you Katie and Bianca in the game, that is just amazing! The data has [*sic*] proven over and over again that some of the most successful companies have a woman's voice. We also see a lot more women playing sports and I think Title IX did everything we hoped it would do when it passed. It's not nearly as foreign an idea as it was a generation ago because you all have grown up with that as your norm.

KK: Completely! To your point Janet Marie about Title IX, Bianca, you played a number of sports at Dartmouth and now you're on the field for the Red Sox. Can you speak to that transition and what made you want to put on a uniform again?

BS: At Dartmouth, I'll admit I was not planning on playing baseball. I played in high school but got hurt my senior year and convinced myself that I wouldn't be good enough to play in college which is why I ended up being a cheerleader instead and walked on to the softball team. One month later, the club baseball team was started. I really wanted to play baseball so I decided to do both!

It was around that time when I knew I wanted to work in baseball, originally in the front office, and in grad school I was shagging balls during BP wearing jeans, shorts, sweatpants and I went through so many pairs of pants that I said to our coach, 'Hey, I need some baseball pants.' Putting the uniform back on and then actually getting to work with the players running drills,

Katie Krall was a member of MLB's inaugural class of Diversity Fellows and now works for the Cincinnati Reds.

throwing batting practice, my position went from your typical Director of Baseball Ops to actually being a coach on the field. That's when it really hit me—I enjoyed working with players and helping them get better.

KK: That is so cool to hear. I love that moment of you putting the baseball pants on and immersing yourself in that world because you knew that was where you belonged. Janet Marie, what do you recommend for women looking to enter the industry?

JMS: You two are probably the perfect examples of this—you have to map your own way. Waiting for a job to be posted or someone to find you is rare. The way I got into baseball is I went to Larry Lucchino who was then president of the Orioles. I knew he wanted to build a park in downtown Baltimore and harken back to the old days to feel like part of the city and I thought that was something I could do. From what I just heard Bianca say and what I know of your career, Katie you've done the same. That's an extraordinary thing to be able to do, to find an opening and a need and figure out how your skillset can fit that need.

KK: Absolutely, taking the initiative and going after your dreams. Bianca, Janet Marie mentioned Larry Lucchino being one of her mentors and taking a chance on her with Camden Yards. How would you say your mentors have supported you?

BS: The mentorship I've received from coaches has helped me feel comfortable enough to actually share my opinion. When you're a new coach, it doesn't matter if it's the major league level or not, any place you go, you hesitate to just jump in because you don't want to be the coach that immediately begins giving instruction. Having coaches who not only encourage you to ask questions, but also answer them and get you involved is really helpful and easier for you to make that transition than trying to figure out on your own, Okay, when am I comfortable enough to start giving my input? Knowing there are so many coaches who have my back and want me to succeed is important too. I'm sure there are plenty of people, even in this industry, who don't want to see women do well. It's a hard truth, but they're there. So knowing that there are people who do have your back is helpful.

KK: Janet Marie, Bianca brought up the art of entering into a conversation and sharing your opinion. How do you know when to add input or hold back?

JMS: I try to find a right balance between staying in my lane and speaking up when I know that I am the

Bianca Smith was hired for the 2021 season to be a minor league coach for the Boston Red Sox.

expert on something or a broader point that needs to be made. I can talk about my projects all day long—what we want the building to be, where we want to take it, everything from the transportation to the graphics—I love talking about those things and I'm comfortable in that role, but then I try to make certain that I don't simply have an opinion on everything. I still even now find it hard to pipe up sometimes on things that aren't neatly in my corner.

KK: That's an interesting philosophy, not necessarily commenting on everything, but when you are the authority being willing to come forward and share what you have to say.

JMS: I think it's really important to add a perspective that isn't already on the table. Sometimes that perspective feels like it's learned by osmosis and that's a harder thing to speak about than if, for example, you're the only one in the room who understands the process for the city approving this project. Whereas for a topic like "How should we react to Black Lives Matter?" I certainly have an opinion and see some aspects of our organization by living in an urban community that maybe others don't, but you want to make sure you have an opportunity to say those things that are totally in your wheelhouse.

KK: As more organizations recognize the benefit of having a diverse workforce, how can teams and the league office create an environment of authentic allyship?

JMS: I really admire the initiatives that MLB has taken. I see candidates come through that [MLB diversity hiring] program as rock stars just like you are. The Dodgers have a summer program that is specifically targeted toward minorities and I've had some fantastic students. I have often said to my team when we hire someone for this, we're not using these 12-weeks to

JANET MARIE SMITH

Janet Marie Smith has been a finalist multiple times for the SABR Dorothy Seymour Mills award and is responsible for many of MLB's best stadium designs.

bring in someone who has already worked for Fox Sports and the Mets. This is meant to be an opportunity for someone who has never had professional experience to be here so that the next time they go to interview for a job, they're able to say that they have that experience. It's the hardest thing in the world to break that first barrier.

BS: Agreed. One thing the league and teams can do is giving minorities responsibilities based on what they actually bring to the table. I speak from experience a bit here, but when a minority is hired for a high profile position, emphasizing why they were hired is so important, not just "we hired a minority for this position." Focus on why you actually hired them. You have to emphasize *this is what they're good at* rather than *this is what they look like.*

KK: The position that they were hired because they were the best coach or analyst in the applicant pool. We're recognizing that they have a different identity or affinity status, but at the end of the day we're hiring them because of what they add to the organization. Who faces the steeper uphill battle—the next Bianca Smith or Kim Ng?

BS: There are different obstacles for both. For women in the front office, there are more role models that you

can look to so more women are going to try for those positions. Kim's the first general manager, but everyone knows she should have been a GM years ago. So as of right now, I think it would be a little harder on the coaching side, but you're still going to face challenges either way.

KK: That's such a balanced answer. I've always found it absurd that for years to be a coach you needed to have playing experience at the professional level in baseball, but for basketball or football you didn't face that same requirement and you could have a high-ranking position. I think it's a dynamic that people cling to, but doesn't necessarily shake out when you look at other sports.

BS: Some of the worst players can be the best coaches, probably because they were the worst. It's not being able to do it yourself, it's translating it for a player and making it effective for them. As long as you can do that, it doesn't matter if you can hit a 100 MPH fastball, just help the player figure out how to do it.

KK: Exactly, you're the teacher. Any final thoughts about the future of women in baseball?

JMS: The fan base for baseball is so evenly split for gender [*sic*] and we should never forget about that. The part of my work that I enjoy the most is positioning things so fans can enjoy the game and create an environment where a rabid fan can count every pitch and keep score, but if he or she is there with other people who just want to experience the atmosphere, they can enjoy that too. I think it's important that as we think about the future of baseball, we consider all levels of being a fan. Youth baseball is particularly important to grow the game and keeping ticket prices at a place where youth can come and families can feel good about bringing their kids to the ballpark. It's not totally in the category of gender, but it is in a way since it impacts 50% of your fans and 50% of your potential fans.

A brief anecdote from several years ago: I had a chance to work on the Dodgers' Dominican facility and we had designed the building to have a women's locker room. When our head trainer Allison Wood got there she was thrilled to see that there was a place for her to shower, dress, have privacy, but she wanted a locker with the men. Allison said I don't want to miss out on the banter, socializing or the occasional conversation that's not scripted, I want to be part of the team. We worked really hard to redesign things so the men could also shower and dress privately, but there would be a way for all of them to be comfortable in the clubhouse and opportunity for those conversations. I hope as we think about facilities going forward we consider the physical space so that women in uniform feel comfortable in that place and feel equal.

KK: That's part of the reason why I think your job is so amazing, Janet Marie, is because you're curating spaces so whether it's a family going to a Dodgers game or Allison, you're helping people fill a specific need. To your earlier point about half of the fan base being female, I wrote a paper when I was an undergraduate at Northwestern on Ladies Day at Wrigley Field in the 1930s. The Cubs couldn't believe the number of female fans who would turn out for these free tickets, many of whom would camp overnight! So you're right, that there has always been a zealous female fan base out there that we need to acknowledge and support because they're an important part of the long-term success of this game.

JMS: You'll have to send that paper to me, Katie!

BS: Along those lines of the fan base being split, I will say that personally as a fan, MLB could do better with things like jerseys. I don't know many women who like a women's cut for a jersey. So something as simple as that is important. Recognizing that women are fans and they're not attending games because of their husbands, fathers, brothers, boyfriends, etc. it's because they actually enjoy the game.

As far as women working in baseball, I'm optimistic. This is my 12th year in the industry and I've seen a lot of growth and change. Yes, there's still a lot to do. Not just getting more qualified women in the game but also keeping them in the game so they feel like they belong. Acknowledging who is in the front office and on the field and figuring out what is the best way that everyone can be comfortable.

KK: Agreed, leaning into the conversation and saying that this is a priority. We recognize it and we're here to make change. ∎

Signs of the Times

Cecilia M. Tan

Jerry slings the baseball to me from his crouch, and I can barely hear his "Come on, Sal!" over the noise of the crowd and the L-Pop walk-up music for the hitter coming to the plate. I'm trying not to look toward first, where a very smug Hector Martinez is trotting up the line, courtesy of the base on balls I just handed to him.

Hector, you smarmy bastard, enjoy being the answer to the trivia question *who was the first batter walked by a female pitcher in the American League?* The Fenway faithful are howling for blood—my blood. They're probably not even sexists, most of them; they'll put down an opposing player for any reason. Heck, most of them even cheered when I was announced. They're baseball savvy. They know they're seeing history.

They still want to win, though. I wander down the back of the mound, rubbing at the baseball. It's a chilly April night; I can see my breath in the stadium lights and the ball feels like ice. The weather shield keeps out excessive heat and wind; it doesn't do anything for the cold. We're up 5–2 in the sixth. The bullpen is gassed from the doubleheader yesterday in which I warmed up four times but never made it in.

I know that's why I'm the first one out of the 'pen today. Matchups, our pitching coach, Oliver Barnes, said when I got to the mound. *It's all about matchups.* But I can't help feeling like the kid picked last off the bench. Little League has allowed girls since my grandmother's era, but when you're the only girl, being last comes with the territory. I remind myself that the way I've made it, at every level, is by succeeding once they let me on the field. Now's not the time to start doubting. This game gives every player a million reasons to doubt themselves, and the ones who succeed are the ones who don't. *Come on, Sal.*

Thank goodness they did away with the "time between pitches" clock in the big leagues, because it feels like I'm taking forever. They replaced it with a rule that once the pitcher's foot is on the rubber, he—the rulebooks literally still say "he," even though the first woman in the National League debuted ten years ago—has to deliver the pitch within 10 seconds or it's a ball. Assuming the batter is in the box, that is. Complicating things further, this year they added back two allowed pickoff attempts per at bat, but anything other than that—sneeze, twitch, whatever—and it's a balk.

No way am I balking Martinez to second. There are two outs already. To put us back in the dugout with the lead intact, I just have to get one guy out.

That guy is Kip Janssen. Of course it is. He's the only Dutch player in the league right now, which makes him kind of an oddity, but they don't use words like *oddity* when you're slugging over .600; they use words like *Ruthian*. He waggles the bat over the plate and does that thing with his tongue I used to think was funny, but now seems downright disgusting. I know he does it to all the pitchers, not just me, but maybe it's no wonder he also leads the league in hit by pitch.

The rest of the pitchers probably didn't have to deal with him bragging to their minor league teammates that he slept with them, though. The only reason the guys believed me, and not the big-leaguer on rehab, was that his shit-talking was already so legendary.

Kip's mouth is moving—talking to Jerry or the umpire. Or both. Probably telling them he knows what's coming because he mentored me when I was coming up through the minors or something. He was only in Louisville for a week, and for the record we did stay late in the VR batting cage one night, but I not only turned down his advances, I didn't learn anything about pitching from him.

Because Kip doesn't know shit about pitching. Jerry knows it. I can see his eyes roll even shadowed by his mask. I come set. The moment my foot is touching the rubber and the batter steps into the box, I hear the little click of Jerry's helmet mic coming on. We get 10 seconds to communicate before I have to throw. I resist the urge to fiddle with my earbug, because that would be a balk, and I'm grateful it cuts down some of the whine from the camera drones overhead. I expect to hear Jerry call the pitch.

But what he says is, "Sally. You got this." Jerry's a good guy. He kind of has to be: backup catchers can't be assholes or they wouldn't keep their jobs. Like me, he went undrafted out of college, and had to prove himself in indie ball. After the major-league expansion of 2030, he made the jump; I signed five years later, but there are critics who'll say the same thing about us both: without expansion diluting the talent pool, we wouldn't even be here. That's what Boston's scouting director told me when they traded me from Louisville to Aberdeen. Maybe he didn't believe it, but he couldn't come out and tell me they were shipping me out because of the "rumor" I'd slept with a teammate. The closest he came to admitting that was some vague, paternalistic "advice" about keeping my wits about me or some horseshit.

Keeping my wits about me right now means keeping my eyes on Jerry. I see his hand move—his pinky extends. Our visual sign for fastball away. There are rumors that the Red Sox have hacked catcher audio at Fenway; why take the chance? I shake him off. I'm a lefty, Kip's a lefty, and I know I can beat him in. Jerry's eyes are incredulous that I'm shaking him off. Rookies aren't supposed to do that to veterans, but I just stare over the top of my glove. Kip's got too much power the other way, he'll just double off the Green Monster…

Except I've got to stop thinking that way or I'll beat myself. Jerry relents: we're coming inside. I pitch like I always do, dropping down sidearm. I give him my best "lefty laredo," but between the unfamiliar mound and my cold, damp fingers—I swear I didn't mean to—I plunk Kip Janssen right in his meaty thigh and he makes a noise like a surprised donkey.

Two men on. This is not the way anyone imagines their big league debut is going to go when they do their positive visualization exercises. I can't even glance toward the dugout. Barny and Kratz, the skipper, must be beside themselves. I don't want to let them down. Barny's been great. He coached a college team once that had a female walk-on player. He told me that to try to put me at ease, I think, like it was no big deal to him who I was, but it only really highlighted to me that women who break through into men's college baseball are still on the rare side. There are 10–20 a year, which sounds like a lot until you realize there are over 10,000 players in Division I baseball alone.

Somehow over the crowd noise and drones and music, I can hear Kip Janssen greeting our team captain, Paul Corso, with a booming, "Hey, Paulie!" as he reaches first base. Of course they know each other from All-Star Games. Corso's been vocally supportive of me in the press, but he hasn't really said much to me personally, outside of when we practiced pickoffs a few weeks ago. You'd think it would chap my ass to see him fraternizing with Janssen at a moment like this.

The tying run is coming to the plate, and my catcher is coming to the mound. I finally do it— I glance at the dugout—but it's only Jerry coming to talk to me, no coaches. Barny and Kratz look stoic over there, wearing their poker faces. Three batter minimum—blessing or curse?

"What's going on?" Jer asks, glove over his mouth so the lipreaders can't see or make a meme out of him. I think they should just make the catcher mic live all the time, but MLB—and some of the catchers themselves—have resisted that. "You nervous?"

"No, I'm giddy as a goat at a square dance," I deadpan, and I can tell his glove is hiding a smile. If I'm doing sarcastic impressions of our Alabama-raised bench coach, I must be okay.

"Attaboy. I mean, girl," he says, and bops me on the shoulder with his glove before he jogs back to home plate.

The mound visit did help me catch my breath. I'm not calm, but I can act like I am, and sometimes that's the same thing. It's hardly the first jam I've had to get out of, right? The next hitter is a guy I saw play as a kid. The ovation for him is deafening. He's a Boston favorite, Xander Bogaerts, currently the oldest guy in the majors and a fan favorite, ever since he returned to the Sox after that disastrous trade to Atlanta. He's 49 years old, one of the last of the guys who got methylation and anti-glycation before anti-aging treatments were outlawed by MLB, and he's more popular than ever.

He's a tall righty, thicker around the middle that he was when I saw him play as a kid. My mom chaperoned my whole travel soccer team to the Northeast regional tournament in Boston when I was ten and took us all to a game at Fenway, back before they built the overhead weather shield. At the time I'd just thought it was cool his name started with the letter X and that Mom let us have real meat hot dogs. I wonder if they still serve those or if they've gone to plant-based dogs like every other park by now?

I try to imagine Xander's got X's for eyes, like a knocked-out boxer in an old cartoon. He's in the box. My foot's on the rubber. Jerry clears his throat but says nothing, just drops a series of signs. They're fake, just there to distract Martinez who's trying to steal them from second. The bop on my shoulder was the signal for what we're going to do.

Kip takes his lead. As a lefty, I can see his every move. He's still jawing away. So is Paulie. That's it. Laugh it up. I turn my head to focus on Jerry.

My high hard fastball isn't as hard as some, but coming from my arm angle to a righty, it looks very tempting. And it is. It tempts Bogaerts to swing.

And miss. Strike one. I hear Janssen bray from first base. Jerry slings the ball right back to me and I get right on the rubber. Bogaerts can't leave the box and we're going to come right after him before his brain has a chance to process my delivery. It's not quick-pitching, not really, but for a guy who came up in the era when every batter tried to make himself a human rain delay, it must seem quick. At least, that's the hope. I change arm angles slightly to spot the pitch on the outer half of the plate. Strike two. Unfortunately, Jerry can't quite hang on and the ball trickles away. Not enough for the runners to advance, but enough that Bogaerts is allowed to step out.

He fixes his batting gloves and does a knee bend and whatever else. I glance over to first again and I see Paulie bop Janssen companionably on the shoulder. I pretend I didn't even see that and I focus on Jerry in his crouch. I'm not even looking at the batter as he steps in. Jerry mouths encouragement. Here goes. Just like we practiced. Here goes.

I step and sling the ball to first. Kip is caught flat-footed, his eyes round with surprise in that split-second where he realizes he's been had. He's been lulled into a false sense of security by a friendly face, not realizing that Corso had it in for him the whole time. Betrayed by someone you thought was your buddy. He dives back, but all he gets is a whack in the face with the tag, his fingers patting the dirt an inch or two shy of the bag. Inning over.

He lies there in disbelief as the rest of us trot off the field. Paulie's grin is genuine as he bangs my glove on our way to the dugout. I grin back. I'll wear my poker face for the media later. I'm sure they're going to ask about the pickoff. I know what I'll tell them. A veteran like Janssen should've known better. Should've been more careful. Should've been more cognizant of the consequences. Gotta keep your wits about you. Right? ■

"This compilation, a distillation of all that is important to the society's members . . .
showcases the SABRite at his or her baseball-loving, stat-obsessed best."
—Paul Dickson, *Wall Street Journal*

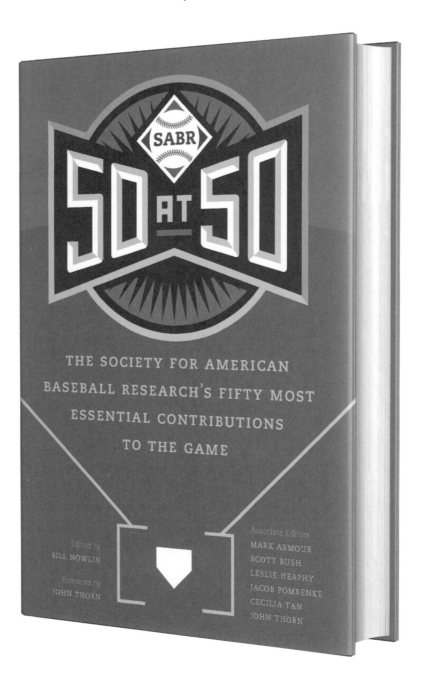

UNIVERSITY OF NEBRASKA PRESS   nebraskapress.unl.edu

OAKLAND ATHLETICS

Water Street & Jack London Square, Oakland, CA 94607

For Immediate Release
January 24, 2027

Contact: Dusty Baker
(510) 555-1901

TRANSGENDER PLAYER SIGNS WITH OAKLAND

(OAKLAND, California)—The Oakland Athletics carved the team's name into the record books Friday by signing Alejandra Gallardo to a minor league deal. Gallardo, a transgender woman, is the first woman to be drafted by a major league franchise and is also the first openly trans player in MLB-affiliated ball.

Gallardo played softball as a freshman at UCLA, mostly at shortstop. She had then requested a tryout for the baseball team as a pitcher, her position in high school, where she had played on her school's baseball team. In three seasons as a reliever and spot-starter for the UCLA Bruins, during which she amassed a 3.51 ERA and 1.08 WHIP in 75 innings, Gallardo went undrafted.

Gallardo said, "This is a huge day for myself, my family, and the LGBTQ+ community. We have finally made a dent in Major League Baseball that should have been made a long time ago."

Athletics Owner John Fisher said, "The Oakland Athletics are honored to bring aboard the first transgender woman of our time into our organization. This is something that has been a long time coming. It was truly our mistake that we didn't think to draft Gallardo initially. However, having the opportunity to pick up her contract and bring her into our organization now is something we couldn't pass up."

Commissioner Tony Reagins said, "This is a huge day for the game of baseball. While we have made inroads in bringing women into the game as coaches and front office executives, including the first female head pitching coach in Jennie Finch for the Pirates a year ago, we have been missing the key element of having a female out on the field. This is a huge step in the right direction for our league and I anticipate the first of many to come."

There has been some backlash surrounding the situation. A player from the Athletics AAA affiliate in Las Vegas where Gallardo will play, spoke under condition of anonymity, telling the San Francisco Chronicle, "Listen, I understand social change. I get it. But what I don't understand is why are we giving handouts and letting a transgender woman into our locker room just because of her sexual orientation. It does not make sense to me, it never will."

The mood around the Athletics locker room was much more positive surrounding the signing. Outfielder Kendrick Jackson said, "I'm honored to be a part of an organization that cares the way the Athletics do. This is history and I'm just proud to be here to witness it."

- 30 -

Baseball and Some Media Futures

Rick Wilber

I'm a science fiction writer who, quite literally, grew up in baseball. My father, Del Wilber, played for the Cardinals, Phillies, and Red Sox before working as a coach, scout, and minor league manager for many years. Dad was a classic baseball lifer and Mom was a baseball wife who carved out her own solid career in radio and public relations. So thinking about the game, the media, and the future is second nature to me.

The family was anchored in St. Louis, where I spent my summers reading juvenile science-fiction novels by the famous writers of the day and listening to Harry Caray and Jack Buck on KMOX radio as they called the Cardinals games. The Redbirds were not often on television in those days, but KMOX brought the games right into our living room and—in April, May, and September—right into my elementary and high school classrooms through those marvelous early transistor radios.

Taffy Wilber interviewing Joe Namath.

We went to the games often, of course—especially in the 1960s, when the Cardinals had some great years and Mom worked in the Cardinals' front office and had box seats as a perk. But even there, those transistor radios brought Harry and Jack right into our ears as we watched Bob Gibson wind up to pitch or Lou Brock take a lead off first as he got ready to try for yet another stolen base.

Cardinals baseball was perfect for radio, with plenty of time for Harry and Jack to wax eloquent about the players and the situation on the field before Gibby would bring in that angry fastball or Lou would take off for second. Perhaps it is nostalgic of me, but often I still listen to my hometown team's games that way, though now it's the Tampa Bay Rays and I get the radio broadcast through my Kindle Fire's At Bat app from MLB.com. I have my ear buds in as I'm reading a science fiction novel from one or another of the writers of the day—Kevin J. Anderson or Fran Wilde or E. Lily Yu or James Patrick Kelly—and I'm listening to the Rays broadcast as Andy Freed and Dave Wills wax eloquent about Tyler Glasnow and his occasional triple-digit fastball or Randy Arozarena's amazing 2020 postseason hitting and can he keep it going this season? Much of that chatter goes by me as I focus on the story and then Freed tells me here's the pitch, and Arozarena gets into that one and maybe he'll stretch it to a triple.

I may be only half-listening—multi-tasking, as we all do so much these days—but in an instant the excitement in the voices of Freed and Wills clues me in. I'm fully engaged as the play takes place, and I am reminded again how good it is to listen to baseball via radio, no matter what device carries it to me.

A week later, I have a game on as I sit at my desk writing. The Rays are hosting the Yankees in what is certainly one of baseball's most heated current rivalries. There's some history of bad blood between these teams and Austin Meadows has just been hit by a pitch for the second time in the game. I'm expecting the dugouts to empty, but the umps intervene and for now the aggression remains mere angry chatter and the game goes on. Good, I'm thinking. Play ball. This isn't hockey. Yet.

I hope we never lose that sense of being there in the booth with the announcer as the tension builds and the moment happens, time after time, inning after inning, game after game, season after season. But new technologies are on the cusp of bringing us even more immersive experiences.

The story I'm writing has a protagonist—an ex-pro basketball player—who's taken up sportscasting and commentary, and who wears a device called a Sweep media system.[1] The Sweep picks up all of his sensory input as he meets with one celebrity or another while interviewing them, takes a few swings at batting practice with the hitter that's flirting with .400, or goes one-on-one with an All-Star shooting guard in the WNBA, or competes with a famous golfer in a hole-in-one contest. Viewers wearing a receiving unit sense what he sees and hears and smells and touches and tastes. They feel as if they're sharing his experience fully, whether he's shooting that three or shagging fly balls during batting practice or having a hot dog at Pink's in Hollywood. They're inside his head, sensing it all, being part of him.

I started writing these stories about the Sweep system twenty years ago, and I set them in the 2030s, which I thought was well into the future, when the technology might well be available. Now we're only nine years away and it's obvious to me that the tech I imagined is nearly here already. New kinds of immersive media are on the horizon, including one where you'll be able to feel as if you are the shortstop turning that dazzling double play or the pitcher hitting the triple digits as he lets a high, hard one fly.

Though I love baseball on the radio—a technology that's been around since the mid-1890s, when Guglielmo Marconi managed to send some signals from one aerial to another on his family's estate in Italy—loving that old technology doesn't mean I don't embrace the new. I'm a simple user, for sure, not a developer; but my smartphone is chock-full of apps, including Ballpark—where the digital Rays tickets are stored that get my son and I into our socially-distanced Sunday matinee games (we're both fully vaccinated, I should add). My wife and I were the first family in the neighborhood to cut the cable cord and start streaming all our television, and were the first, too, to bring Alexa into our house, where it not only answers our questions and keeps track of things generally, it also runs the three—count 'em, three—Roombas that zoom around keeping things clean. This fascination with new tech prompted me to apply to be a Google Glass Explorer back in 2013. Google said yes to my application and I spent $1500 on Google Glass, a technology that was ahead of its time and suffered from privacy problems, but is still around, as you'll see. I try to stay current; my excuse is that it's necessary research for my science fiction, both for background details and as a reminder of how fascinating (and worrisome) the future can be.

So I fancy myself a futurist and I'm willing to take an educated guess at how the media will present the game of baseball to us in the coming years, both at the ballpark and in the new ways to bring the game right into our living rooms. Let's start with some technology that's available now or will be very soon, and then look forward into the future, with technology that's being talked about but isn't here yet.

Virtual Reality (VR) is here right now and rapidly improving. This technology brings you into a three-dimensional artificial environment where you interact with that environment in any number of ways, competing in a next-generation video game, flying an airplane, soaring over the Great Wall of China or the Grand Canyon, attending a rock concert or, if you're into baseball, taking your swings against a very realistic pitcher. VR typically requires a headset and controllers for your hands.

Baseball video games have been around for a long time. The best of them, like R.B.I. Baseball, coming from Major League Baseball's Advanced Media group. Putting those games into a three-dimensional virtual word takes them to a new level of seeming verisimilitude. The technology is so realistic that there are training apps out there now that you can use to help your inner big-league ballplayer take on some serious pitching. One that some players are said to have used during the 2020 hiatus is the WIN Reality on the Oculus 2, where you choose your pitching level, hold the controller (and maybe a bat with it) and step up to the virtual plate.[2]

A new wrinkle in this virtual reality environment is MLB.com's streaming service of live games, now presented in 3D. One of the most popular VR headsets is the self-contained Oculus Quest 2 and with that headset and your subscription to MLB.com you can stream out-of-market games through your Oculus, zooming around the field and into the dugout, seeing all the live action, even replaying favorite games back to the 2018 season.[3] You get pitch-by-pitch data visualization and other stats in overlays when you want them, and 360-degree video highlights. All of this from the comfort of your couch at home. At the 2021 SABR Analytics

Del Wilber spent eight seasons in the big leagues with the Cardinals, Phillies, and Red Sox.

conference, developers from MLBAM hinted that by using software extrapolation, soon they hope to be able to offer angles on plays as if from a player's perspective to Oculus and other VR platform users.[4]

This all makes great sense to me if you're not able to attend games in person and if you already use the Oculus for gaming and other entertainment. Is the enhanced 3D imagery and the ability to manipulate your viewpoint worth wearing the bulky Oculus headset to watch major-league games that never include your home team (only out-of-market is available because of media rights deals) worth the $300 price tag? That's up to you.

Augmented Reality Glasses, or Smart Glasses, are here now, too, though the best of them are pricey. Most pairs, which look very much like a regular pair of glasses, can present information to you about what you're seeing. You choose whether to focus on the live action in front of you or the information. They are typically voice actuated: you "tell" the glasses what information you need. You can take pictures or videos, too, and share them immediately through email or through social media apps like Facebook or Instagram.

At their simplest, smart glasses are very much as if your smartphone became a pair of glasses. Will fans use them? Take a look around at the next game you're able to attend and see how many people look at their smartphones during the game, checking their email, taking a quick picture and posting it on Facebook, looking up the stats on the next hitter or checking into some arcane fact about the action on the field. You can do all of that through smart glasses, even as you converse through texts or messages or, soon no doubt, by voice with others online, perhaps at the same game, sharing videos ("Hey, look at this, I got a great video of that Kiermaier catch at the wall!").

Baseball has always been about conversations, right? You talk to those around you, high-fiving with the fans in the rows in front and behind you when a good thing happens, and moaning with them when your cleanup hitter takes a called third strike. With smart glasses you're able to watch the action live and see chats from fans from all over the park, or all over the world, depending on your tech and settings. You can also easily connect to the radio broadcast of the game, so the announcers are in your ear while you're glancing at the stats, perhaps, while watching the action on the field.

I wouldn't be surprised to find out that Major League Baseball Advanced Media is already working on its own kind of smart glasses, perhaps on a team by team basis. You could purchase preset glasses at the ballpark or download the app that would provide your existing smart glasses with the relevant information, like the pitch by pitch feed for your team's home games. Additionally, these smart glasses take pictures and videos, so you could tell your glasses to take a video of the next pitch. Maybe you'll capture the perfect bunt, or the home run, or the great catch in center field.

The downside for augmented-reality smart glasses is the price. The top of the line models, like the Microsoft HoloLens 2 or the Magic Leap One, cost thousands of dollars, and even the less expensive ones run $500 or more. Some of the glasses also use haptic technology in gloves you wear. With haptic technology, when your glasses show you a virtual object you can have the sensation of touching it via the gloves.

As an early adopter of Google Glass back in 2013, I found that early device clumsy to use but was fascinated by its potential. I shared it with my students, I wore it on long bike rides and to baseball games and walks on the beach. It worked. It took surprisingly good pictures and videos, but it was those pictures and videos that were problematic for people. If you were wearing Google Glass all you had to do was blink and the device took a picture. This felt intrusive, for sure, since those around you never knew when you were taking their picture. That privacy concern became a major knock on Google Glass, and a deserved one.

Google Glass is still around, as Glass Enterprise Edition 2, and still expensive, at more than $1000. The Enterprise Edition 2 is aimed at industrial and other professional training, allowing management and employees to learn dangerous jobs in a safe environment.

Immersive reality—in the way I'm using it here for purposes of predicting how the media may work with baseball in five or ten years—may be some variation on the fictional future I've predicted in my novels and stories. My fictional Sweep system can have, let's say, a baseball star who is willing to be connected very directly to his fans, transmit his sensory input to those fans. They'll feel the wind on his face as he's racing toward third for a triple. They'll not only see the third baseman put his glove up waiting for the ball, they'll feel the dirt on their faces as our player slides head-first, touches the bag, and a half-second later, feel the tag on their shoulder. Safe.

Players, coaches, and managers have already taken the first step in this direction when they've agreed to be miked up during games, which happens now with some frequency. Once mostly done as a Fox or ESPN game-of-the-week gimmick, hot mikes on players have become a staple of MLB's own YouTube channel.[5] All the fans get now is the player's audio and some ambient noise, but what if the player were also wearing smart contact lenses that could capture what he was seeing and transmit it to the fans?

Smart contact lenses are already available in their early stages of development for health and vision purposes. They show promise, in the years to come, to be able to do almost everything that smart glasses do, including heads-up displays of information. An article published online by The American Academy of Ophthalmology predicts that, in the years to come, smart contacts will have the same visual displays as smart glasses.[6]

Will our miked and lensed player wear these tools only during a game, or might he build a large fanbase by wearing them at home, or when he's out for dinner, or at an awards ceremony, or with his wife, playing in the front yard with their children? And will he consent to having haptic connections for touch, too, when such connections are possible? And for taste? And for smell? I'm guessing yes. Many ballplayers are already active on Twitter and other social-media platforms; they seem to enjoy the celebrity. Can Sweep media be far behind? I suspect not.

For now, I'm waiting for the price to drop on those smart glasses, so I can see the stats and watch the live action and, just like the good old days, listen to the radio broadcast as my team, the Tampa Bay Rays, try to earn their way back to the World Series. ■

Notes

1. In my long-running S'hudonni Empire series of stories and novels. The most recent, *Alien Day*, was published by Tor/Macmillan in June 2021.
2. Information page for Win Reality baseball VR training program, https://winreality.com/baseball.
3. "MLB VR," Specs page for the MLB VR feed for Oculus Quest VR devices, https://www.oculus.com/experiences/quest/2873640696088444.
4. Graham Goldbeck, Marc Squire, Sid Sethupathi, "MLB Statcast Player Pose Tracking and Visualization," Presented at SABR Analytics Conference, March 14, 2021.
5. In 2020 MLB's Youtube channel introduced a recurring video series entitled "Mic'd Up," and in 2021 a series of videos entitled "Play Loud," featuring mic'd up players on both benches in a game.
6. Reena Mukamal, "High-Tech Contact Lenses That Go Beyond Correcting Vision." February 5, 2020, American Academy of Opthalmology website, https://www.aao.org/eye-health/tips-prevention/smart-contact-lens-tech-beyond-vision-correction.

Democracy at the Ballpark
Looking Towards a Fan-Owned Future

Stephen R. Keeney

Think about your favorite baseball team. Think about the many times a sports team you root for made a baffling decision. Think about the roster rebuild that never seems to end. Now imagine something new. Imagine buying a membership in your favorite team. Imagine voting on who runs the team or on how to finance stadium upgrades. Maybe you should even run for election to the board of directors. You would go to the ballpark knowing that every dollar you spent would go back into the team. Imagine how much better every hot dog and every beer will taste! "Get another round, we need a new shortstop!" you tell your friends, while you ponder that day's scoreboard stumper.

This may seem like a fantasy, but it could be the future of baseball. Fan-ownership of sports teams works. The fan-owned Green Bay Packers are one of the most prestigious teams in the National Football League. In Europe, fan-owned teams dominate the top soccer competition. Moving Major League Baseball teams to a fan ownership model can lead not only to success on the field, but increased democracy, increased transparency, and a stronger sense of community and investment for fans.

WHY FAN OWNERSHIP?

Currently, when franchise decisions are made, there is no community involvement. Decisions are made by wealthy owners. And the interests of the fans and the interests of the owner are not always the same. This has many wondering if we need owners at all.[1] As one writer put it, "Our sports franchises are public assets that we have allowed to be owned by private rich people."[2]

Fan ownership means that fans control the goals, finances, and on-field product. If fans decide to pay profits back to members, then that's up to the fans. If the fans decide that the profit margin is too big, they can make games more affordable for the average fan; this happens in Germany, whose fan-owned soccer teams generally have lower ticket prices and higher attendance than other countries.[3] They can also decide to increase prices and how to spend the profits: in making the team better on the field and/or improving their communities with scholarships, grants, or other charitable or developmental enterprises. MLB teams currently do offer various forms of community support and charitable giving, but with fan ownership these become meaningful decisions made by the community.

THE STAKEHOLDERS

The ownership structures of sports franchises should be centered on the interests of all stakeholders. In the current structure, owners are the only stakeholders with any meaningful input. That interest is primarily a business one: turning a profit.

The most important stakeholders in professional sports are the fans. While the players make sports possible, fans make sports profitable. A franchise's fans are customers, advertising audience, neighbors, community, and soul. Sports without fans are just exercise.

Another crucial stakeholder is the local community. Businesses around the stadium often rely on gameday revenue, but other businesses and organizations struggle to compete with sports. A stadium without sufficient parking can cause businesses to lose foot traffic from parking congestion during games. Fans are usually local citizens who get a sense of belonging and identity from following the local franchise, celebrating successes and mourning losses as a group. Local governments benefit from tax revenue from the stadium and players' income, but they are also often strong-armed into giving taxpayer-funded stadiums to billionaire owners. Taxpayer funding means that even non-fans in the local community have an interest in how a franchise is run and how the local government interacts with it.

Players also have an interest in franchise decisions. They train their whole lives for a very short career. Therefore, players need to make as much money and win as much as possible in just a few years. Players have the same interest in the franchise as other workers: They create the business's value, so they deserve a say in decision-making.

FAN OWNERSHIP MODELS

Current models give us insight into how future fan-owned teams might look. There are two dominant models. The most common model looks similar to a corporation, where fans purchase some sort of buy-in that gives them voting rights. Some models give fans more to vote on, but the basic structure is that fans purchase voting rights via stock shares or membership fees, and then vote for directors who oversee franchise operations. Less common is direct, municipal ownership by the local government. In the second model, fans get voting rights from citizenship.

The most famous example of the corporate model in American sports is the Green Bay Packers. Packers fans buy in when new "shares" are issued. Shares give them the right to vote for team directors, who then elect a committee to make the operational decisions by hiring a GM, who runs the day-to-day operations. While reasonable minds can disagree on how much say this really gives fans, the fact is that most American sports fans lack even that much say in their team's operation. In 2011 the Packers announced a plan for a $146 million stadium improvement, paid for with a new round of stock offerings instead of strong-arming the local government to use tax dollars.[4]

There are similar examples in affiliated baseball's minor leagues. The Syracuse (NY) Chiefs of the International League were a fan-owned team from 1961 until 2017. They originated as a fan-owned team after multiple owners moved teams out of Syracuse. Fans bought shares which allowed them to vote for directors, with no person allowed to vote more than 500 shares, no matter how many they owned. Financial trouble hit in the 2000s, and in 2017, after a bizarre series of events, the team was sold to the New York Mets.[5] The team took a loan from a group of directors in exchange for 600 shares plus control of the board.[6] The group installed their own general manager, then reported about one-third of all shares (representing more than half of all shareholders) as abandoned property to the State of New York, increasing the per-share profit of the remaining shares from the sale to the Mets.[7] Over 900 people had to reclaim their shares to get a share of the profits from the sale.[8]

Another fan-owned team that went private recently was the Wisconsin Timber Rattlers. The High-A team, along with its Fox Cities Stadium and sister team, the Fond Du Lac Dock Spiders, were owned by the Appleton Baseball Club—a fan-owned venture that operated minor-league baseball in Appleton, Wisconsin, since 1939.[9] The club failed financially due to the cancellation of the 2020 season during the COVID-19 pandemic.

The club was purchased by Third Base Ventures, a group headed by Craig Dickman, a long-time Appleton and Green Bay Packers director, for an undisclosed fee.

Other examples of this style of ownership are on display at the highest levels of European soccer. In Germany's Bundesliga, all clubs must follow a 50 + 1 rule, requiring the club to hold at least 50% plus one of all of its own shares. The club is run by presidents and directors who are elected by the members—fans who pay a membership fee. This means no private owner can take control of the club away from the fans and put profits ahead of fan interests.[10] The prices of membership are affordable for average fans. Membership fees for Germany's largest and most successful club, Bayern Munich, run just 60 Euros (~$72) per year.[11] The second most successful and third biggest club, Borusia Dortmund, only costs 62 Euros ($75) per year.[12] Because the focus is on the fans and the team rather than profits, Germany has some of the lowest ticket prices and highest attendances in all of Europe.[13]

Spanish soccer also gives us examples, where the two richest and most successful clubs are fan-owned: Real Madrid and FC Barcelona. Under Spanish law, soccer clubs must be privately owned, with four clubs (Real Madrid, Barcelona, Athletic Bilbao, and CA Osasuna) being grandfathered in as fan-owned clubs.[14] For these clubs, fans buy a membership, which gives them the right to vote on directors, president, and various other club items. Membership costs a Real Madrid fan about 150 Euros (~$181), and an FC Barcelona fan 185 Euros ($224).[15] The membership structure ensures that these clubs cannot be purchased by private owners.

Critics of the fan-ownership models in soccer say that teams need rich, private owners to put in the

Green Bay Packers fans, sporting cheese-wedge hats, one of which reads "OWNER."

money necessary to compete in Europe. This criticism fails both in regard to team success and fan happiness. In Spain, Real Madrid, Barcelona, and Athletic Bilbao have combined to win 68 of 89 league championships (76%).[16] From 2010 through the 2020 campaign, Real Madrid, Barcelona, or Bayern Munich have won 8 of the 10 UEFA Champions League titles.[17] In fact, Real Madrid, Barcelona, or a German team have won 26 of 65 tournaments (40%), with Real Madrid having the most wins ever (13), Bayern tied for third (6), and Barcelona fifth (5).[18] These three teams also lead all of Europe in their UEFA Club Coefficient, a stat measuring a team's success in European competitions over the past five years.[19] This success, combined with the fact that German soccer continually has the best league-wide attendance numbers across Europe, shows that fan-ownership can deliver trophies, fan empowerment, and financial stability.

A less common method of fan/community ownership is the direct ownership of a team by a local government entity. The best example of this was the Double-A Harrisburg (PA) Senators. The private owners of the Senators threatened to move the team unless the city gave them a new, publicly-funded stadium. Faced with the choice between an unreasonable demand and losing their local team, the City of Harrisburg decided to buy the franchise outright in 1995. The purchase price was $6.7 million, with $1.25 million coming from capital reserves and the remaining $5.45 million coming from a bond issue.[20] Facing budgetary issues, the city sold the team in 2007 for $13.25 million plus a guarantee to keep the team in Harrisburg for at least 29 years.[21]

The fact that Harrisburg bought their team with public money, nearly doubled their investment in just over a decade, *and* kept the team in town shows that municipal ownership can work. In this model, a sports team could operate much the same way as a municipal "enterprise fund," where certain activities are paid for and run in ways similar to what a private business might do, except that public service, rather than private profit, is the driving motivation. For example, many cities or counties own their water or electricity distribution services. They provide the water or power to citizens and businesses and charge fees for distribution and usage. Often, the money paid to the water or power system is put into its own account, separate from the government's "general fund," but still under the control of local elected officials. That money is then used primarily to improve those services, but can also be moved to the "general fund" under certain circumstances to accomplish other government objectives.

The issue of municipal ownership has come up in the major-league baseball context as well. When McDonald's founder and owner of the San Diego Padres Ray Kroc died in 1984, his widow Joan Kroc inherited the team. She tried to donate the team to the City of San Diego, but an owners' committee persuaded her to drop the idea, and she sold the team in 1990.[22] When Major League Baseball took control of the Dodgers from the feuding McCourts, sports journalist Dave Zirin advocated for the team to be given to the fans, while also lamenting the lack of public pressure to do so.[23] These examples show the single largest obstacle to any meaningful development in fan ownership is the leagues themselves. All major American sports leagues, including Major League Baseball, now prohibit anything but private, for-profit ownership of teams.[24]

FAN-OWNED vs COMMUNITY-OWNED MODELS

As we think about a future of fan-owned baseball teams, we have to consider what features are necessary to achieve ownership that is democratic, transparent, and representative of fan interests. To see what this looks like, consider the two dominant forms already discussed: community ownership, which would be ownership by some level of government, and fan ownership, which would be ownership by fans who buy some sort of voting rights share.

Community ownership is a straightforward concept. The city, county, or state would take over the team and appoint employees to operate it under the same laws and regulations that other government agencies have to follow. The teams could be run like other "enterprise funds," such as municipal power, water, or other services with their own budgets and oversight.

The government entity could purchase the team the way Harrisburg did when it bought the Senators, or it could forcibly purchase the team from the current owners with Eminent Domain. Eminent Domain is the legal principle stemming from the Fifth Amendment of the US Constitution, which provides that the government can take private property as long as the owner receives due process and fair market value in return, and the property will be for public use. Usually in sports, property is taken from low-income residents and given to wealthy owners on the premise that having the team is a public purpose, even if the taken property becomes private.[25] In this case, the taking would turn the business into public property.

This form of ownership has several advantages. First, the decisions, finances, and inner workings of the team would be required to comply with the principles of democracy, community input, and transparency (sunshine laws, open meetings laws, etc.) that governments are subject to under state, federal, and local law. This is a benefit to all in the community who currently have no say and little access to information about team operations. Second, this method puts all community members on equal footing, regardless of fanhood. Finally, the community would own a profit-generating asset whose proceeds are used to benefit the citizens. Cities could decide to keep profits low by keeping ticket prices low, which is good for the fans, or it could decide to use the profits for public services. Imagine profits from beer and hot dogs at the ballpark being used to fix roads, hire more firefighters, or provide better public education.

There are cons to this method of ownership. Not all fans live within the city, county, or state where their team sits. My hometown Cincinnati Reds, a small-market team, have fans not only in Cincinnati, but in other counties in Ohio, Kentucky, and Indiana. Those fans would be left out of any say in or benefit from a community ownership model. Another issue is deciding which level or levels of government should own the team. While cities like Harrisburg, Pennsylvania, can afford to buy a Double-A team, how many large cities can afford to buy a major-league team? Surely cities like New York, Los Angeles, or Chicago could find the money. But cities like Cincinnati, Cleveland, Kansas City, or Milwaukee may not have the money or operational capacity. With smaller cities, the county's or state's help might be needed. However, as one author pointed out several years ago, sometimes cities spend more on stadiums to give to teams than it would cost to buy the team outright.

Fan ownership using a Board of Directors is another approach. In this case, the teams would have to be bought by—or given to—the new entity from the previous owner. We have seen examples of shareholder and membership models. A shareholder model like that in Green Bay and most other American examples is a step in the right direction, but the membership model holds more promise as a way to allow more fans to participate and to prevent private owners from taking the club back.

As we saw with the Syracuse Chiefs, allowing individuals to buy more shares gives those individuals more voting power. That is how a few directors with outsized voting rights privatized a fan-owned team. When the vote to approve the sale to the Mets took place, about 100 of the approximately 4,000 shareholders voted, but almost two-thirds of the shares were voted. Some methods to limit this power by wealthy individuals would be to make the shares unable to be cashed out, as the Green Bay Packers have done, or to have a Board of Directors made up of a minority of shareholders, with the other seats on the Board held by local government representatives and player representatives. An absolute limit on the number of shares that any one person or entity can vote is essential for this type of ownership to be any different from current ownership.

By contrast, the membership method with a one-member-one-vote setup allows far more people to participate in the decision-making, and prevents a few individuals from wielding outsized influence. This prevents individual members from being "owners" in a legal sense, which means that there is no incentive for them to seek profit from membership. As we saw with the European soccer examples, a reasonably priced membership can be affordable for the average fan where stock shares might not be. A membership system also breeds participation because once someone stops being a member, their voting rights cease. Votes will not be tied up by people whose parents bought stock and lost the certificate in the attic decades ago, as was the case in Syracuse. Since there is no vested property interest there is nothing to sell, transfer, bequeath, or inherit, except maybe season tickets. For those reasons, a membership model is better than a shareholder model for increasing fan participation and ensuring democratic control by the most important stakeholders.

In any ownership model, it would be a mistake to shut out the players or the local government from decision-making. In either fan-owned model, a set number of director seats should be reserved for members/shareholders, a set number for the local community, and a set number for players. The players are the ones who make sports what they are. They deserve a voice in how each team is run.

HOW TO GET THERE FROM HERE
The road to any sort of fan-ownership model for Major League Baseball will likely be long, winding, and fraught with danger for municipalities brave enough to take on billionaire owners. The first hurdle is the current owners. An owner giving a team away to a community or a fan group would be simple enough, at least in theory. Fans of the English soccer team Newcastle United have started taking pledges of money from fans to buy an interest—however small—in the club if the owner sells the team.[27] But taking a team by force would be a whole different ballgame. In theory, cities or states could use the power of eminent domain

to take ownership of sports franchises. This has been tried in the past, but never succeeded for different reasons. The City of Baltimore tried to use eminent domain to take over the Colts, but a court later ruled that Bob Irsay snuck out of town just in time, and since the team was no longer there, the city could not take over the team.[28] The City of Oakland also tried to use eminent domain in the 1980s to prevent the Raiders from moving out of town. Eventually, a California appeals court held that the city taking over the Raiders would violate the US Constitution's commerce clause because it would interfere with the interests of the other league owners.[29]

That notion brings up the next hurdle, the leagues themselves. As previously mentioned, every major sports league in the United States prohibits non-profit ownership among its members. Additionally, because Congress has granted the leagues exemptions from anti-monopoly statutes (except for Major League Baseball, whose exemption is from the Supreme Court), there is little that can be done outside of an Act of Congress to force the leagues to accept municipal or non-profit owners. In theory, Congress could again raise the specter of eliminating those protections to strong-arm the leagues into changing their rules. They have tried it before, but the law failed in the end.[30] Congress could also, potentially, simply make such provisions in the league charters illegal. With the lobbying power of the leagues and their owners, this route would be a long-shot without a massive amount of popular mobilization on the part of sports fans and affected citizens across the country. We are simply not there right now.

Perhaps a foothold is all that is needed. The Packers and soccer giants Real Madrid and Barcelona show that you do not need rich, individual ownership to succeed on the field. But right now, a fan-owned or community-owned team would have a massive uphill battle just to get on the field. This creates a chicken-and-egg question for supporters of fan-ownership: will there be a chance to show that these models can work within the leagues and slowly change more teams from private to fan-owned over time, or must there be a critical mass of cities or fan groups ready to make a move at once to even get in the door?

A FAN-OWNED FUTURE

What both fan-owned models share is that decisions will more likely be made in the interests of the club. By removing the profit motive, the focus becomes the short-term and long-term health and success of the team. One con is that in both models the people who end up in charge are usually just different wealthy people. And while that may not be ideal for a truly democratic team operation, the fact that they are held accountable to the rest of the voters means they are less likely to act out of self-interest than unaccountable private owners.

None of this is to say that current owners are all bad. There are plenty of owners out there who put a good product on the field, support the local community, and are willing to pay good money for good players. But in a sports franchise, just as in any other business, the profit motive is always there. That motive can be aligned with the interests of the fans and the local community, or it could run counter to those interests.

A future with more fan-owned teams is a future with a better fan experience. Bringing more democracy to professional sports teams means more value for and more input from the most important stakeholders. The current owners will be fine. Some might give the team

Table 1. Ownership Model Comparison

	Community-Owned (Government)	Fan-Owned (Shareholders)	Fan-Owned (Membership)
Pros	All local residents have a say, even non-fans	Financing comes from willing fans	Financing comes from willing fans
	Team decisions and operations subject to public oversight law	Fans from anywhere can have voting right	Fans from anywhere can have voting right
	Community owns a profit-generating asset	Conveys a legal property right in the team	Fan buy-in for participation is lower than shareholder mode
	One person, one vote		One person, one vote
Cons	Initial funding could be difficult for small-mid markets	Easily dominated by a few wealthy shareholders without voting limits	Lack of legal ownership
	Out-of-town fans have no input	Cost could be barrier to entry	
	Multiple levels of government could fight for ownership	Raising capital requires fans to pay more up front	Raising capital requires fans to pay more up front

to the community as Joan Kroc tried to do. Some might be bought out at a profit. Others might lose the team via Eminent Domain, meaning they would be paid fair market value for the franchise, almost certainly at a profit. But unlike many fans, these former owners won't spend season after season despairing over decisions made by people who care more about profits than the team or the community. A fan-owned future means truly being part of the team. ■

Notes

1. Henry Druschel, "Imagining a Fan-Owned Team," September 27, 2017, BeyondtheBoxscore.com, https://www.beyondtheboxscore.com/2017/9/27/16367428/public-ownership-baseball-teams-socialism-universal-basic-income. Ben Burgis, "Sports Team Should be Owned by the Public," JacobinMag.com, December 28, 2019, https://jacobinmag.com/2019/12/nfl-cowboys-jerry-jones-football-owners-public-ownership.

2. Harvey Wasserman, "The Real Solution to Scumbag Sports Owners," CounterPunch, April 30, 2014, https://www.counterpunch.org/2014/04/30/the-real-solution-to-scumbag-sports-owners/?fbclid=IwAR2569-v52qPgY_tTliQ-ImftGEBZc8uPjZqrTfWq_C42WEoR7giR3YHnD0.

3. Raffaele Poli, Loic Ravenel, and Roger Besson. "Attendance in Football Stadia (2003–2018)," CIES Football Observatory Monthly Report No. 44, April 2019 (International Centre for Sports Studies), available at https://football-observatory.com/IMG/pdf/mr44en.pdf.

4. "Green Bay Packers Shareholders," Green Bay Packers, accessed April 3, 2021, https://www.packers.com/community/shareholders.

5. Lindsay Kramer, "Syracuse Chiefs Shareholders Approve Sale to New York Mets," Syracuse.com, November 17, 2017, https://www.syracuse.com/chiefs/2017/11/syracuse_chiefs_shareholders_approve_sale_to_new_york_mets.html.

6. John O'Brien, "To Escape Fiscal Crisis, Syracuse Chiefs' Board Considers Offers: One for $500,00, Another For $1 million." Syracuse.com, September 30, 2013, https://www.syracuse.com/news/2013/09/syracuse_chiefs_board_considering_two_investment_proposals.html.

7. Roger Cormier, "No, The New York Mets' Acquisition of the Syracuse Chiefs Did Not Go Smoothly," GoodFundies.com, December 17, 2017, https://goodfundies.com/no-the-new-york-mets-acquisition-of-the-syracuse-chiefs-did-not-go-smoothly-dbacbd34b5cd.

8. Ricky Moriarty, "More Than 900 Syracuse Chiefs Owners to Get Back $2 Million in 'Abandoned' Stock," Syracuse.com, December 1, 2017, https://www.syracuse.com/business-news/2017/12/more_than_900_syracuse_chiefs_owners_to_get_2_million_in_abandoned_stock_back.html.

9. "Wisconsin Timber Rattlers, Fox Cities Stadium Sold," The Business News, January 23, 2021, https://www.readthebusinessnews.com/features/merger_acquisitions/wisconsin-timber-rattlers-fox-cities-stadium-sold/article_e1756586-4fb2-11eb-ba26-ff31134e2efe.html.

10. "German Soccer Rules: 50+1 Explained," Bundesliga.com, accessed April 3, 2021, https://www.bundesliga.com/en/news/Bundesliga/german-soccer-rules-50-1-fifty-plus-one-explained-466583.jsp.

11. "Pricing: Membership Fees," FC Bayern, accessed April 3, 2021, https://fcbayern.com/en/club/become-member/pricing.

12. "Apply for Membership," Borussia Dortmund, accessed April 3, 2021, https://www.bvb.de/eng/BVB/Membership/Apply-for-membership.

13. Poli, Ravenel, and Besson, "Attendance in Football Stadia."

14. Khalid Khan, "Cure or Curse: Socio Club Ownerships in Spanish La Liga," Bleacher Report, June 11, 2010, https://bleacherreport.com/articles/404511-cure-or-curse-socio-club-ownerships-in-spanish-la-liga#:~:text=Spain's%20Sports%20Law%2C%20Ley%2010,93%20season%20of%20Primera%20Divisi%C3%B3n.

15. "Types of Card," Real Madrid FC, accessed April 3, 2021, https://www.realmadrid.com/en/members/member-card/types-and-prices; "Become a Member, FC Barcelona, accessed April 3, 2021, https://www.fcbarcelona.com/en/club/members/become-member/registration-of-adult-members.

16. "Spain—List of Champions," Rec Sport Soccer Statistics Foundation, accessed April 3, 2021, http://www.rsssf.com/tabless/spanchamp.html.

17. "History," UEFA, accessed April 3, 2021, https://www.uefa.com/uefachampionsleague/history/.

18. "History: Winners," UEFA, accessed April 3, 2021, https://www.uefa.com/uefachampionsleague/history/winners/.

19. "UEFA Club Coefficients," UEFA, accessed Aril 3, 2021, https://www.uefa.com/memberassociations/uefarankings/club/#/yr/2021

20. Megan O'Matz, "Harrisburg Strikes Deal for Senators, City Will Pay $6.7 Million to Keep Baseball Team," The Morning Call, July 8, 1995, https://www.mcall.com/news/mc-xpm-1995-07-08-3055425-story.html.

21. "Harrisburg Senators Sale Announced," MiLB.com, May 16, 2007, http://www.milb.com/gen/articles/printer_friendly/milb/press/y2007/m05/d16/c244716.jsp.

22. "Panel Blocked Bid to Give Padres to City of San Diego," LA Times, July 30, 1990, https://www.latimes.com/archives/la-xpm-1990-07-30-sp-1027-story.html.

23. Dave Zirin, "Baseball's Blues: It's Not Just the Dodgers," LA Times, April 22, 2011, https://www.latimes.com/sports/la-xpm-2011-apr-22-la-oe-zirin-dodgers-20110422-story.html.

24. The Green Bay Packers avoid this requirement because they were grand-fathered in. They existed before the current rules were created, which apply only to new owners (known as "members" in the NFL Constitution, Article 3.2). The Packers were formed in 1919, the NFL (under a prior name) was formed in 1920, and the current NFL constitution dates back to 1970 when the AFL-NFL merger was completed.

25. For example, Eric Nusbaum, Stealing Home: Los Angeles, the Dodgers, and the Lives Caught in Between (New York: Hachette Book Group, 2020).

26. Neil deMause, "The Radical Case for Cities Buying Sports Teams, Not Sports Stadiums," Vice.com, December 29, 2014, at https://www.vice.com/en/article/vvakva/the-radical-case-for-cities-buying-sports-teams-not-sports-stadiums.

27. "Newcastle United: Supporters Set Up a Fund to Buy Part of Premier League Club If Sold," BBC.com, April 8, 2021, available at https://www.bbc.com/sport/football/56673354.

28. M. & C. Council of Baltimore v. B. Football C., 624 F. Supp. 278 (D. Md. 1986), available at https://law.justia.com/cases/federal/district-courts/FSupp/624/278/2305222/.

29. City of Oakland v. Oakland Raiders, 174 Cal.App.3d 414 (Ct. App. 1985), available at https://www.leagle.com/decision/1985588174calapp3d4141559.

30. Neil deMause, "The Radical Case for Cities Buying Sports Teams, Not Sports Stadiums," Vice.com, December 29, 2014, at https://www.vice.com/en/article/vvakva/the-radical-case-for-cities-buying-sports-teams-not-sports-stadiums.

Under Coogan's Bluff

Harry Turtledove

They open the door. They're opening thirty doors at once, but I can only talk about mine. Air from 2040 goes out, and air from 1905 comes in. The first thing I do is cough. It smells like horseshit and coal smoke and a locker room after an Atlanta doubleheader. In 1905, New York City only—only!—has 4,000,00 people, but I don't think any of 'em took a bath in the past week.

I figure it'll be cold in the portal building, but it isn't. It's always 72 inside the portal itself, and the 1905 air in the foyer feels about the same. I step out into the past. To either side of me, the other Angels do the same. We're all in slacks and jackets, shirts and ties. We'll still look funny to the locals, but less than if we wore our usual 2040 clothes.

On the street, the men are in workmen's clothes or gloomy wool suits with too many buttons and tiny lapels. Some wear cloth caps, others derbies. The women... It's sad. Skirts down to the ground, blouses and jackets that cover the rest of 'em, hats like you wouldn't believe.

A white-bearded guy stumps by the front window. I mean stumps—he's got a peg leg like you'd see in a pirate movie. Keyshawn Fredericks, who'll pitch for us tomorrow, stares. "Whoa!" he says. "I bet he fought in the Civil War!"

He's probably right. Where we are, when we are, smacks me in the face like a giant salmon. Guys who've done this before told me how it is. But living it... The difference between hearing it and living it is like the one between a picture of a steak dinner and eating a steak dinner.

Eddie Morales gets out in front of us. He's the manager; it's his job. "Three o'clock local time," he reminds us. "The buses'll be here any minute to take us to the hotel. We'll have dinner, get as much rest as we can, and then head for the Polo Grounds. We've got another game to win. Been a hell of a long year, but this one'll give us something to brag about."

We have to stand around for ten minutes before the buses show up. Yeah, plural—they have six-horse teams. Carriages, wagons, men on bikes, a few cars... Traffic in 1905 isn't the same as it will be two lifetimes on, but there's a lot of it.

We go out through the big open doors and climb on the buses. They're painted on the sides—LOS ANGELES ANGELS, 2040 CHAMPIONS. People will know who we are anyway, from our clothes and because we average a lot bigger than they did in 1905. Somebody yells, "Matty'll clock you clowns!" A big cheer goes up.

They yell other things, too. We got warned about that, and it's true. It'll be worse—louder, anyway—tomorrow at the Polo Grounds. That word we don't say now? They scream it. Keyshawn and three or four other guys are African American, and Thabo's from South Africa. They probably think he's from South Carolina. They yell at him like he is.

Some of our Latinx players are dark, too—Adilson Bivar, especially. He's from São Paulo, where a lot of the fireballers around the league are from. He takes the crap in stride. If we have a lead tomorrow, he'll close.

The crowd doesn't know what to make of Kaz Fukushima or Pong-ju Pak. They call them Chinamen or something like that but worse. Japan? Korea? Not on their radar, not that they have radar.

Kees was born in Amsterdam, and Ralph's from Melbourne. The downtime people can't tell that by looking, though, so they just hoot at them for being from 2040.

The buses start rolling, heading uptown. When traffic's easy, we go a little faster than a walk. When it's heavy, we move a lot slower. No traffic lights. Cops at big intersections. At the others? We're on our own. Fun!

Keyshawn and I sit next to each other. He stares out the window. "It's so white, man!" he says, and he's not talking about the smoky air or the soot-stained buildings. "So white. My people, they're still down South picking cotton, I guess. Not slaves, but they might as well be."

"My own great-great-greats come through Ellis Island about now," I answer. "They finally see one Russian pogrom too many."

"One what?"

"Race riot. Or religion riot. Whatever. 1905 Russians like Jews the way 1905 Southerners like black folks."

He nods. "Gotcha."

We go up Central Park West. Central Park looks like… Central Park. I've been there when we play the Yankees. Only big difference is what people wear.

When we go past 72nd, Keyshawn points to the fancy building on the west side of the street. "That's the Dakota."

I know what the Dakota is. "John Lennon lived there."

"Yeah, him, too," Keyshawn says. I look at him. He looks back at me. *Time and Again*, man." I saw some of the Netflarx stream, but Keyshawn reads science fiction. Old science fiction, even. What do you expect from a left-hander?

In Harlem I think I hear Spanish, but it's Italian. The hole-in-the-wall shops and restaurants don't look too different from how they will 135 years on—minus the LEDs and neon—and like Keyshawn said, everyone's White.

We stop in front of the Mount Morris Hotel. We hop down from the buses, kinda stretch, and go inside to check in. The lights are electric, but dim.

LIBRARY OF CONGRESS

Christy Mathewson and John McGraw

The room… Bed's okay, I guess. A glass and a basin and a pitcher on the dresser. Toilet? Bathtub? End of the hall. Line forms on the left!

No WiFi. No TV. No radio. Not even a landline. All we can bring back is our clothes, a change or two, and our uniforms. They superscan us before we enter the portal, same as at airports.

Gym? Weight room? Nope. The Giants won the toss. We came back. They didn't come forward. When we play 'em, it's by their rules. We make money off it. So do they. They think it's a lot. Well, to them it is. And there's the whole pride thing, on both sides of the time gap.

If we don't die of boredom before we play. What do people do in hotel rooms like this? Chances are they go out and drink and screw. We can't even do that. Or we're not supposed to. That guy on the 2038 Orioles in 1909 Pittsburgh… No, no names. But they monitor us closer now.

Coaches bang on our doors at six. We troop down to the dining room. Nutrition isn't everything it should be. But roast chicken, peas, and a baked potato… That's not too bad. The bird's even tasty. And one bottle of beer. Budweiser. Some things don't change. Yeah, it tastes the way it's supposed to.

Then back to our rooms. The coaches keep an eye on us. What else are coaches for?

I look out the window. It looks dark. Street lights aren't everything they're gonna be. I lie down on the bed and stare at the ceiling. After a while, I doze off. Nothing else to do.

I wake up an hour later. Down on the street, an oompah band—trumpets and tubas and bass drums—is playing as loud as it can. They warned us this kind of crap happens. Here-and-now people help the Giants however they can. If the guys from 2040 don't get any shuteye, maybe they won't play so good.

Uptime, we'd call the police. Here? Now? Half the chavs in that horrible band're probably New York's finest.

Eventually, they shut up and go away. Even more eventually, I fall asleep again. Two hours later, they come back. Sweet night, uh-huh.

* * *

Breakfast? Bacon, eggs fried in bacon grease, hash browns. Horrible for you, but it tastes good. Lots of coffee. We need coffee.

We board the buses again and head for the Polo Grounds. Eighth Avenue and 157th, across the river from where Yankee Stadium'll be. Not this one, the one before. Only that one's not there yet, either.

They haven't started letting fans in, but there's already a crowd up on Coogan's Bluff waiting to watch for nothing. They boo us when they spy the buses. Keyshawn waves, just to rile them up some more. We go on in. The visitors' locker room isn't big enough to swing a cat. We jostle each other when we put on our unis.

Then we get our gear. The catcher's masks are okay. The wire's strong, and they even come down to protect the throat. No helmets to wear underneath, though, or at the plate. The catcher's mitts are thick leather pancakes. No shinguards, dammit; Kaz shakes his head. Balloon protectors.

First baseman's mitts are longer, flatter versions of what the catchers use. Fielders' gloves? They're gloves, like a soccer 'keeper wears, only with baby webs between the thumb and first finger.

A bunch of bats to choose from. Louisville Sluggers, different lengths and weights, but all heavy and thick-handled. "Never get any whip with these sorry things," Mel Sturgeon grumbles. He hit 48 out this season, so he knows about whip.

"Just square it up. It'll do what it does. That goes for everybody," Eddie says, raising his voice a skosh. "Ball won't jump, either. Did you look? Nobody on the Giants hit more than seven. Nobody in the Show even got into double figures."

They're little guys. They don't know about launch angle. Even so, there's a difference between seven and 48. Just a bit.

We go out to loosen up, get used to the 1905 equipment. My great-grandpa went to the Polo Grounds in the 1960s, when the Mets were new. He told me about it. This park is the one before that, though. It's wood, with Y-shaped pillars every fifteen feet or so holding up the roof over the second deck. No fence in center field, just white posts holding up a waist-high rope or wire. People in carriages or cars can watch the game. They won't see well—has to be 500 feet out there. Real short down both lines, though, same as in the park my great-grandpa saw.

The Giants are warming up, too. They eye us. We eye them. They're wearing their Series uniforms, black with white caps and socks and a big white NY on the chest. Baggy wool flannel, but classy anyway. No numbers—nobody's thought of those yet.

They look like they know what they're doing. Well, they should. They went 105–48, then beat the A's in five in the all-shutout World Series. Mathewson threw three of them. Won't his arm be dead, facing us a few days later? I hope so.

I start playing catch to get loose. The third time Dave Bowyer, our third baseman, throws me the ball, I drop it. Never would with the glove I'm used to, but these tiny little things from 1905 give you no margin for error.

Eddie sees me do it. "Two hands, guys!" he yells. "Remember, two hands! Gotta make the plays!"

I feel like a jerk. And I feel even lousier when the Giants' manager snickers at me. John McGraw— I looked him up online. Little stumpy guy; looks mean. He's only thirty-two, so he might still play, but he's put on weight.

The umps watch both teams warm up. Only two, not the six we'd have at a postseason game. No automated strike zone. No replay, either. Whatever they call, everybody's stuck with it.

When I take grounders, the infield grass seems okay. The dirt… They'll rake it before we start. Even so, it's raunchier than anything I've played on since Little League. Same with the outfield: bumps and divots everywhere. You'll get some exciting hops. Yeah, a few.

Look up old-time stats, you'll see the 1905 Giants fielded .960. You think: Stone hands. That's what I figured till I went back there. Put on one of those gloves, trot out on that field, and you don't want to laugh at them any more. You want to tip your hat.

They've razzed us nonstop from Coogan's Bluff since we arrived, but those guys are far enough away, we can pretty much ignore 'em. It gets harder after the stands start filling up. I wonder if any of my great-greats have figured out that baseball is a pretty good game and come uptown to watch. They wouldn't know I was descended from them; not like Kaplan's a rare name. It'd be pretty funny if they were here anyway, though. Anybody who isn't White, the people in the seats scream at him. Some of what they scream… We've come a ways since 1905. We aren't where we ought to be, but we aren't where we were, either. Thank God.

Ladies? They're worse than the men, or maybe just shriller.

And some of those people, maybe even screaming so they fit in, are recording the game with little tiny devices the folks from 1905'll never notice. They'll go up through the portal again afterwards, just like us. And the FOXSPN techs will stitch the footage together and stream it at a couple of benjamins a pop. Playing against the past is fun. Monetizing it? That's profit!

Eddie and McGraw exchange lineup cards. The umps go over the ground rules. The PA announcer has a megaphone, not a mike. He bawls out the lineups to the crowd. The Giants take the field. Twenty-five or thirty thousand people scream their heads off.

"Play ball!" Hank O'Day says. He's working the plate. Jack Sheridan handles the rest of the field.

"Dave Bowyer, third base!" Megaphone Man booms. And it's a game.

* * *

Dave steps in. I'm hitting second, so I crouch on one knee swinging a bat in the on-deck circle to see what Mathewson's throwing. Bresnahan, the Giants' catcher, doesn't crouch down as far as guys do now. He's farther behind the plate than they perch now, too. O'Day stands right in back of him, looking over his head, not his inside shoulder.

Mathewson's first pitch is a batting-practice fast-ball...except it's right at the knees on the outside corner. Unhittable. "Strike one!" O'Day yells. As soon as Matty has the ball back, he winds up and fires again. This one's maybe two miles an hour faster, and maybe—maybe—an inch outside. O'Day gives it to him. "Strike two!"

You see right away why he's so good. Take a little off, put a little on, send it exactly where you want to... Old-timers go on about Greg Maddux. Like that.

Dave leans over the plate a little. Mathewson's next one's up and in. Then he hits that outside corner again. Dave gets the bat on it, but dribbles one to second.

"Joshua Kaplan, second base!" the PA man shouts. I step into the left-hand box against a Hall of Famer. Weird.

He throws the first one right at my hipbone. I start to buckle—and it breaks back over the inside corner. O'Day calls it a strike. Well, it is. Bresnahan chuckles as he tosses the ball back to Mathewson. "Never seen a fadeaway before, huh?" he says. Then he says another word, the one Jews like just as well as black people like the one the crowd's been screeching at Keyshawn.

"We call it a screwball, ya dumb mick shithead," I answer. I'd never do that in 2040. I know better. If you think we're messed up now, though, going back in time shows you how we got that way.

People don't throw the screwball much any more. It tears up your arm. Nobody enjoys microsurgery every couple-three years. But Matty has a good one. Two pitches later, I fly out to center. I think I've hit it hard, but it doesn't go anywhere. Dead ball, yeah.

"Batting third, Mel Sturgeon, left field!"

Mel's a lefty, too; he's 6–4, 225. He makes you thoughtful when he digs in, in other words. Mathewson gives him one low and away, and Mel goes with it. He flips it down the left-field line. Only about 280

there, so it lands in the seats. He trots around the bases with a big grin on his face. We're up a run.

Matty kicks the dirt once. He waits for them to throw the ball back out of the stands, which they sure don't in my time. Then he gets Pong-ju to ground to short. In come the Giants. Out we go.

"Roger Bresnahan, catcher!" the PA guy says. The catcher leading off? Okay.

Bresnahan steps in. He stares at Keyshawn. "Watcha got?" he asks, and adds that other word, the one you don't say in 2040.

Keyshawn fires a fastball, maybe 94, at his belly button. Bresnahan folds up like a clasp knife. Ball one. Bresnahan looks out again. Keyshawn puts a curve on the outside edge. Bresnahan flails. He can't hit it, any more than you can eat soup with a fork.

And Keyshawn gives him full gas, 99 or so, right at his coconut. I don't know how Bresnahan falls out of the way, but he does. As he's picking himself up, a little at a time, Keyshawn says, "You don't want to call me that again, White boy."

Bresnahan takes half a step toward him. He stops even before Kaz can get in front of him. He's 5–9 or so, 190 or 200. He's giving away ten inches and sixty pounds. He may be a racist so-and-so, but he doesn't have a death wish.

O'Day also hustles out there. He's an ump who works hard. Good for him. "Knock it off, both of you," he says. "Roger, you knew they played Negroes. Get back in the box." He turns to Keyshawn. "Enough from you, too. You made your point."

Baseball starts again. The American game, right? Two pitches later, Bresnahan bounces to me. I make sure I watch it into my tiny glove, and I throw him out. The next guy fans. Mike Donlin, who hits third, would be the MVP if they have one in 1905. He gets good wood on a fastball, but lines out to Sturgeon.

We put a guy on in the second—bad-hop single over Art Devlin's head at third—but don't do anything with him. They get their first hit in the second, when Bill Dahlen pokes one past me. I just touch it. With a real glove, it's an out, but not with the toy I'm using. Keyshawn catches Devlin looking to strand Dahlen.

Then Keyshawn hits. No DH in 1905. He looks dangerous up there. Maybe he is, if he makes contact. He doesn't. Mathewson does: he politely sticks one of those 78 mph fastballs in Keyshawn's ribs. Keyshawn drops the bat and goes to first without even looking at him.

Dave hits into a fielder's choice. Gilbert's throw is going to first before Keyshawn gets close. Just as well. I single into right. Dave stops at second. Up comes Mel with ducks on the pond.

Bresnahan trudges up the dirt path from the plate to the mound. Yeah, like the parks in Phoenix and Detroit and Philadelphia now, trying to look old-timey. I know what he's telling Mathewson. Don't let this guy beat you. Matty nods. Bresnahan swats him on the butt and gets behind the plate again.

Mathewson stretches, fires. Bresnahan's mitt pops. "Strike one!" O'Day yells. Mel steps out. I don't blame him. That isn't well-placed junk. That's gas, not quite as fast as Keyshawn but awful close. Christy's got the big arm. With the dead ball and the big field, he just doesn't use it all the time. He saves it for when he needs it.

Mel gets back in. More heat, this time two inches off the plate. Silk O'Day calls it a ball. Bresnahan jaws at him without turning around. Mathewson throws that fadeaway. Mel fouls it back onto the roof. It rolls down and they put it into play again. It's scuffed? Dirty? They don't care.

The next one makes Mel skip rope. Even count. Matty paints the outside corner, has to be 95. Mel's frozen. The ump punches him out. He shakes his head as he goes back to the dugout. Pong-ju hits the first pitch hard, but Donlin runs it down in left-center.

Keyshawn gets a quick out in the bottom of the third. When Matty steps in, they look at each other for a second. They both know what's coming. And it does. Keyshawn drills him in the butt, not too hard. Christy takes his base without a word. He gets away with hitting Keyshawn, and Keyshawn gets away with hitting him. Yeah, baseball.

Bresnahan's sitting dead red when the count gets to 1–2. Keyshawn throws him a slow curve straight from one of the Dutch Spinners. Probably learned it from Kees. Roger almost comes out of his shoes swinging, but he's a foot and a half out in front. He slams down the bat and cusses all the way to the dugout. George Browne, the right fielder, flies out on the first pitch.

Keyshawn's due up again in the fifth. Eddie asks, "Got one more in ya?" Keyshawn nods. Eddie says, "Go get 'em, Tiger." Keyshawn fans. They don't pay him to hit.

Bottom of the fifth, the Giants put two on with one out. An error, a sharp single. Our pen heats up. The crowd laughs; they don't play that way in 1905. Billy Gilbert, the Giants' second baseman, grounds one up the middle. I dive. I get lucky—it sticks in the glove. I give Pong-ju a backhand flip from my belly, and he turns the DP. Inning over.

A split second after Pong-ju throws to first, Devlin, who's running, knocks him sideways. In 2040, that ain't kosher. It is here. The 1905 guys got warnings beforehand. So did we. Pong-ju just gets up and goes in.

Devlin picks himself up, too. "Hell of a play," he says to me, and then, "Asshole."

"Up yours, too," I answer. He barks an almost-laugh.

Top of the sixth, Mel smacks one into the gap in right-center. Donlin can't get it. Neither can Browne. It goes almost to the rope. Mel's big, but he can motor. He zooms through a stop sign and beats the throw home. Insurance run.

Last four innings, we whipsaw the Giants: righty-lefty-right-lefty. They can't get used to anybody. They put a couple of guys on, but don't really threaten. McGraw lifts Mathewson in the eighth. Matty's no automatic out, but Sammy Strang's a real hitter. He works a ten-pitch walk, in fact; the game slows down while they throw back the foul balls. Doesn't help, because Bresnahan pops up.

Joe McGinnity pitches the ninth. We get one more run on two singles and a sac fly. The second single's mine, so I feel good.

Adilson closes out the bottom of the ninth in order. Fans start filing out unhappily. Coogan's Bluff empties. "Final score, Los Angeles Angels from 2040, three; New York Giants, nothing. Winning pitcher, Fredericks. Losing pitcher, Mathewson," the PA announcer bellows. He's never heard of saves. Adilson gets one anyhow.

We clean up. We change. The Giants want nothing to do with us: McGraw's a sore loser. We go back to the hotel. Can't wait to pass through the portal again. The past is kinda interesting to visit, but you wouldn't want to live there. ∎

How Climate Change Will Affect Baseball

Dr. Lawrence Rocks

What does climate change have to do with baseball? There are various factors: First, the relationship of climate to athlete health; second, the relationship of climate to analytics; third, the relationship of fans to the weather; and fourth, the relationship of weather to the business of baseball, as new construction of ballparks will have to take climate into account.[1]

In the past, many fans, rather than attending in person, have opted to watch games via video, whether on TV or streaming at home, or in local venues offering the broadcast, such as bars, resorts, etc. But in the 2020 season we saw the first time MLB fans had no in-person option. The COVID-19 pandemic mandated social distancing, resulting in the closing of schools, theaters, stadiums, restaurants, and other places where people gather. The 2020 season start was delayed, and when games finally did resume it was for a truncated 60-game season, played in empty stadiums. This was a first for Major League Baseball, where fans were forced, for the first time, to endure a period with no baseball at all not because of economic work stoppages or weather, but because of a pandemic, and then when the season started, to watch their favorite teams on TV only.[2] Some stadiums were filled with cardboard cutouts instead of real people.[3] Perhaps having seen the disruption on a grand scale that a global phenomenon like a pandemic can wreak on baseball, we are ready to envision what climate change might require of the sport.

MYSTERIES OF CLIMATE CHANGE

Before we get into baseball specifics, let us establish some basics about climate that will be relevant to our discussion. In 1972 I said that "a hotter world climate due to the 'greenhouse effect' will happen by the year 2030."[4] I am now adding to it a prediction of a "windier" climate. Why? There are contradictory forces at work on the future of weather. First, Nature has its own cycle of climate change, and second, human activities are changing the atmosphere. Let us consider Nature vs. Human contributions to climate.

Carbon dioxide concentration in the atmosphere has risen by 40% in the latest half-century due to human activities. However, atmospheric temperature for this time period has risen only a few percent, not anywhere close to 40%. This is a non-correlation between carbon dioxide concentrations and temperature of the Earth's atmosphere. Other forces must be at work. What could they be? The study of ice cores from the Greenland ice cap suggest that the Earth has previously experienced four "ice ages," and that we are "overdue" for another one. The layered structure of the ice cores includes layers that go back 400,000 years. The ratio of isotopes of oxygen in the ice—namely oxygen-16 to oxygen-18—reveals the existence of these previous "ice ages." The ice core data are compelling evidence that some large-scale changes in Earth's climate are natural phenomena.[5] Nature's climate changes occur in periods of tens of thousands of years. We can't make climate policies based on such long periods of time. It is apparent that in the near-term, the direction of the change will be towards a hotter climate, and that's what we must concern ourselves with.

My judgment is that the forces of Nature are getting ready for an ice age in the long term, in spite of human greenhouse gas emissions. But for the near term, we are due for unstable weather patterns, as the Earth's climate does a rollercoaster ride down into an ice age, due to arrive in a millennium or more. There will be warming spells that suddenly change into cooling spells—and vice-versa—where these spells last for hundreds of years, thus making both "changeable" and "unalterable" seem to be correct judgments about climate.

It seems self-evident that more information is needed about the temperature and the cloud cover of the Earth. For this reason I have made the following proposal for a weather observatory on the moon, which Topps commemorated with a special edition baseball card on January 27, 2021.[6]

THE NEXT FRONTIER: WEATHERSTATIONMOON OBSERVATORY

As I wrote in 1972, the "real value of Space will come in the area of special technologies and scientific research."[7] As it relates to harnessing space exploration for purposes of climate study, "the fabrication of special electronic components, the relaying of TV and other communication media by satellite, measurements of the Earth's resources by infrared photography, surveillance of weather by satellite…are Space's possibilities."[8] I have suggested that NASA deploy an unmanned weather station on the Moon to track climate changes. WeatherStationMoon would take the Earth's true temperature, in totality and in its regions, by telescopic observation of the infrared light emissions coming from the Earth. This will measure "climate warming." The station would also measure the Earth's cloud cover, in totality and in its regions, by telescopic observations of the visible and ultraviolet light reflections from the Earth's cloud cover (the Earth's "albedo"). An increase in cloud cover will make the Earth's climate colder.

An increase in greenhouse gases and an increase in cloud cover are opposing forces to each other. It is uncertain which will prevail. However, I believe that the opposition of these forces will make the near-term climate unstable, and likely more windy. This may or may not determine the future of climate. However, if a WeatherStationMoon was in operation, it could contribute to answering the question. Heat Energy is the flow of thermal energy between bodies of different temperatures; thus there is a distinction between heat energy and temperature.[9] The earth is likely to experience an overall temperature rise, but it could happen without an equal distribution of heat. Thus, the poles could become warmer and the equator cooler, without any overall temperature rise, or vice versa. This is yet a question for WeatherStationMoon to answer, if allowed to come to fruition.

Both detailed temperature mapping and detailed cloud cover movements would aid weather forecasting. Obviously, better long-range weather forecasts greatly help in commerce, shipping, air travel, virus and pathogen movements, military strategies, and planning all outdoor sports. The unmanned WeatherStationMoon would only need a small telescope, a solar array to generate electricity, and a battery pack to store electricity for the Moon's night, which is 14 Earth days long. The proposed WeatherStationMoon could be placed on the Moon by remote control, as the Mars vehicle was, or placed there by the astronauts of Project Artemis—which will send a mission to the Moon in 2024. From any landing site on the Moon, the Earth appears 3.5 times bigger than a full Moon appears from the Earth, changing phases of full-to-new Earth every 28 days. A moon-based observatory will

A Topps/Allen & Ginter commemorative card of Dr. Rocks.

see all the continents every day, and give a total picture of the Earth, as well as detailed parts of it, providing critical climate data to the United States and the Paris Accord Nations, who are in the process of drawing up economic solutions to climate change. I call upon the Paris Accord scientists to support such a project, whether by NASA, some other country, or private enterprise. Climate change should not become politicized. Observations from the Moon, if taken over years, should yield important data that could show whether the Earth's climate changes are mostly due to Nature's forces or human activities, and could serve to measure the effectiveness of government policies in the wake of the Paris Accords.

CLIMATE CHANGE EFFECTS ON BASEBALL

Now that we have some understanding of the large scale picture of climate change, let us talk about how the hotter and more volatile climate we will experience in the coming years will affect the sport of baseball. Did you know that as an elastomer, a baseball will lose elasticity in high temperatures, thus there is an optimal temperature range for the baseball's flexibility?[10] As we are learning, even small changes in the ball can have large effects on the field.[11] But the coming warmer climate will likely adversely affect the player (and spectator) more than the baseball. Baseball, as an industry, will need to make the following adjustments:

- **Baseball stadiums will need new roof design**
  Sudden adverse weather events will become more frequent in our near-term climate. Roofed stadiums will be a defense against such events as dust storms, very high temperatures, and very

high humidities, all of which can reduce attendance. The domed stadium has been a developing design since before the climate change issue arose. These roofs should incorporate solar energy. I wrote in 1980 that "possibly no single energy system has greater public support than solar heating. It is desirable, ultimately inevitable, and presently capable of conserving conventional heating fuels. Solar heating may have the potential to displace almost half the present consumption of natural gas and about 10% of oil-derived fuels."[12] Solar architecture will be the wave of the future for stadium construction.

• **Player facilities should be "on the roof" instead of in the basement**
Present stadium designs place most player facilities deep underground, and that is injurious to the health of the players. Such facilities as locker rooms, training gyms, medical stations, physical rehab facilities, and conference rooms can be

---

The Sequence of Chemical Events Causing Respiration Stress

1. Pollutants inactivate both lung enzymes and hemoglobin in red cells.
2. Oxygen blood-levels drop, in consequence.
3. The involuntary nervous system responds to increase the breathing rate.
4. Heart and respiration rates increase to raise oxygen blood-levels.
5. Adrenalin is released to activates the hormone system of the brain.
6. The voluntary nervous system is activated to help in respiration.
7. Extra breathing produces extra body heat.
8. Extra body heat is dissipated by lung evaporation of water.
9. Lung cooling causes even more work for the cardiovascular system.
10. Muscle-oxygen levels require the absorption of extra oxygen.
11. An exhaustion is felt at the conscious level.
12. Muscle coordination, from eyesight to movement, is impaired.
13. Physical performance, and emotional moods, become impaired.
14. A heart attack becomes increasingly more likely.

---

difficult to ventilate. This can lead to poor air quality from viruses, bacteria, dust, cleaning agents, and other chemicals, leading to headaches, mood changes, and airborne illnesses.

• **Ventilation will be more important than filtration**
It has been well established by air quality studies that in closed or indoor spaces, "ventilation" of air is far more important to health than is the "filtration" of air. Ventilation, which brings in fresh air, has less "air drag over persons" than does filtration, which recirculates air. The latest studies have come from COVID-19-related research on eliminating viruses from hospitals, restaurants, schools, and so on.

• **Rebuilding and retrofitting of stadiums should be done quickly**
And it can be. The 1950s is an example. During the 1950s the major leagues expanded across America from 16 teams located mostly in the American Northeast, to what is now teams spread across the continent. Almost every team built a new stadium during the "epoch of expansion." We now face another reason for the physical reformation of stadiums in baseball, which might be called the "epoch of climate adaptation."

• **Regional contests should be favored**
In the future, fans may consider "regional contests" more interesting than East coast vs. West coast games. From a historical perspective, many of the most fierce baseball rivalries have been from teams with regional proximity: Yankees/Red Sox in the Northeast, Cubs/Cardinals in the Midwest, and so on. In the heyday of the 1950s there were fierce "crosstown" rivalries between the Brooklyn Dodgers, New York Giants, and New York Yankees—and the Dodgers and Giants continue that rivalry on the West Coast today.[13] Thus, regionalism could be good for MLB's economics, not only because it would require teams to make less cross-continental travel, but because of heightened fan interest.

• **Long-Stay Scheduling will be economically favored**
In an age of unsettled weather, air travel will need to be reduced for reasons of safety and economics. This would favor long-stay scheduling, with regional teams playing in blocks of 5 to 7 games, instead of the 2- to 4-game series the

schedule currently favors. If weather conditions are unpredictable, and rescheduling becomes increasingly expensive, why wouldn't team ownership elect long-stay scheduling?

- **Spring Training sites may need to relocate**
  If the weather in Florida becomes too humid and Arizona too hot, MLB teams will need to relocate their spring training sites, and rather quickly. Many teams have already made the move from Florida to Arizona recently, as well as consolidating their Arizona facilities nearer to Phoenix. Teams would need to coordinate their moves, as well, since each team needs others to play exhibitions against. But to where? California could become too dry, etc.

- **Players may experience loss of muscle power**
  As temperature rises, the body will need to cool itself more. Most body cooling is accomplished by water evaporation from the lungs, not by sweating as is commonly believed. This will increase cardiovascular work of respiration, and that, in turn, will reduce body energy available for playing ball. Even if there is just a few percent drop in skeletal muscle energy the professional athlete will feel it.[14]

- **Player stats will be affected**
  A generally hotter climate will lessen air density. This will cause fly balls to travel further, fastballs to be faster, curveballs to curve less, and spin rates of pitches to be higher. These factors will cause pitchers to change their usage percentages on their pitch selection, and probably continue to fuel MLB's "launch angle revolution."

- **Eras in baseball will become statistically incomparable**
  Baseball statistical comparisons will change. In addition to the changes mentioned above due to hotter air, if player health is chronically impaired even by a small amount, "metrics" will follow the decline in their health. This affects the ability of teams to project success for players and draft picks, for coaches and players seeking to improve or diagnose the cause of slumps, and of fans to enjoy the performance of their favorite players. If the statistical record becomes meaningless for comparing players across eras (and some would say it has already become so), perhaps the "intangibles" of character, "clutch" performance, and teammate support will become

---

A Broadcast from the Future

Hello, everybody! The game is about to start. Looking at the scoreboard weather conditions, I see:

Temperature 98 degrees Fahrenheit, **Wind** 15 MPH, Humidity 60%, and the **Air Quality Index** at 26 "Good." But the big picture **Weather Map** shows a chance of a wind storm coming our way. The **Caution Sign** says a roof closure may be announced shortly.

Well, here comes the first pitch. Ball one. A 103 MPH fastball. Next pitch. There's a fly ball to dead center field, and over the 415 mark for a home run. It must have gone 500 feet. Well, that's the thin air for you, balls are thrown faster, and balls are batted further.

Next batter. An inside pitch. A curve ball that didn't curve much. It had high spin rate, but it didn't grip the thin air, so it didn't curve. Here's the next pitch. A ground ball past shortstop for a single. Wow. That grounder had speed. The hard infield made for a grounder too fast to field. Next batter stands in. Wait. A stolen base. Man on second base. Runner calls time. Needs to catch his breath. In high humidity he needs to breathe more for body cooling, and he needs to regain his oxygen level. Okay. Here's the pitch. A line drive to right center field, one bounce and off the wall for a double. One run in. It certainly looks like we're in for yet another high scoring game, folks.

Hold it. Folks, the wind is picking up. The umpire is coughing so much he has to call time. It looks like that wind storm is arriving. The roof will take ten minutes to close. It's getting dark and dusty in here. The air conditioning will take time to cool and clear such a big volume of air as our ballpark holds. So, let's count on a 20 minute delay.

---

more important in comparing players of the future with players of yesteryear?

- **Personal pollution-detection devices will become popular**
  Health concerns will foster a new industry for wearable pollution-detection devices. These are solid-state devices the size of a wrist watch that measure particles and gases in the air. They can be plugged into a cell phone for data transmission to others. In theory, millions of people could monitor our environment in real time. Many companies are making such devices. The technology is already here, but the popularity of the devices remains to be created. (If the capability were built into one of the name-brand

"smart" watches like the Apple Watch or Fitbit, the technology would instantly gain millions of users.[15])

• **Teams must prepare to handle an increase in respiratory illnesses**

As the Earth moves into more unstable weather, it will become windier. A windier climate will mean more dust in the atmosphere, and more respiratory stress for players (and spectators). Inhaling very fine dust particles inactivates the cilia in a person's mucous membranes, allowing the particles to enter the lungs. Asthma, or chemical emphysema, will result. Will the longevity of career necessary to reach the Hall of Fame be attainable for the players of the future, if air quality is so negatively affected?

CLIMATE POLICIES NOW

The question remains: if we want to mitigate the circumstances outlined above, what can we do? I have proposed an energy policy for the United States that will lessen human contribution to climate instability. This policy is the result of some fifty years of involvement with energy and environmental issues, beginning with my book *The Energy Crisis* in 1972. Among the steps we should take:

Nuclear electricity should be developed by making small reactors of no more than 300 megawatts.

Wind electricity should be harnessed by a "North American Off-Shore Wind Alliance" between Canada, the United States, and Mexico.

Solar power is best harnessed in "solar architecture" for heating and cooling of homes.

Abandon biofuels since they take more energy inputs than they yield as a fuel.

Recycling capabilities must be included in manufacturing to lessen resource consumption and to lessen waste disposal sites.

I believe that lessening the human contribution to climate change can only begin in meaningful ways when we have more accurate information about the Earth's temperature and its cloud cover dynamics. That's the best way to get consensus among the peoples of the Earth for policy-making support. ■

Notes

1. Hot Stove, "DeJong, Dr. Rocks discuss climate," MLB Network, January 28, 2021. https://www.mlb.com/video/dejong-dr-rocks-discuss-climate.
2. Bob Nightengale.,"Coronavirus: Doctor says baseball can 'lead the way' on coronavirus response," *USA Today*, March 18, 2020.
3. I was one of them. Ken Davidoff, "The drastic 2021 changes MLB teams should make to combat COVID-19," *New York Post*, December 9, 2020.
4. Lawrence Rocks, Richard Runyon, *The Energy Crisis* (New York: Crown Publishers, 1972), 177.
5. Jessica Stoller-Conrad, "Core questions: An introduction to ice cores," NASA Jet Propulsion Laboratory, August 14, 2017. https://climate.nasa.gov/news/2616/core-questions-an-introduction-to-ice-cores.
6. Topps Now WeatherStationMoon commemorative baseball card, January 27, 2021. https://www.topps.com/cards-collectibles/topps-now/weather-stationmoon-mlb-topps-now-regcard-wsm-1.html.
7. Rocks, Runyon, *The Energy Crisis*, 129.
8. Rocks, Runyon, *The Energy Crisis*, 129.
9. Lawrence Rocks, *Developing Your Chemistry Fundamentals* (Tulsa: PennWell Publishers, 1979).
10. CBS New York. Steve Overmyer report. November 9, 2017. "Cardinals' DeJong, Renowned Scientist Test Effects of Heat on Baseball."
11. Meredith Wills, "How One Tiny Change to the Baseball May Have Led to Both the Home Run Surge and the Rise in Pitcher Blisters," The Athletic, June 6, 2018. https://theathletic. com/381544/2018/06/06/how-one-tiny-change-to-the-baseball-may-have-led-to-both-thehome-run-surge-and-the-rise-in-pitcher-blisters.
12. Dr. Lawrence Rocks, *Fuels for Tomorrow*. (Tulsa: PennWell Publishers, 1980.)
13. Carl Erskine, Burton Rocks, *What I Learned from Jackie Robinson*. (New York: Mc-Graw-Hill, 2005).
14. John Brewer, *Run Smart: Using Science to Improve Performance and Expose Marathon Running's Greatest Myths*. Bloomsbury Sport, 2017. https://research.stmarys.ac.uk/id/eprint/2102
15. Emily Vogels, "About One in Five Americans Uses a Smart Watch or Fitness Tracker," Pew Research, January 9, 2020. https://www.pewresearch.org/fact-tank/2020/01/09/about-onein-five-americans-use-a-smart-watch-or-fitness-tracker.

For Immediate Release
March 13, 2030

Contact: Dusty Baker
dbaker@nashstars.com

NASHVILLE STARS JOIN MEXICO CITY AS 32ND TEAM IN MLB

(NASHVILLE, Tennessee)—Major League Baseball announced Monday that the Nashville Stars will be the second expansion team joining the league for the 2032 season.

After announcing in January that the Mexico City Matadors would become MLB's first expansion team since 1998, the league has evened the total number of teams at 32 with the arrival of the Stars. With the Russell and Ciara Wilson-owned Matadors announced as an American League team, the Nashville Stars are slated to be a National League team.

The decision was made by new MLB Commissioner Tony Reagins after Rob Manfred stepped down from the position in December.

Commissioner Reagins said, "This is a significant day in the history of Major League Baseball and the great city of Nashville. After landing a team in a city on the rise in Portland, we have decided expansion made the most sense in a city with culture that has already had a presence with our minor league system. Nashville has seen a significant rise in its population and the tourism numbers continue to reflect the growth of the city. We are thrilled to establish the Stars as a key element in the expansion of America's National Pastime."

With the announcement, the American and National Leagues will be split into a total of eight divisions, following suit with the NFL's current set-up of West, North, South, and East divisions. It has not yet been confirmed what teams will be moving into the newly implemented North and South divisions in both leagues.

Following the debates surrounding the cuts of minor league organizations—the fallout from which many believe contributed to Manfred's decision to step down—expansion was a top priority for Commissioner Reagins to address.

The Nashville Stars ownership group stemmed from the Music City Baseball group with the likes of former General Manager Dave Dombrowski, Managing Director John Loar, as well as Memphis native and 10-time Grammy winner Justin Timberlake. The Nashville organization agreed to pay $2 billion to enter the league after the Mexico City Matadors paid $1.9 billion to do the same two months ago.

Los Angeles Dodgers outfielder Mookie Betts said, "It's great to see Major League Baseball expanding to my hometown. It may be the Music City, but that is also a great sports town."

- 30 -

The "Natural"

Marty Resnick

Here we go. Logan was all nerves, with a touch of relief, as he walked from the on-deck circle to the right-handed batter's box. Styx's *Mr. Roboto* began playing over the PA. Logan smirked and accepted his new walk-up song and apparent nickname courtesy of his team, the Nashville Stars.

He had been playing this game for sixteen seasons, but it felt like his first at bat in the major leagues. Sixteen years ago he had been a lanky, olive-skinned twenty-year-old—a five-tool prospect. Now he was thirty-six, with a body that was more ripped than ever before, with one single tool—pure bionic power.

He completed his usual pre-bat routine, loosening and tightening his grip on the bat with his natural left hand below the hand of his synthetic right arm. Logan stood in, slightly bent his knees with a wide stance, and stared intently at the pitcher. Logan's natural left eye was transfixed on the pitcher, while his augmented right eye had one goal: track the ball. Most people couldn't tell the difference between the new eye and the one he'd lost, unless they caught a glimpse of the slight glow as the tracking software kicked in.

Logan needed to clear his mind, not think about what happened in the past, and focus on the at bat, but that was near impossible. *Two men on, two outs, bottom of the ninth, last chance to get two runs in, he thought to himself.*

Unfortunately, Pete "Predator" Perez was pitching and he was well known for throwing the fastest ball in the major leagues, especially because he threw up and in. Predator had put three batters on the Injured List this season already.

"Strike One!" the umpire exclaimed.

A fastball clocked at 106.5 MPH pounded the catcher's mitt. Logan had just stared at it.

What am I doing here?

A little over a year ago, Bridget had been by his side in the hospital. Pieces of their car had been removed from his eye, while his arm had been removed from his body.

Only to be replaced with cybernetic parts. He hadn't been sure he'd even make it back onto a field, much less to the big leagues. Now he was here and... "Ball!" The umpire's hand signaled the pitch was high.

Ten months of the team executives, the commissioner's office, and the MLB Players' Association debating if he was even eligible to play. Some felt strongly that he wasn't, throwing around words like *Freak*, *Cheater*, and *Has-been*. Logan had felt in his bones that his career was over.

"Strike two." The umpire looked at him as if wondering if Logan was actually going to swing at a pitch.

I'm wondering the same thing, Blue.

Logan had spent a month on a rehab assignment at Double-A Mexico City. Every day he'd stepped into the clubhouse, he'd expected to be told it would be his last. Most of his teammates accepted him. Some weren't sure what to make of a "part man, part machine player" but, to those minor leaguers, Logan was a legend. His opponents, on the other hand, seemed to protest every hit, every play, every game. It was exasperating.

Meanwhile, lawyers and the powers that be fought over whether he was ineligible by dint of his unfair advantage, or for liability concerns, or whatever other reasons they cooked up. They seemingly had so many options to put a stop to it, but they hadn't—yet.

"Ball!" the umpire declared, with another emphatic indicator the pitch was outside. "Two-two!" He was enjoying calling balls and strikes a bit too much.

Logan looked over his shoulder and saw the group of kids from the hospital rehabilitation center who encouraged him through his recovery. Logan had arranged tickets for all of them as a thank you. They were all clapping and yelling—still encouraging him right to this moment.

"Ball three." Logan barely heard the umpire as he hit the deck; the ball had nearly grazed his face. Predator clearly wanted to make Logan his fourth victim of the season.

This guy is insane! The crowd must've thought so, too, as an angry murmur spread through the stadium.

Logan climbed slowly to his feet.

Then he heard what the rehab center kids in the stands had started chanting: Hero. That's what Bridget

44

ALIAKSANDR MARKO

had called Logan. That's what the doctors called him for agreeing to take part in the experimental tests, for going through with the life-altering technologies for "architecting athletes" they'd been developing. *Hero* was how minor league teammates had referred to him.

The rest of the crowd was starting to pick up the chant from the kids. "Hero! Hero!" they cheered in one voice.

Full count. Time to focus. Logan looked to his third base coach. The sign was clear. Swing away.

The Predator's wind-up was a bit exaggerated, but Logan knew the heat was coming.

As the pitcher released the ball, Logan's augmented eye locked on to it. The 150 milliseconds any hitter has to respond to the pitch seemed like plenty of time, like the ball was in slow motion. The brain-computer interface coordinated Logan's eye and hands perfectly. The trajectory of the bat was right on. The launch angle, perfection.

The bat on ball made a sound that could be heard in the farthest reaches of the upper deck.

The pitch came in at a record 108.2 MPH. The ball left the building at a record 135.4 MPH. ∎

The Astrofuturism of Baseball

Harrie Kevill-Davies

In October 2019, three American astronauts aboard the International Space Station played baseball to mark the final game of the World Series, in which the Houston Astros were participating. In a video shared on Twitter, Jessica Meir pitched a 17,500 mile-per-hour fastball, which Drew Morgan hit with a makeshift bat, a flashlight.[1] Christina Koch, in the position of catcher, remarked that "as we prepare to send the first woman and the next man to the surface of the moon, we say we are proud to be from Houston, home of the astronaut corps."[2] Despite the novelty of this event, we can trace the history of baseball in space right back to the early Cold War. Even if space travel is not yet living up to the visions of science fiction, baseball being played on the ISS suggests life is imitating art. In this article, I trace the threads of connection between baseball and space from the mid-twentieth century to the present. I suggest that as we look to the future, if we are to have a truly international and collaborative presence in space, we must consider how—or whether—we can disentangle it from iconic signifiers of American culture such as baseball.

In 1951, the Bowman Gum Company of Philadelphia released a set of non-sports trading cards named *Jets, Rockets, Spacemen*. The set, released seven years prior to the launch of NASA, presented its readers with a vision of what space travel might look like in the near future. The card set features a young cadet blasting off into space for the first time from a base in Manhattan. Our hero works for the United States in concert with the United Nations and the so-called Solar League in the defense of universal peace, hinting at the spirit of the Truman Doctrine. Invoking the concept of light years, card number 91 of the set, "Videoscope," shows astronauts who have journeyed across galaxies watching "a baseball game that the Indians and White Sox had played eight years before."[3]

In "Videoscope" it is assumed that, even in outer space, astronauts will want to watch baseball. This implies future astronauts are from the United States, where baseball reigned as the national pastime at the time of the card set's issue.[4] In the context of contemporary non-sports cards, many of which taught American history, baseball takes its place within visions of America's future as well as within commemorations of America's past. Even in entirely non-sports sets, baseball makes several appearances, and cards featuring players proved particularly popular both at the time and among later collectors. By including baseball in cards that both look back at America's past and forward to its future, it is assumed not only that baseball will be endlessly present, but also that it is consequential to the development of American history and identity. The fact that Bowman's primary business was baseball cards may explain this inclusion; the firm wished to promote its most lucrative product. However, even in arenas other than trading card markets, the idea that baseball has a role to play in the maintenance of global democracy was not uncommon in this period. In his famous book, *Coca-Colonization and the Cold War*, historian Reinhold Wagnleitner cites an American general in Berlin in 1945 as saying, "We only have to teach German kids how to play baseball—then they'll understand the meaning of democracy."[5]

The idea that control of space might be critical to the global (or even galactic) spread of democracy was prevalent in this period, with space technology being developed primarily to preempt undeclared nuclear strikes. Although the early development of the space program was driven by the concept of the "free skies," according to which no nation could lay claim to portions of space, it was generally assumed that American technological supremacy would prevail, and that such policy could contain perceived nefarious plans for space on the part of the USSR[6]. However, during this earlier period of space development, scientists and science fiction writers known as astrofuturists used popular science and science fiction to promote the public interest in manned space travel, partly in order to increase support for the nascent space program.[7] These astrofuturist evangelists included both science fiction writers and actual scientists, including some of the rocket scientists who had come to the United States

91.   **Videoscope**

One day King Trunion took us to the brain people's observatory, where we saw a videoscope with which Krotonion astronomers often probe the Milky Way. The instrument had powers of magnification that cannot be expressed in Earthian terms. The King focused it on rays of earth-light that had traveled through space for eight years. The next moment we were looking at a baseball game that the Indians and White Sox had played eight years before.   Continued on Card 92

JETS ☆ ROCKETS ☆ SPACEMEN

© Bowman Gum, Inc., Philadelphia, Pa., U.S.A.
Reprinted 1985 WTW Productions

In one of the 1951 Bowman trading card sets, *Jets, Rockets, Spacemen*, visitors from Earth watch a baseball game beamed from Cleveland years earlier via alien technology.

from Germany after World War II to develop rocketry for missiles and space travel. The most famous of these, Wernher von Braun, was a staunch astrofuturist, whose plans for space travel were recorded in serial format in *Collier's Magazine* in 1952 and 1953, illustrated according to von Braun's plans by Chesley Bonestell. Von Braun painted his vision of the space future in decidedly suburban terms, with an emphasis on "professional activity and middle-class luxuries," placing himself "within a context of industrial activity and suburban domesticity, thereby offering his readers a fair example of how astrofuturism could make sense during the 1950s."[8] In essence, space was shown as a natural extension to postwar suburban affluence—an affluence that had itself been driven by the scientific and technological developments that had brought about victory in WWII, the nuclear program, and the idea of sending men to space.[9] Although space was indeed the final frontier, in the eyes of astrofuturists, the point of getting there was to replicate the prosperous mode of living of the postwar United States.

In this context, we can see how baseball, as a critical component of the American Way of Life, might fit neatly into visions of intergalactic travel. Today it is striking how suburban many of the places visited by the hero of *Jets, Rockets, Spacemen* appear. Although the space settlements are referred to as cities, they follow regular layouts like tract housing (and in the early days of the postwar suburbs, tract housing plans were also "advertised and perceived" as cities.)[10] Space stations are connected by curving highways and railways, resembling those advertised by Bohn Aluminum and Brass Corporation, Vanadium Corporation of America, and contemporary engineering firms. Space buildings and ships alike have picture windows, providing wide vistas over the galaxy, while ships also have "telescreens," just as suburban homes had televisions, their "windows on the world."[11] The design of ships closely

resembles that of contemporary cars and futuristic imaginations of other modes of transport in contemporary advertising, as well as domestic appliances. They feature the "bulbous streamlined forms" common to the period, and as such would have been familiar to targeted boy readers not only as staples of science fiction but also as everyday items.[12] Therefore it is not surprising that in the Videoscope card, astronauts use a machine that bears this kind of design to watch that most American of sports, baseball.

This collapsing of outer space with familiar Americana can also be seen clearly across depictions of baseball in space. Another case study is the popular Hanna-Barbera animated show, *The Jetsons*. This cartoon gave us a glimpse of how baseball might be played in the future. In the 1985 episode "Team Spirit," the consummate organization man George Jetson appears as the star pitcher for his firm, Spacely Sprockets, in a game of Spaceball against its rival, Cogswell Cogs.[13] Both companies rely on robots to play the game, with Cogswell warming up against a robot pitcher, George Jetson attended by a remote-controlled robot valet, and other robots participating as players. This vision of baseball, coming at the height of the Reagan presidency, and in the wake of the Strategic Defense Initiative (also known as "Star Wars"), tapped into contemporary ideas about the possible future of the United States in relation to space exploration.

During the 1980s, despite a number of catastrophic, tragic setbacks, NASA was invested in building reusable space shuttles that could run service missions to space telescopes, and could build and populate an international space station in orbit. In this sense, the 1980s space program was heightening the mundanity of space travel, converting it from a monumental effort to achieve a single, defined mission, to a routine transportation and habitation system. The fact that *The Jetsons* was revived during this period fits with this ethos—space travel was a hot topic, but was presented in terms of setting up daily life and routine there, with All-American home comforts, including baseball. *The Jetsons* showed us what it might be like to live, work, and play baseball in other galaxies, fueling the expansion of the American Dream into new frontiers.

The initial run of *The Jetsons* was launched in 1962, during a time when space fervor was all the rage, just a year after President John F. Kennedy's "Moon Shot" speech, in which he spoke to a Joint Session of Congress about the nation's aspirations for the mastery of space.[14] The first episode aired a mere 11 days following Kennedy's well-known speech at Rice University in which he said, "I regard the decision last year to shift our efforts in space from low to high gear as among the most important decisions that will be made during my incumbency in the office of the Presidency."[15] In that speech, Kennedy framed manned space travel as a *fait accompli*, the natural conclusion to centuries of scientific research. He also famously likened space exploration to earlier American frontiers, presenting it as a place to be conquered, tamed, and inhabited. As Kennedy primed both Congress and the population for the excitement of space travel, astrofuturists had been doing just that for a decade or more, using popular science and science fiction, partly in order to increase support for the space program among the public. As De Witt Douglas Kilgore points out, astrofuturist boosters depicted space as "not an impossible Arcadia but as a feasible movement into new territories that conformed to established and predictable laws," and showed visions of space composed of "familiar tools and mundane, lived spaces."[16] If we take up this claim, *Jets, Rockets, Spacemen* and *The Jetsons* can be seen as astrofuturist pieces, in that they both demonstrate life in space as a normal extension of American family life, with all the same routines and relationships one would expect in an archetypal suburban American town. Both artifacts assume that manned space travel will occur, result in an expansion of the American Dream, and look like American life—complete with baseball.

These examples show that for all the talk of collaborationist ideals, the inhabitation of space has been seen as an American project that would spread American values across the world and even across galaxies, and the presence of baseball in space marks American cultural dominance during the Cold War. However, by the late 1980s, baseball faced a potential demise; in a 1988 episode of *Star Trek: The Next Generation* set in the twenty-fourth century, we learn that the popularity of baseball spread across the world, then waned. An episode of *Star Trek Deep Space 9* confirms that the last ever World Series was played in 2042.

Given the highly collaborative and internationalist (and even intergalactic) vision of space put forward by the Star Trek franchise, the diminishing presence of such a strong signifier of American cultural dominance makes sense. That said, baseball does appear in several episodes, most notably the Deep Space 9 episode "Take Me Out to the Holosuite" in which the crew of the space station are challenged to a game of baseball by visiting Vulcans. Although baseball is supposedly no longer popular by the twenty-fourth century, and the DS9 space station is inhabited by humans from other nations than America, and by other species, the game still appears as a manifestation of American culture, once again showing us that space is an American venture. The space station Commander, Sisko, is portrayed as an American who nostalgically enjoys playing baseball with his son Jake. In the show, baseball is described as "a contest of courage, teamwork, and sacrifice" and one that requires "faith" and "heart," all of which could reasonably be described as values associated with the American way of life. Although most of the crew have never played baseball before, and have to read the rules to understand even the most basic tenets of the game, the space station holosuite is able to recreate a baseball stadium with bleachers and a working scoreboard, while all the players wear standard twentieth-century baseball uniforms. Therefore, even in a vision of space that is highly progressive in its approach to inclusivity and diversity, baseball remains a signifier of an American culture to which all residents of the space station have access. Even in a distant space station, the hegemonic sway of American culture is seen as privileged.

Likewise, when we see astronauts aboard the International Space Station playing baseball in space in 2019, we are reminded that even in this collaborationist venture, American cultural norms are highlighted and broadcast around the world. The video provided a fun promotion for the World Series, and an entertaining view for viewers on Earth of life aboard the ISS. Moreover, it gave us a glimpse of how both Major League Baseball and NASA have made strides toward equity and diversity in the twenty-first century. MLB has increased its outreach to young female players and female fans, while NASA is sending increasing numbers of women to space. However, even amid twenty-first century pushes toward equity, when we put men and women into orbit, the ways in which we imagine it happening have often been foreshadowed by science fiction. Even on the final frontier, we aim to replicate the comforting signifiers of American culture that proliferated in the postwar period. As we look forward to 2040, and as SpaceX works toward Elon Musk's goal of colonizing Mars, the idea of playing baseball in space becomes less far-fetched. But the fact that we have this idea at all has its roots in Cold War American expansionism and science fictional visions. Despite the noble twenty-first century aims of inclusivity, and the inherent collaborationism of projects like the ISS, it has become difficult to envision the future of space as anything other than dominated by the United States, and one way in which this is signified is the existence of baseball in space. ■

Notes

1. Jennifer Leman, "Watch NASA Astronauts Throw a 17,500 mph Fastball" in *Popular Mechanics*, October 31, 2019. https://www.popularmechanics.com/space/satellites/a29655302/nasa-astronaut-fastball (accessed March 24, 2021).

2. Tweet by @MLBonFOX, October 25, 2019, including video from the International Space Station and the text "Ever wonder what it would be like playing baseball in space? Take a look at our friends from @Space_Station enjoying the game we love!" https://twitter.com/MLBONFOX/status/1187914643991220224?s=20.

3. The specifics of the game are not mentioned, but the Indians played the White Sox 22 times in the 1943 season, including several (6) double headers.

4. The astronauts could plausibly be Korean, given that baseball was popular there from the nineteenth century, but we are reminded that baseball was introduced to Korea by missionaries, placing it firmly within the notion of baseball as part of a mission to civilize the racial or cultural other.

5. Reinhold Wagnleitner, *Coca-colonization and the Cold War: the cultural mission of the United States in Austria after the Second World War*, E Book ed. (Chapel Hill, NC: University of North Carolina Press, 2000), 1. https://search.library.northwestern.edu/discovery/fulldisplay/alma9917669754202441/01NWU_INST:NULVNEW.

6. See R. Cargill Hall, "Origins of U.S. Space Policy: Eisenhower, Open Skies, and Freedom of Space," in *Exploring the Unknown: Selected Documents in the History of the U.S. Civil Space Program*, ed. John M. Logsdon et al., The NASA History Series (Washington D.C.: National Aeronautics and Space Administration NASA History Office, 1995). and Roger D. Launius, "Space Technology and the Rise of the US Surveillance State," in *The Surveillance Imperative: Geosciences During the Cold War and Beyond*, ed. Simone Turchetti and Peder Roberts (New York, NY: Palgrave MacMillan, 2014).

7. Several texts discuss early astrofuturism among science fiction writers, like Robert A. Heinlein and Arthur C. Clarke, as well as scientists associated with the early space program, notably rocketry scientist Wernher von Braun. These texts include McCurdy, Howard E., *Space and the American Imagination*. 2nd Ed. Baltimore, MD: The Johns Hopkins University Press, 2011, McCurdy, Howard E., and Roger D. Launius. *Imagining Space: Achievements, Predictions, Possibilities, 1950–2050*. San Francisco, CA: Chronicle Books LLC, 2001., Kilgore, Douglas De Witt, "Astrofuturism: Science, Race, and Visions of Utopia in Space," University of Pennsylvania Press, 2003, and Geppert, Alexander C.T. (ed), *Imagining Outer Space—European Astroculture in the Twentieth Century*, Palgrave Macmillan, 2018.

8. "Astrofuturism: Science, Race, and Visions of Utopia in Space," University of Pennsylvania Press, 2003, https://www.upenn.edu/pennpress/book/13909.html.

9. There is a wealth of writing on how technological advances of the wartime period both powered and infiltrated design, appliances, and daily life in the postwar suburbs. For more, see Whitfield, S.J. 1991. *The Culture of the Cold War*, Baltimore, MD, The Johns Hopkins University Press., Colomina, B., Brennan, A. & Kim, J. (eds.) 2004. *Cold War Hothouses: Inventing Postwar Culture, from Cockpit to Playboy*, New York: Princeton Architectural Press and Cohen, L. 2003. *A Consumers' Republic: The Politics of Mass Consumption in Postwar America*, New York, Vintage Books.

10. Barbara Miller Lane, *Houses for a New World: Builders and Buyers in American Suburbs, 1945–1965* (Princeton, NJ: Princeton University Press, 2015), 13.

11. For more on how television operated as a window on the world, see Lynn Spigel, *Make Room for TV: Television and the Family Ideal in Postwar America* (Chicago: University of Chicago Press, 2013/11/26/, 2013). http://www.amazon.com/Make-Room-TV-Television-Postwar-ebook/dp/B00ICQO8AM/ref=mt_kindle?_encoding=UTF8&me=.

12. Laura Scott Holliday, "Kitchen Technologies: Promises and Alibis, 1944–1966," *Camera Obscura* 47, no. 16:2:87.

13. *The Jetsons*, season 2, episode 31, "Team Spirit," directed by Art Davis, Oscar Dufau, Carl Urbano, Rudy Zamora, Alan Zaslove, written by Gary Warne, aired November 11, 1985, in syndication. https://www.imdb.com/title/tt1287171.

14. John F. Kennedy, The Decision to Go to the Moon, Speech before Joint Session of Congress, delivered May 25, 1961, National Aeronautics and Space Administration NASA History Office, https://history.nasa.gov/moondec.html (accessed March 22, 2021).

15. John F. Kennedy, Address at Rice University on the Nation's Space Effort, delivered September 12, 1962. https://www.jfklibrary.org/learn/about-jfk/historic-speeches/address-at-rice-university-on-the-nations-space-effort (accessed March 22, 2021).

16. Kilgore, "Astrofuturism: Science, Race, and Visions of Utopia in Space," 3.

Baseball in 2040
The Digital Viewer

Allison R. Levin

There is no denying that baseball is getting more expensive, with fans being priced out of watching games in person.[1] The result is fans struggling to recreate an in-person experience at home through so-called "third venues."[2] These may include setting up multiple screens to get as many different perspectives as possible—from social media to Statcast to camera views not provided on the over-the-air-broadcast. Fans are also texting, Face Timing, posting on social media, or otherwise communicating with friends during the game to maintain a communal feel. Unfortunately, it is nearly impossible to replicate the unique feeling one gets from attending a game—the atmosphere, smells, and excitement just don't exist when watching from your living room. All of this means that fans are frustrated, and many are tuning out of baseball.[3] Luckily, fundamental changes will emerge over the next twenty years, driven by technology, that will bring at-home fans back into the game. The various advances will center around two main features—the fan's desire to watch the game on their terms and replicating a communal feel. By 2040, fans will be fully immersed in the game through advances in artificial intelligence (AI), augmented reality (AR), virtual reality (VR), and 4D effects (4DX).

To understand how the viewing experience will change, we must examine how second screens or double screens are used in 2021. Further, I will look specifically at millennials and Gen Z to predict how the technology will grow, because these populations will become the core audience watching the games as well as the ones to develop and create the technology we will be using in 2040. Currently, second or double screens allow fans to establish social connections and interactions while watching games live.[4] This technology is essential for millennials, among whom only 31 percent report they prefer to watch the game alone.[5] Since younger fans crave a shared sport experience even when watching at home, fan interaction will become a significant focus beyond what currently exists.[6] Growth in this area will begin by expanding the devices and platforms people can use, in order to make it easier to watch what you want, how you want, and where you want. Athlete- and team-generated content is also rapidly increasing, which helps fans feel a stronger tie to both brands and build a shared community with people who are enjoying the same content.[7] These expanded content opportunities will lead to fans enjoying multiple interactive experiences while watching the game.[8] Over 55% of millennials report that they currently use social media to get updates on their favorite team and players while watching the game.[9] Currently, these interactive experiences include fans watching a game on a television (or streaming the broadcast to a digital device) while connecting on social media platforms to communicate with fellow fans (in real time) as well as getting to know the team and players through their content. The trend of combining the consumption of the broadcast with social media interaction is growing. As the interactive experiences continue to expand, so will the fans' desire to augment what they are watching live through these third venues.[10] As the ones researching and developing these technologies while also making up the core audience, millennial and Gen-Z fan preferences will translate into what we will be using by 2040. Fans should expect the second screen process to become more streamlined, allowing more options to replicate an in-venue experience, including the all-important sense of community.

This streamlining will occur through a complete overhaul in the presentation of games incorporating AR, AI, VR, and 4DX to give fans a fully personalized and immersive experience. First, we must understand what each of these terms means for baseball coverage. The most logical place to start is with AR, as we already see great strides in this technology with Statcast. Specifically, AR is how technology enhances parts of the viewer's physical world with digital content.[11] We are witnessing the start of this revolution with over-the-air broadcasts overlaying launch angles and home-run distances over the plays on the telecast. This is only the cusp of the potentional for AR. The other three, AI, VR, and 4DX, are not nearly as developed in the context of baseball; however, all four working

A young boy does "the Wave" as a digital spectator to a baseball game, from his own couch at home.

together will be crucial to the future of our digital viewing experience.

For our purposes, AI is building systems using human reasoning as the model to create better products and services.[12] In other words, it is not what we typically think of, so-called strong AI, where the goal is trying to achieve a perfect replica of the human mind. Instead, it is about creating more intelligent technology that assists the consumer—or, in this case, the viewer—in meaningful ways.[13] AI can be used to predict what at-bats a viewer would want to see and alert them when those players are at bat, to respond to questions, or even make in-game purchases or place bets.

VR is not a new concept, but it has not been fully explored in the context of baseball yet. Virtual reality is a computer-generated simulation where a person interacts with an artificial three-dimensional world, typically using cumbersome goggles and gloves. However, technology is advancing to where soon people will need only a special pair of glasses to access the virtual world.[14] VR will allow viewers to feel like they are at the game from wherever they choose to watch. We mustn't confuse VR with AR. VR provides an immersive experience, while AR enhances the world we view by providing graphical overlays.[15]

The final element of the technology that will change how we view games is 4DX. 4DX is not new, but it is not widely used outside theme parks and high-end movie theaters. If you have ever been on a ride or gone to a movie where your seat has moved in time to what was occurring on the screen, you felt the appropriate weather (warm or cold air, wind, rain) and experienced scents that matched what you saw on the screen; you have experienced 4DX.[16]

Now that we understand the basic idea of how these four technologies work, we can begin to imagine how they all will work together to revolutionize how we will watch the game in 2040. It is easy to imagine somebody deciding to watch baseball and sitting in their 4DX chair to enjoy the game. They would put on their simple, lightweight VR frames (by 2040, we will no longer need the cumbersome goggles and gloves) and be transported to the stadium of their choosing. They can select any view from the stadium to enjoy the game—from the bleachers to the front row to the dugout—there are no limits. Even better, by simply turning their head or asking the AI for a different angle, they can have a 360-degree view of the game.[17] The 4DX chair will allow the fan to replicate the in-person experience by providing the same conditions those in the stadium feel and smell. The chair will be fully customizable, with fans choosing what in-person elements they want to experience—perhaps choosing to experience all the smells but forgoing the weather, so they don't have to experience the rain, freezing cold, or heat and humidity.

But that is just the start of the experience. Through the VR frames, one can seamlessly move from game to game in the snap of a finger, and when we add in AI and AR, the experience becomes truly personal. Through AI, fans will be able to invite friends to join them in the interactive experience with a simple voice request (akin to today's "Hey, Siri/Alexa/Google"). Even better, everyone can be present and enjoy the social element of baseball, even if they are not all watching the same game. If you want a friend to see something exciting in one of the games, you just ask them to move over to it (again just by directing the

AI), and everyone can watch it together. In essence, many people worldwide will have all that day's games at their fingertips, available for simultaneous play.

Another change that will develop out of this technology is fans choosing what announcers they are hearing. While subscribers to MLBTV through MLB.com can already swap the audio on many streaming video broadcasts, including alternate languages, and Amazon has started exploring this option in their NFL broadcasts, it will continue to become more prevalent and easier to accomplish.[18] If a viewer wants to change announcers, all they'll do is ask the AI to switch it. We also expect there will be personal replay capabilities, including the ability to listen to the same play again but with a different set of announcers. Viewers will also customize their experience by controlling (through AR) what shows up on the screen during the broadcast. Instead of being stuck with the universal "score bug" we have in the corner of our screens now, they will have access to a near-unlimited choice of options, including what statistics they prefer to see, what Statcast overlays appear, and how the screen is formatted.

Further, using a combination of VR and AR, the fans who like to check social media or online discussion during the game will no longer need to juggle multiple devices or screens. They will easily be able to swipe their social feeds into the main viewing area, check what others are saying, and then move them back out of the direct line of sight. The AI's excellent voice recognition will make it seamless for fans to post when they want to, regardless of whether the feed is up on the screen. If a favorite pitcher strikes out the side, it will be as simple as saying, "post the Cardinals are dominating." The AI will also provide notifications when replies or messages arrive, or if friends or favorite accounts post. The user can have them read aloud or swipe them onto the screen, as well as choose where these feeds appear, ensuring the game remains visible.

Through the capabilities of AR built into the VR experience, fantasy players will be able to see the statistics of their active players overlayed on the game broadcast. Through AI technology, the fans can be alerted when their fantasy players are coming up to bat or pitching in other games throughout the league(s), and potentially see that action instead of—or in addition to—the game they are already watching. Miss a key play? No problem, just ask the AI for a replay, and it will pop up on the screen. Since its legalization in the US, sports betting is a rising trend being embraced by Major League Baseball, with

commissioner Rob Manfred telling reporters in 2019 that he sees it as a "great source of fan engagement."[19] By 2040, it's possible the AR will allow fans to access the biometric profile of the player, giving them more insight into the player's fatigue level, perhaps helping the fan make more informed betting decisions.[20] And much like our current fantasy sports experience, one will easily be able to access any daily bets and place in-game wagers, only these will be through the accessible AI features built into the viewing experience.

With this technology, fans will be able to call up plays that happened in other games, or years or centuries ago, by asking the AI for the footage, much like fans today can use the MLB Film Room launched by MLB in 2020, only incorporated into their 4DX display.[21] If somebody wants to see a replay of a play that just happened, they can have it show up on the screen and view it from 360 degrees to make their own decision about the call. If a team is bringing in a pitcher to face a particular batter, one can easily ask the AI to see a replay of every time that pitcher and batter have faced each other. If fans argue about a particular historical play, they simply ask the AI to access it and share it with everyone, hopefully deciding the argument. Further, it is easy to imagine a situation where one disagrees with a replay or where a hitter goes against their trend versus the pitcher and simply asking the AI to switch to "video game mode" to replay it in the VR frames to see if the result is any different.

Fans are craving the best possible experience when watching from home while not losing the human, communal element of watching the game with friends.[22,23] These technological advances are on the way. Allowing fans to watch anywhere without the need for anything other than a pair of VR frames with incorporated AI and AR technology (the 4DX chair adds to the at-home experience), baseball will fully adapt to the wants and needs of the next generation of fans. There is already an indication that these advances will increase viewership. More than 40 percent of the next generation of fans point to AR as something that would increase their desire to watch the game, and 54 percent say that VR would increase the likelihood of them watching a game.[24] By 2040, the at-home viewing experience will have changed significantly. In the process, the fans who are currently reluctant viewers will be drawn in through the complete customization and integration of their interests and desires. ∎

Notes

1. Josh McHugh, Ethan Watters, and Po Bronson, P. (Eds.). "The Future of Sports." (September 2015). Retrieved from http://www.gannett-cdn.com/usatoday/editorial/sports/The-Future-of-Sports-2015-Report.pdf.

2. McHugh, Watters, Bronson, "The Future of Sports."

3. Dave Zirin. "Why No One Watches Baseball Anymore." *The Nation*, July 2, 2019, www.thenation.com/article/archive/why-no-one-watches-baseball-anymore-mlb-red-sox-yankees.

4. Adam Deutsch, Kat Harwood, Lee Teller, and Chad Deweese. "The future of sports broadcasting: Enhancing digital fan engagement." (2019). Retrieved from https://www2.deloitte.com/us/en/pages/technology-media-and-telecommunications/articles/enhancing-digital-fan-engagement.html.

5. Deutsch, Harwood, Teller, and Deweese, "The future of sports broadcasting."

6. McHugh, Watters, Bronson, "The Future of Sports."

7. Oren Simanian, Tomer Yehudayan, and Nathan Moyse. "Top 9 tech areas that are changing sports in 2021." (February 1, 2021). Retrieved from https://www.calcalistech.com/ctech/articles/0,7340,L-3890794,00.html.

8. Pietro Marini. "The future of AI in sports for players, broadcasters and fans." (June 25, 2020). Retrieved from https://thefutureshapers.com/the-future-of-ai-in-sports-for-players-broadcasters-and-fans.

9. Deutsch, Harwood, Teller, and Deweese, "The future of sports broadcasting."

10. Marini, "The future of AI in sports."

11. "What Is Augmented Reality?" The Interaction Design Foundation, July 22, 2020. https://www.interaction-design.org/literature/topics/augmented-reality.

12. Bernard Marr. "The Key Definitions Of Artificial Intelligence (AI) That Explain Its Importance." *Forbes*, February 14, 2018. https://www.forbes.com/sites/bernardmarr/2018/02/14/the-key-definitions-of-artificial-intelligence-ai-that-explain-its-importance/?sh=51dd2ed84f5d.

13. Marr, "The Key Definitions Of Artificial Intelligence."

14. Cory Mitchell. "Virtual Reality." Investopedia, November 21, 2020. https://www.investopedia.com/terms/v/virtual-reality.asp.

15. Mitchell, "Virtual Reality.".

16. "WHAT IS 4DX?" 4DX. Accessed April 2, 2021. https://www.cj4dx.com/aboutus/about-us.php.

17. McHugh, Watters, Bronson, "The Future of Sports."

18. Deutsch, Harwood, Teller, and Deweese, "The future of sports broadcasting."

19. Greg Ryan, "MLB's Rob Manfred on Sports Gambling, Disney, and Trump," *Boston Business Journal*, March 6, 2019. https://www.bizjournals.com/boston/news/2019/03/06/mlb-s-boss-on-sports-gambling-disney-and-trump.html.

20. Marini, "The future of AI in sports."

21. Thomas Harrigan, "Best Way to Binge Baseball? MLB Film Room," September 8, 2020, MLB.com. https://www.mlb.com/news/mlb-film-room-launch.

22. Darryl Morey, Jessica Gelman, Bill James, Nate Silver, and Katie Nolan. "Sports in 2040: Hindsight is 2020." (March 6, 2021). Retrieved from https://www.sloansportsconference.com/event/sports-in-2040-hindsight-is-2020

23. Marini, "The future of AI in sports."

24. Deutsch, Harwood, Teller, and Deweese, "The future of sports broadcasting."

Artificial Intelligence, Machine Learning, and the Bright Future of Baseball

Brian Hall

Baseball is a sport steeped in tradition, but there are relatively new and rapidly developing technologies that are already impacting baseball and will continue to shape its future: artificial intelligence ("AI") and machine learning. We are currently living in the midst of a technological revolution powered by AI and machine learning. Six out of seven Americans carry an AI-powered assistant with them everywhere—their smartphone.[1] With Google Translate, we have a universal communication device that 15 years ago we thought was something we could only see on *Star Trek*. There are many other uses of AI and machine learning in industry that have far reaching impacts on our society, such as the coronavirus vaccines that were developed in record time, aided by new techniques powered by machine learning. Few people could have predicted how quickly and seamlessly AI and machine learning have become part of our lives. I suspect we will also underestimate how quickly it will be integrated into baseball and other sports.

For a baseball team, poor decision-making can lead to costly mistakes in terms of dollars, performance, and wins. Knowing this, teams have turned to the science of decision-making, viewing decisions as being the product of an interplay between two parts of the mind: "System 1"—a person's quick, instinctual response, and "System 2"—rational analysis that is a product of slower, thoughtful reasoning.[2] When a person is asked to complete a task requiring cognitive effort, that person may inadvertently rely on an instinctual response (System 1) rather than expend the mental energy needed to make the best rational decision (System 2).[3] Naturally, sabermetricians are champions of System 2 thinking. Sabermetrics, with its goal of better, quantitatively supported decision-making, has also led to large amounts of new data to analyze. However, the human mind and traditional statistical techniques can only process new information up to a point before being overwhelmed.[4] In contrast, the strength of AI and machine learning is that large amounts of data are its rocket fuel, and the larger the dataset the better.[5] Baseball has created new sources of data (such as Statcast) and statistics (spin rate, barrel, etc.). Seven terabytes (7 TB) of data are gathered by MLB at each game.[6] Machine learning and AI can detect patterns in these otherwise overwhelming mountains of new data, and teams will be able use these insights to improve their decision-making.

What kind of decisions are teams looking for AI and machine learning to help with? With the growth of player data, these tools can be used to try to crack the nut of predicting player performance.[7] It is hard enough to try to predict a player's future performance with years of high school, college, and minor league stats. But what about adding more contemporary statistics such as exit velocity, barrels, launch angle, spin rate, OAA, extension and arm strength? And how does that interact with a player's age, weight, build, running speed and other measures of athletic ability? To analyze this information, machine learning models can be built using the data of past players. Based on what the computer learns from these past players during this "training" phase, it can build a model to predict how well players will perform in their careers. The accuracy of these models is then judged by setting aside some prospects that the computer has not seen before, and having the computer predict how bright the future is for these players. If these prospects are players from the past, with the results of these careers already known, they can be used as "test" data to judge how well the machine learning model performed in predicting the future performance of these players. The models that do well can be used by teams to better project the careers of current prospects, while those models that do poorly in the "test" phase will be discarded.

The batter and pitcher match-up has always been a chess match, but each side can now be aided by insights produced by an AI-assistant. Currently, it is becoming more common to see players in the dugout studying analytics on their iPads intently when new pitchers come into the game. Within two decades, expect wearable devices to become widely adopted, with perhaps "smart" glasses or contact lenses conveniently providing such information. Such advice could include the probability of the location and type of the next pitch.[8] Elon Musk, through his Neuralink project, expects to take this further by developing implantable brain-machine interfaces. While it may seem outlandish today, it may be common (and more cost-efficient) to upgrade our brain chips than computers or phones, which require external displays. If information is no longer accessed through an iPad on the bench, but through wearables or implants, AI could be paired to help provide advice. Of course, MLB would need to make a decision as to whether players would be allowed to access information while in a game. When making such a decision, it is important to remember that ultimately it is up to the player to throw the pitch, make contact with the bat, catch the ball and throw it. An AI assistant would not enhance a player's physical abilities, only aid the player's judgment.

Recent advances in machine learning have also aided pitchers in training, detecting patterns in pitching mechanics—previously unobservable to the human eye—to avoid arm stress as well as potentially increase a pitcher's velocity, movement, or spin rate.[9] There are hundreds of biomechanical variables that could influence pitcher arm health. Consider the linking of the joints that start at the ankle, move to the knee, hips, shoulders and elbow before ending at the wrist (the "kinetic chain"). Previously, it was difficult to determine which of hundreds of variations in body movement were responsible for creating arm stress. However, with a machine learning approach, the causes of arm stress can be better identified without needing to sacrifice performance, such as arm velocity.[10] Given this, expect pitcher velocities to continue trending upwards.

Even data on the neural activity of batters and pitchers are being used to measure, among other things, the impact of pressure on performance.[11] For example, by measuring electrical activity in a batter's brain during the time between the pitcher releasing the ball and the ball crossing the plate, researchers are starting to quantify how cognitive activity is correlated with on-field metrics (OBP, SLG, and OPS). In the coming years, it should be possible to use machine learning to detect more granular patterns in cognitive activity. This would allow for the creation of new player statistics that are not a measure of the player's external performance, but a measure of a player's inner world. For example, a statistic could be created to measure how well a batter or pitcher's brain handles stress or how quickly a batter's brain can react and adapt to different pitches. These new "brain" statistics

could be valuable in identifying the progression of talented players and could become an important statistic to help predict which players are likely to succeed.

Previously, player injuries could be seen as largely unpredictable and a result of bad luck. Recent work relying on data based on player age, body type, usage and playing style has attempted to better identify risk factors impacting a given player's risk of injury.[12] European soccer currently appears to have taken the lead in creating new sources of player data for use with AI injury predictions models. Researchers were able to improve their predictions on the risk of injury for a soccer player using machine learning and these data related to average playing time, position, age, body mass, quality of sleep, fatigue, and various neuromuscular factors such as joint range of motion, balance, strength of the hip adduction, core stability, and knee flexion.[13] If soccer teams are successful in reducing injury rates by utilizing these techniques to decrease the playing times of players flagged at higher risk, expect baseball teams to develop and adopt similar techniques.[14] By detecting patterns to injuries that could be avoided by decreasing playing time or the training workload—whether for a couple hours or days—AI may be able to help fans avoid the heartbreak of losing their favorite player early in a season to injury.

Umpiring could be helped as well. The home plate umpire has the tough job of determining the position of a pitch down to a fraction of an inch when the ball is being hurled ever faster and with more movement. One recent study found that umpires made the wrong call on average 30% of the time when a batter had two strikes.[15] MLB has been experimenting in the Atlantic League with "Robo-Umps"—an Automatic Ball-Strike system that employs TrackMan's 3D-doppler radar system to determine the position of the ball.[16] While this works for calling balls and strikes, a human eye is still needed for checked swings and calling runners safe or out. In the past ten years, advances in a computer vision system known as Deep Learning has allowed machines to see the world and make decisions with ever increasing accuracy.[17] To further improve Robo-Umps in the coming years, Deep Learning technologies could allow computers that are processing video of the game in real time to determine whether a player has foul-tipped, checked a swing, or is safe or out. This should reduce errors in calls and speed up the game, perhaps by putting an end to heated conversations between umpires and players/coaches. The Robo-Ump in the digital cloud won't have the ears to hear the complaints.

Technology changes rapidly, making it difficult to predict further into the future of baseball, AI and

Using machine learning, AlphaGo taught itself the game of Go, and in 2016 beat 18-time world champion Lee Sedol. Pictured here is Go professional Michael Redmond providing a play-by-play commentary on the AlphaGo/Sedol match.

machine learning, but there are clues when one looks at breakthroughs that have occurred in other games. In 1997, IBM's Deep Blue became the first computer to defeat a world chess champion, using early artificial intelligence algorithms.[18] More recently, in 2016, a Google computer called AlphaGo, taught itself the rules of the game of go using a modern type of artificial intelligence called reinforcement learning, and used this knowledge to defeat the world champion. That this feat could occur so quickly surprised many, as go was seen as far more complex than chess, and AlphaGo employed novel moves that go champions had never seen before, despite the game's closely studied ~2,500 years of history.[19] Today, if you must win a chess or go game over an opponent, you could always consult AI for the best moves, moves better than any human has been able to make for several years now. The game of baseball, similar to the games of chess and go, can be broken into a series of strategic data-driven decisions made by a team's management and its players. One day a savvy baseball team will rely on AI in those must-win games.

But even if this information were available, the question arises as to how to communicate it in the middle of a game to players on the field. This is tricky because AI can also easily intercept and understand a team's signs. If you have your doubts, just watch a video by Mark Rober, a popular YouTube content creator, entitled "Stealing Baseball Signs with a Phone (Machine Learning)."[20] The video demonstrates how simple it is to use a phone to crack the code behind baseball signs. With

signs so easy to decipher with machine learning, a future scandal involving a team using this technology may make us long for the simple days of trash cans. A machine learning cheating scandal could also push MLB to revise its rules on how to communicate information between coaches and players on the field and from catchers to pitchers. If rules are changed, and electronic communication becomes permitted, it would make it much easier for pitch-by-pitch insights generated from AI to be deployed to players.

The groundbreaking AI and machine learning technologies in our phones and our homes have been produced by some the best tech companies in the world, whose idea of top talent is superstar professors and graduates recruited from a handful of elite universities in the world. Sports teams have another sort of star talent that they primarily need to spend their resources on, and the tech and financial industries can snap up the best AI and machine learning talent in the world. This poses a problem for sports teams who want to capitalize on AI and machine learning, as there are few people in the world who can create innovative products based on the mathematics and software engineering underlying AI and machine learning. But that hasn't stopped some fans, whose love of the game has motivated them to create new innovative applications in baseball. And, if SABR is any guide, baseball has a brighter future when fans get involved in baseball research. By 2040, we will have taught AIs much about baseball, and it will be exciting to see what they will teach us in return. ∎

Notes

1. Pew Research Center, "Mobile Fact Sheet," April 7, 2021, accessed June 16, 2021. https://www.pewresearch.org/internet/fact-sheet/mobile.

2. Daniel Kahneman, *Thinking, Fast and Slow*. Farrar, Straus and Giroux, 2011; Joe Lemire, "This Book is Not About Baseball. But Baseball Teams Swear by It," *The New York Times*, February, 24, 2021.

3. Lemire, "This Book is Not About Baseball."

4. Donald E. Farrar and Robert R. Glauber, "Multicollinearity in Regression Analysis: The Problem Revisited," *The Review of Economics and Statistics*, vol. 49, no. 1, 1967: 92–107; Kahneman, *Thinking, Fast and Slow*.

5. On the other side of the coin, for simple problems with smaller datasets, traditional statistics may be more useful then machine learning or AI.

6. Barb Darrow, "Live from Fenway Park: a behind the scenes look at MLB's Statcast," *Fortune*, September 4, 2015. https://fortune.com/2015/09/04/mlb-statcast-data.

7. Arlo Lyle, *Baseball prediction using ensemble learning*, PhD thesis, University of Georgia (2007).

8. Phuong Hoang, Michael Hamilton Hien Tran, Joseph Murray, Corey Stafford, Lori Layne, & David Padget, *Applying machine learning techniques to baseball pitch prediction*, International Conference on Pattern Recognition Applications and Methods, 2014.

9. Kristen Faith Nicholson, "Predicting Pitching Arm Stress With Machine Learning Models," SABR Analytics Conference: RP18, 2021. SABRVideos Youtube channel: https://www.youtube.com/watch?v=krZRI6o6wkw.

10. Nicholson, "Predicting Pitching Arm Stress."

11. Jason Themanson, "Contextual Influences On Neural Activity to Pitches and Feedback: Psychology and Performance at the Plate," SABR Analytics Conference: RP8, 2021. SABRVideos YouTube channel: https://www.youtube.com/watch?v=gjWtOTlzjD8.

12. Matt Manocherian and John Shirley, "Modeling Injury Risk Using In-Depth Injury Data," SABR Analytics Conference: RP2, 2021. ABRVideos YouTube channel: https://www.youtube.com/watch?v=g_iPVOY6TiU;

Georgios Kakavas, Nikolaos Malliaropoulos, Ricard Pruna, and Nicola Maffulli, "Artificial Intelligence: A tool for sports trauma prediction," *Injury*, August 19, 2019. https://doi.org/10.1016/j.injury.2019.08.033.

13. Alejandro López-Valenciano, Francisco Ayala, et. al. "A Preventive Model for Muscle Injuries: A Novel Approach based on Learning Algorithms," Medicine & Science in Sports & Exercise: May 2018, Volume 50: Issue 5: 915–27. https://pubmed.ncbi.nlm.nih.gov/29283933.

14. Mark Ogden, "Soccer looks to AI for an edge: Could an algorithm really predict injuries?" ESPN.com, February 4, 2011. https://www.espn.com/soccer/blog-espn-fc-united/story/4306701/soccer-looks-to-ai-for-an-edge-could-an-algorithm-really-predict-injuries.

15. Mark T. Williams, "MLB Umpires Missed 34,294 Ball-Strike Calls in 2018. Bring on Robo-umps?" *BU Today*, April 8, 2019. https://www.bu.edu/articles/2019/mlb-umpires-strike-zone-accuracy.

16. Katherine Acquavella, "Robot umpires: How it (*sic*) works and its effect on players and managers in the Atlantic League, plus what's to come," CBS Sports, August 27, 2019. https://www.cbssports.com/mlb/news/robot-umpires-how-it-works-and-its-effect-on-players-and-managers-in-the-atlantic-league-plus-whats-to-come.

17. Anne Bonner, "The Complete Beginner's Guide to Deep Learning: Convolutional Neural Networks and Image Classification," *Towards Data Science*, February 2, 2019. https://towardsdatascience.com/wtf-is-image-classification-8e78a8235acb.

18. Larry Greenemeier, "20 Years after Deep Blue: How AI Has Advanced Since Conquering Chess," *Scientific American*, June 2, 2017. https://www.scientificamerican.com/article/20-years-after-deep-blue-how-ai-has-advanced-since-conquering-chess.

19. *AlphaGo*. Directed by Greg Kohs. Moxie Pictures, 2017. Film.

20. "Stealing Baseball Signs with a Phone (Machine Learning)." YouTube, uploaded by Mark Rober, June 30, 2019. https://www.youtube.com/watch?v=PmIRbfSavbI&ab_channel=MarkRober.

At the Intersection of Hope and Worry

How Baseball and Society Learn from History

Alan Cohen

Sixteen months ago, we were stuck in our homes wondering if, or under what circumstances, baseball would return. To some degree, as I began this essay in April 2021, things had not changed.

There were encouraging signs during the summer of 2020. Once, as I was walking my dog, Buddy, we happened on a batting cage at the rear of the local high school. The sound of bat on ball was unmistakable, and before long the kids were playing games. The big leagues had an abbreviated season, and there were even a limited number of fans in the stands during the World Series.

There is continued optimism in 2021. I have been a datacaster since 2013, entering pitch-by-pitch information into a computer system used by MLB-affiliated teams. I was in Florida at the end of March and worked at four spring training games. Minor league ball in Hartford, Connecticut, recommenced on May 11.[1] On May 23, my wife and I celebrated our 50th wedding anniversary partially with a day at the ballpark. (Frances performed the National Anthem and, with attendance restrictions lifted, more than 5,000 fans were at the game.)

For this researcher, the past 15 months have been spent thinking about the future and remembering the past, with equal parts hope and worry.

Upon receiving the task of writing about "The Future According to Baseball"—a daunting prospect at the very least—I looked back on my years as an insurance underwriter, something I do not do often. An underwriter's goal is essentially to predict the future by looking in the rear-view mirror. Often, the rear view is not pleasant—like the flashing lights of a police car, or an ambulance. The future, then, is a traffic ticket or a hospital stay.

The one essential thing I have learned is that baseball research has as much of a chance of being compartmentalized as society in general, which is to say none. Baseball, society, history, and the future are all interwoven. And I have learned that there is a special challenge in maintaining the balance between the elements of thought and the elements of baseball.

I have also discerned that in a society that is litigious, baseball will most assuredly be part of that equation. In the early part of the twentieth century, issues such as baseball's status with the anti-trust laws were grabbing headlines. A century later, disputes in baseball are still finding their way into our nation's courtrooms and legislative bodies.

In terms of baseball, what is in our rear-view mirror and what does it mean for the future?

As historians, we do look back, but we also have the task of making our stories relevant. And baseball has great relevance to our society as a whole; the relevance of Jackie Robinson and the all-too-slow integration of baseball which, in actuality, is yet to be complete; the impact of larger than life characters such as Babe Ruth on the world as defined by entertainment; the players who by happenstance serve as the role models that many children lack in their everyday lives.

All of this has been underlined by the events of the past 15 months—as a medical crisis like the COVID-19 pandemic has social, economic, and political consequences, with the trauma stretching from Minneapolis to New York to Atlanta to Chicago.

What impacts and is relevant in society often has affected baseball. Take Sunday baseball, for example. The United States, in its formative years, saw "Blue Laws" enacted in several states and base ball, like most endeavors, rested on Sundays in a religious society.[2] But economic and social pressures to allow Sunday baseball arose in the final two decades of the nineteenth century. Indeed, part of the motivation for the American Association was the desire for Sunday baseball in cities west of Pennsylvania.[3] In the twentieth century, the pressure increased until the final bans were lifted in Pennsylvania prior to the 1934 season. What does this rear-view have to do with the future in 2021?

Across the land, society is changing and behaviors once restricted are gaining in favor. One such behavior is gambling. Whereas a century ago, eight Chicago players were banned from baseball for life for their involvement with gamblers during the 1919 World

Series, and as recently as 32 years ago Pete Rose suffered the same fate for gambling on the outcomes of his own team's games, the taboo against gambling seems to be dissipating. Sports gambling is becoming legal in more and more states.[4] It has become commonplace to see sports betting advertisements during televised baseball broadcasts. As the integration of baseball 75 years ago set the path for desegregating other American institutions and the eradication of Jim Crow, the eradication of the line between gambling interests and baseball is symptomatic of a society that currently accepts gambling in everyday life. (Whether or not this is beneficial to baseball in the short or long run is debatable, but I believe a future betting scandal is inevitable.)

I stumbled on Sunday baseball when researching another topic. My very first two biographies for the SABR BioProject resulted in explorations ranging from the trivial (players homering in the same ballparks as minor leaguers and major leaguers[5]) to the obscure (the Hearst Sandlot Classic and youth baseball), to the challenging and rewarding (Negro baseball). Looking back while researching these stories over the past 15 months, I also gained a glimpse of the future as I stared into my computer.

I, like others of my generation, learned baseball from my parents. One generation passing on its love of baseball to another generation was, in my youth, a part of American culture. Opportunities given in baseball to persons of color have resonated and often set the stage for opportunities given to the previously disenfranchised population in other aspects of the American society.

During the years when America's written and unwritten policies regarding segregation kept persons of color from availing themselves of educational, economic, and social opportunities, including the chance to participate in organized baseball, there was a flourishing of Negro baseball. There arose, in Black America, not only a love for the game but also parallel institutions to "mainstream" ball, including leagues and newspapers covering the games. But the Black newspapers were weekly publications, and thus the exploits of heroes such as Josh Gibson and Satchel Paige lacked the daily, detailed documentation given to their White counterparts. Black audiences flocked to games. To them, baseball was more than just statistics and what happened on the field.

Entertainment was a higher priority than statistical analysis. Box scores and the like were secondary to spectators having fun while cheering on their favorite players. So our rear-view mirror on the Negro Leagues is obscured by a bit of dirt, with the fun and spectacle shining through.

For decades, researchers like Larry Lester, Gary Ashwill, and Neil Lanctot, to name just three, have been scraping away at that dirt. Although Blacks and Whites play on the same field, the stories of how they got there—or anywhere else in society—are anything but similar. In the future, steps will continue to be taken to complete the chronicle of Negro baseball and that chronicle will be there for all people to share and understand.

In my research into the Hearst Classic, I have come across some unsung role models including Victor Feld in New York, Oscar Vitt in San Francisco, Ottie Cochran in Pittsburgh, Bunny Corcoran in Boston, and the Wrambling Wrecks in San Antonio, Texas. These adult leaders and sponsors have, in their time, assured not only the future of baseball but also the futures of men and women who will benefit society in the years ahead—the future.

WHO ARE THESE PEOPLE?

In New York, the Greater New York Sandlot Athletic Alliance traces its origins to the *New York Journal American* Sandlot Alliance.[6] Those involved in the program were, at the time that they participated, the future of baseball. A teenage Joe Torre, for example, was in the program in 1958.[7] He was National League MVP a few years later and now serves as Special Assistant to the Commissioner of Baseball.

Adult leadership from *New York Journal-American* sports editor Max Kase to early program director Rabbit Maranville to Tommy Holmes guided the New York program in its first 20 years.[8,9] Victor Feld is the current president of the GNYSAA. A member of the New York State Baseball Hall of Fame Class of 2020, with induction ceremonies slated for August 25, 2021, Feld is being honored for a lifetime of working with area children.[10] Each year, boys and girls are awarded scholarships by the GNYSAA, and the current head of the Parade Grounds League, Ruben Ramirez, was MVP in the GNYSAA All-Star game in 1968. He has spent the entirety of his adult life in the field of education.[11]

In this instance the sight in the rear-view mirror has been remarkable! A baseball institution from a bygone era, the Heart Classic, has paid current dividends.

Another view takes us to San Antonio. In 1949, a group of disabled World War II veterans banded together to lend a hand in the city's annual youth All-Star game. Each of the veterans' disabilities—from missing limbs to paralyzed bodies—was such that the veterans were on full government support. Each year, the game was the highlight of the summer, and the two top ballplayers were sent to New York to participate in the prestigious Hearst Sandlot Classic.[12]

After sponsoring the all-star games in conjunction with the American Legion in 1947 and 1948, the *San Antonio Light*, in 1949, began an affiliation with the disabled veterans. Known as the Wrambling Wrecks, the group had been formed by Bill Harrell (who had lost his hands in the war and used hooks to navigate his way during his post-war life) to help other disabled veterans to remain active.[13] The affiliation continued through 1992, when the newspaper stopped publishing. The Wrambling Wrecks continued to hold games through 1998. Not only did the games determine the players to go to New York for the Hearst Games (through 1965), but they also raised funds for charities supported by the Wrambling Wrecks.

With each passing year, the event grew bigger and better, and over the years, greats of the game such as Joe DiMaggio, Ted Williams, and Frankie Frisch were on hand, along with scouts from every major-league team.[14,15,16] Stars from the entertainment world, including actors Joe E. Brown (star of the baseball films *Elmer the Great* and *Alibi Ike*) and Dan Blocker (Hoss Cartwright on television's *Bonanza*) also appeared. There was entertainment for the whole family (tickets were $1), and kids got in free. One lucky spectator drove away in a new automobile. Writer Harold Scherwitz chronicled the "Wrambling Wrecks" event from 1949 through 1970, and even the most obscure of players were included in his coverage—because on that night really nobody was obscure and each of the players had stars in his eyes. He wrote these words in 1962:

Insignia of the Wrambling Wrecks, the group of disabled veterans that sponsored youth games in San Antonio, Texas.

Fourteen years of contributing some fun to the local athletic scene has brought these men (the Wrambling Wrecks) banged up in World War II, before the public as good citizens as well as good soldiers. Most of them were athletes before the loss of legs, arms or eyes, paralysis or other war injuries put them on the sidelines as competitors. The Wrambling Wrecks have dived into the task of setting up the game, selling the tickets, and handling most of the details. The tasks assigned to various members have snapped them out of natural unhappiness over their war injuries in many cases. The sense of accomplishment and the realization that they are paying their way and doing something for their organization has turned out to be a beneficial therapy that can't be bought. Their organization has gained a standing in the community with the best. Baseball has benefited, and Texas has been supplying topflight ballplayers as its representatives in the New York game.[17]

Although only five of the 39 players from the Texas games who represented San Antonio in New York over the years went on to the major leagues (including Davey Johnson, who was still in uniform 54 years after his first San Antonio appearance), many of the stories involve players who did not make it to the Show. They, like the Wrambling Wrecks, contributed, often off the playing field. And the spirit of the Wrambling Wrecks was very much in evidence in February 2021 as veterans were among the coalition that brought help to those in Texas impacted by the terrible winter storms. With the Wrambling Wrecks around, the future of baseball and society is bright.

In Pittsburgh, insurance executive Austin T. "Ottie" Cochran[18]—who had played some good quality semi-pro ball—headed up the Greater Pittsburgh Amateur Federation, and his efforts were chronicled by Andy Dugo in the Hearst publication in that city, the *Pittsburgh Sun Telegraph*. Mentoring the young all-stars were former Pirate players including Pie Traynor, Lee Handley, and Wilbur Cooper. The most successful of the young players was Dick Groat, who represented Pittsburgh in the Hearst Games in 1947 and 1948. A couple of the ballplayers who played in the area All-Star games had their futures in football. Joe Walton from the 1953 game and Mike Ditka from the 1958 both went on to successful careers in the NFL and were on opposing sides in the 1963 NFL championship game.

In San Francisco, the call went out to Oscar Vitt to head up the *Examiner* Baseball School. A veteran of

Ossie Vitt, as a young Tiger, being pushed in a wheelbarrow by Jack Onslow, 1912.

the game, Vitt had teamed with Ty Cobb, roomed with Babe Ruth, and managed Bobby Feller. In the ensuing years, Vitt would be joined by former Pacific Coast League players and area high school and college coaches in a selection caravan that went throughout northern California. In 1952, he saw a young Frank Robinson try out at Oakland.[19] Each year at the New York game, where he served as the manager of the US All-Stars from 1949 through 1961, Vitt would characteristically say that "this year" he had the best players ever.[20] His teams in New York included Hearst MVP Al Kaline in 1951 and catcher Ron Santo in 1958.

In Boston, the youth were encouraged to dream about playing at Fenway Park in the city's annual All-Star game, most often lining up as the Records versus the Americans, as the game was sponsored by the *Boston Record-American*. The force behind these games was Arthur "Bunny" Corcoran, who organized tryouts and selected players, more than 30 of whom, over the 25-year history of the Boston event, would move on to major league baseball. The Red Sox were very much involved in these games as they saw the games as an opportunity to scout the players of the future while giving thousands of boys each year the opportunity to try out for one of the 30 slots in the big game in Boston. Hearst MVP Bill Monbouquette (1954[21]) and Tony Conigliaro were such players.

But most of the players, of course, did not make it to the majors. Their stories provide the tapestry of baseball and the optimistic outlook that characterizes players and fans alike, an optimism that is as American as the game. The selection process involved tryouts in several locations in the Boston area. In 1971, the year of the last of these All-Star games, one player would not be denied.

The young man was from Everett, Massachusetts, and his story is the stuff from which legends are made. He went to tryout after tryout before finally being selected, at the very last tryout, as one of the 90 semi-finalists. At the time, he was a 16-year-old infielder.[23] Then came the time to whittle down the 90 to 30, for the two 15-man team rosters in the final game. In the morning game on July 29, he went 1-for-2, scored the winning run, made the best fielding play of the game, and was selected as one of the 30 finalists.[24] The personification of persistence, he eventually became far better known for his ice hockey skills, and Mike Eruzione captained the United States Olympic team to the Gold Medal in the Miracle on Ice in 1980.

WHAT MIRACLES DOES THE FUTURE HOLD?

As we emerge, as a nation, from the darkness of the pandemic, baseball is not so much a National Pastime as a common attitude. The American spirit is best shown when we endure the shared moments of frustration and spring forward with optimism and achievement. We saw this in baseball when a team down by three games in a Championship Series came back to advance to the World Series and win its first World Series in 86 years. Many saw it when a country, after years of economic insecurity in the 1930s, saw prosperity two decades later. Moving forward with a shared purpose is what America should be about and what success in baseball has always been about.

We have been there before. As the decade of the sixties ended, a decade known for much challenge and frustration, from the outcry of the civil rights movement to the disillusionment of Vietnam to the emergence of a generation accompanied by the crescendo of music from rock to country to folk to Motown, people from many different walks of American life all got glimpses of one another. Unfortunately, that glimpse did not lead to unity. The shared sense of accomplishment when humankind walked on the moon was as fleeting a moment as the time it takes a home run to travel from home plate to the stands. And in subsequent decades the desire for "security" outdistanced the desire for societal cohesion.

Since the moon landing, baseball has changed, too. Expansion to new markets, the designated hitter, and free agency have all had both supporters and detractors. Some speak with a reverence for the past, a time when things were different. But they weren't necessarily better. Yes, baseball was "integrated" at the major league level in 1947. But in the thirteen seasons through 1959, only 124 players of color had entered the game.[25] That was less than 10% of all players entering the game during those years.[26] It would be decades before Black managers became accepted in dugouts with the likes of Frank Robinson, winning the Manager of the Year award and Dusty Baker and Dave Roberts leading teams to the World Series.

A spirit of giving back to the game has helped baseball and society at large. From the likes of Rabbit Maranville and Tommy Holmes and Oscar Vitt being involved in youth games; to Black legends like Buck O'Neil (unknown to most White fans before 1994) getting involved in the Negro Leagues Baseball Museum; to Roberto Clemente's dedication to humanitarian aid—that is a great history of the past and tapestry for the future.

Some see the big money being paid to today's athletes as a barrier that will keep the players from giving of themselves in the years to come. A look in the rear-view mirror finds that for decades and decades, salaries were deemed too high, but that did not get in the way of the likes of Babe Ruth and Ty Cobb offering their time to work with kids.[27] As long as there are challenges in the community at large, look for ballplayers and teams to come forward with help and direction. In 2020 alone, baseball players and teams stepped up to the plate with initiatives ranging from the Players Alliance dedicated to fighting racial inequity, to teams like the Dodgers with their COVID-19 Community Relief program.[28]

The future of baseball and society as we enter the third decade of the twenty-first century seems at times to be outside the realm of predictability. During the past year, after being isolated in our homes, we stepped out to encounter our neighbors and got to know each other better. In the broader sphere, after generations of racial injustice, America is on the verge of confronting the true impact of segregation, more than 70 years after baseball took those first steps towards integration.

Frankly, the situation remains, in society as in baseball, anything but predictable. There is, however, the eternal battery of hope and enthusiasm, blended with worry and fear, defining America. Just as they define baseball on Opening Day. ■

Sources

In researching the "rear-view mirror" that is a major part of this story, the author used articles from the following:

Baseball-Reference.com
Boston Record-American/Sunday Advertiser
Pittsburgh Courier
Chicago Defender
New York Daily News
New York Journal American
Philadelphia Inquirer
Pittsburgh Courier
Pittsburgh Sun-Telegraph
San Antonio Light
San Francisco Examiner
New York Journal American
Philadelphia Inquirer

Notes

1. Dom Amore, "Goats Win Home Opener in Latest Sign Normal Life is Returning," *Hartford Courant*, May 12, 2021: 3–1.
2. Alan Cohen, "Never on a Sunday: Baseball's Battles with the Blue Laws in Rochester," in Don Jensen, ed., *Base Ball 10: New Research on the Early Game* (Jefferson, North Carolina, McFarland Publishers, 2018), 190–202.
3. Charlie Bevis, *Sunday Baseball: The Major Leagues Struggle to Play Baseball on the Lord's Day, 1876–1934* (Jefferson, North Carolina, McFarland Publishers, 2003), 34–50.
4. Christopher Keating, "Connecticut Senate to Debate Passage of Online Gambling," *Hartford Courant*, May 26, 2021: 7.
5. With the Pandemic, two more ballparks (Buffalo, NY and Dunedin, FL) joined the list.
6. Dwelling on the program at length is doable for the author but unappetizing to most readers. See my previous articles on the Hearst Sandlot Classic. The author's published articles on the Hearst Sandlot Classic include: Alan Cohen, "The Hearst Sandlot Classic: More than a Doorway to the Big Leagues," in Cecilia M. Tan (editor), *The Baseball Research Journal* (Fall 2013), 21–29. Alan Cohen, "From Sandlot to Center Stage: Pittsburgh Youth All-Star Games," in Cecilia M. Tan (editor), *The National Pastime: Steel City Stories* (2018), 60–63. Alan Cohen, "Bats, Balls, Boys, Dreams, and Unforgettable Experiences: Youth All-Star Games in New York (1944–1965)", in Cecilia M. Tan (editor), *The National Pastime: New York, New York: Baseball in the Big Apple* (2019), (2017), 85–88.
7. Alan Cohen, "Joe Torre" for SABR BioProject.
8. Michael Friedman, "Max Kase Cited for Youth Work," *Yonkers* (New York) *Herald Statesman*, August 27, 1970: 35.
9. Arthur Daley, "Sports of the Times, The Rabbit," *The New York Times*, January 7, 1954: 34.
10. *The Hall Monitor: The Official Newsletter of the New York State Baseball Hall of Fame*, November 12, 2020: 3, 6.
11. Dylan Kitts, "Restoring a Classic: Dormant Summer Sandlot Showcase is Revitalized on Diamonds," *New York Daily News*, August 11, 2009: 25.
12. Harold Scherwitz, "Sportlights," *San Antonio Light*, June 5, 1949: D1, and Raul Dominguez, Jr., "All-Star Game Continues Despite Waning Interest," *San Antonio Light*, July 22, 1989: H-7
13. Scherwitz, "Sportlights," *San Antonio Light*, June 5, 1949: D1, and Raul Dominguez, Jr., "All-Star Game Continues Despite Waning Interest," *San Antonio Light*, July 22, 1989: H-7
14. "Alex, Knutson Named for Trip To Hearst Sandlot Classic," *San Antonio Light*, July 22, 1959: 46.

15. "Ted Shows How It's Done," *San Antonio Light*, July 14, 1961: 32.

16. "Tigett, Myer Picked for Hearst Start Game," *San Antonio Light*, July 29, 1960: 42, 46.

17. Scherwitz, "Worthy of Support." *San Antonio Light*, July 24, 1962: 12

18. "Ottie Cochran Dies at 62 Playing Golf," *Pittsburgh Press*, April 30, 1967: 3–2.

19. Walter Judge, "Examiner School Returns Gomez to Old Haunts to Instruct Kid Pitchers," *San Francisco Examiner*, June 24, 1952: 27.

20. Morey Rokeach, "Vitt High on U. S. Stars After Drill," *New York Journal-American*, August 16, 1960: 25.

21. Bill McSweeney, "Yawkey Finds Talent in Hearst Sandlot," *Boston Daily Record*, August 16, 1961: 34.

22. David Cataneo, *Tony C.: The Triumph and Tragedy of Tony Conigliaro* (Nashville, Tennessee, Rutledge Hill Press, 1997), 28

23. Kevin Mannix, "Ten More Players Added to RA-A Sandlot Squad," *Boston Record-American*, July 17, 1971: 30.

24. Kevin Mannix, "Red Sox Host RA-A Sandlot Game," *Boston Sunday Advertiser*, August 1, 1971: 21.

25. Larry Moffi and Jonathan Kronstadt (editors), *Crossing the Line: Black Major Leagues, 1947–1959* (Jefferson, North Carolina, McFarland Publishers, 1994), was shown as a source in "Integration and the "Barrier Breakers": Back Baseball 1945–1960 ("Charting History") a lesson plan developed by Negro Leagues Baseball Museum. The list showed 119 players. Another five players have been determined to have been inadvertently excluded from the list.

26. Per Baseball-Reference.com, Jackie Robinson was the 7,942nd player in the major leagues. When Tommy Davis made his debut on September 22, 1959, he was the 9,309th player in the major leagues, although those figures include the non-major-league National Association.

27. Al Warden, "East Defeats West 5–4 in Esquire All-American Tilt," *Ogden Standard Examiner*, August 29, 1945: 12.

28. Press release, "MLB, MLBPA JOINTLY COMMIT $10 MILLION TO THE PLAYERS ALLIANCE," September 21, 2020. https://www.mlbplayers.com/post/mlb-mlbpa-jointly-commit-10-million-to-the-players-alliance; "Relief Efforts, Dodgers team website, MLB.com, accessed May 27, 2021. https://www.mlb.com/dodgers/community/relief.

The Rules They Are A-Changin'

Cecilia M. Tan

Before we can talk about the future of the rules in baseball, we ought to have a peek at the past. But more importantly we should acknowledge that the reason we're so interested in the future of the rules right now is because in 2021 anxiety over Major League Baseball's rules is running high. The owners and Commissioner Rob Manfred believe the long term health of the game is in jeopardy from loss of fans, and the commissioner is trying to address that loss through rules changes, imposed unilaterally if necessary.[1] On the part of the fans, the anxiety stems from change itself. (Indeed, it follows that die-hard fans of a sport that so highly touts its traditions would be traditionalists.)

Nonetheless, major rules changes have been implemented successfully at the major-league level before without the sky falling. Some of the seemingly most drastic have come within living memory for many fans. The mound was lowered and the strike zone shrunk significantly after the pitching domination of 1968.[2] The designated hitter was finally adopted in the American League (after having been debated since the nineteenth century[3]) in 1973.[4] Video replay review was first introduced in 2008 in a limited way, then expanded in 2014.[5] But the pace of change has accelerated in the Manfred Era, leading Manfred himself to say of purists who have decried the rules changes under his watch, "Their logic, I believe, is: 'He wants to change it, therefore he doesn't love it.' My logic is: 'I love it, it needs to be consummate with today's society in order for people to continue to love it, and therefore, I'm willing to take whatever criticism comes along in an effort to make sure the game is something Americans will continue to embrace.'"[6]

THE MANFRED ERA

Before Rob Manfred became commissioner in 2015, he had been working in and around Major League Baseball since 1987, including representing the owners as outside counsel in the 1994–95 labor negotiations.[7] For purposes of this article, though, we'll consider the Manfred Era as beginning on September 28, 2013, when he was named Chief Operating Officer of MLB by then-commissioner Allan "Bud" Selig, a move that cemented Manfred's role as Selig's heir apparent. Baseball being criticized for being "slow" is nothing new.[8] But under Manfred, MLB began to beat the drum that something had to be done about the slow pace of play, lack of game action/balls in play, and over-three-hour game times, because the league was losing fans.[9] Some rules tinkering got underway by 2014, when a 20-second pitch clock was imposed in the Arizona Fall League, and by 2015 had spread to the Double and Triple A levels of the minor leagues.[10] In February 2015, Manfred had been in the commissioner's chair for less than a month when MLB announced new rules intended to speed things up.[11] These included a clock on the inning breaks, the ability of managers to call for a replay challenge from the dugout instead of having to come on the field, and a mandate to enforce Rule 6.02(d) which requires hitters to keep one foot in the batters box during an at-bat.

Batters were not thrilled about the sudden enforcement of a rule that they had been flouting at will for decades.[12] Umpires didn't seem particularly invested in enforcing the rule, either, and although the average time of game dropped by six minutes from 2014 to early 2015, the time began to creep right back up, lengthening from around 2:53 at the start of the season to 2:56 by the end.[13] By 2016, games averaged three hours again. (See Table 1.) In 2017, the intentional walk rule was changed to allow managers to simply tell the umpire to give first base to the hitter, eliminating the need to pitch the four largely ceremonial

Table 1. Average Time of an MLB Game

Year	Time
2014	3:02
2015	2:56
2016	3:00
2017	3:05
2018	3:01
2019	3:06
2020	3:07

SOURCES: AP, CBS Sports[14]

balls to the catcher. No one expected that to save a lot of time, and it didn't: the average time of game rose again to 3:05, so even more changes were introduced before the 2018 season, including a limit of six mound visits per nine-inning game, new time limits on inning breaks, and putting time clocks on pitching changes.

In 2019 mound visits were trimmed from six to five, and new inning break limits were introduced, with local games' break time reduced from 2:05 to 2:00, and national games from 2:25 to 2:00—eliminating an entire advertising slot!—and the commissioner's office warning that for the 2020 season they "retained the right" to reduce the inning breaks to 1:55 in both local and national games.[15] By far the most contentious of the changes, though, was the rule requiring relief pitchers to face a minimum of three batters, which many argued would have the opposite from the intended effect. Cliff Corcoran of The Athletic wrote that "the three-batter minimum is rife with irony—a rule intended to make games shorter will likely make them longer; a rule intended to save fans from enduring mid-inning pitching changes will only make them more desperate to see them."[16]

Of course in 2020 the novel coronavirus pandemic forced MLB to renegotiate the entire existence of the season with the MLBPA, including new rules governing travel, health, and safety, as well as "emergency" rules that had on-field effects such as the universal DH in both leagues, seven-inning doubleheaders, and an extra innings rule that placed a runner at second base to start each half-inning. Somehow in 2021, seven-inning doubleheaders and the extra innings rule have remained, despite the easing of the pandemic and the derisive clap-chants from the Yankee Stadium bleachers to "Play-Real Base-Ball!" every time the extra runner on second appears.

A much bigger rule "change" in 2021, though, is MLB's crackdown on "sticky substances."[17] Although it has been illegal to "doctor" the ball with Vaseline or any other substance since the last legal practitioner of the spitball, Burleigh Grimes, retired from the game in 1934, for years it has been an "open secret" that a majority of pitchers used some kind of substance (other than the approved rosin) at least some of the time to improve their grip. With the crackdown ongoing as this paper is being written, it remains to be seen just what rules changes might come out of it. Some have suggested that a substance be made legal for pitcher use similar to rosin. Others have suggested that all pitchers and their gloves, hats, and uniforms be inspected before every inning. History suggests that the sticky substance crackdown is akin to the steroid crackdown: a problem that was allowed to grow unchecked for more than a decade before MLB decided it had to step in. Where the sticky substance debate seems to differ is that fans seem to be less angry over sticky stuff than they were about steroids, as if cheating with performance-enhancing goop is somehow less egregious than performance-enhancing drugs.

Is part of the muted reaction to "sticky stuff" on the part of fans—especially when compared to steroids, or even the Astros recent trash-can banging cheating scandal—because fans accept "sticky stuff" as part of baseball's status quo? When trying to project what baseball's rules will look like in 2040, it's one of the questions we must ask. But sometimes it's tricky to determine what "feels like baseball" and what doesn't.

That's where play-testing comes in.

THE ATLANTIC LEAGUE EXPERIMENT(S)

Many of the rules changes that have been considered and/or implemented by MLB under Rob Manfred were not cooked up in the commissioner's office; they've already been used somewhere. For example, the Southeastern Conference (SEC) has been using a pitch clock in college baseball since 2010.[18] And then there's the Atlantic League. This unaffiliated independent baseball league was already trying some rules innovations on their own before MLB made them an official testbed.

At the time when Rick White became president of the Atlantic League, MLB had just started investigating pace of play. In 2014, MLB created a blue ribbon Pace of Game committee.[19] That same year, the Atlantic League just went ahead and began enforcing both Rule 6.02 (batters cannot step out of the box) and Rule 8.04 (pitchers have 12 seconds to deliver the ball after receiving it), limited teams to three 45-second "time outs" per game—including mound visits, reduced warmup pitches from eight to six, and started calling the rulebook strike zone (including the high strike). Reportedly, time of game immediately dropped by eight minutes.[20]

"We took it upon ourselves to take an initiative to reduce the time of play and the pace with which the game was played," White said when asked. "And we openly shared our data with MLB. They never asked for it; we just did it."[21] The relationship between the Atlantic League and MLB developed over time. White and Manfred had known each other from the era when White had founded Major League Baseball Properties and Manfred had been working on MLB labor issues. When White and a group of Atlantic League owners met with then-COO Manfred in 2014, their main hope was to reach an agreement governing the transfer of players from their league to MLB. "We anticipated he was going to become the commissioner," White explained. "We wanted to introduce the league to him, and I don't think that he had a real conscious thought about who we were and who composed our league, especially on the playing side. But in that meeting, we talked about the quality of play in our league and we threw out—you know, as an opportunity—the idea for us to beta test initiatives. We really didn't think that was going to go anywhere."

But Manfred saw in the Atlantic League an ideal place to experiment with rules changes. The Atlantic League is a better test environment than the affiliated minor leagues because of its nature as a "second-chance league." The Atlantic League is populated with experienced players—80% with major league or Triple AAA experience, according to White—and its teams are not controlled by major league clubs. This means the competition is more analogous to major-league play than one finds on a Double A team being forced to play the 0-for-35 prospect whose multimillion dollar signing bonus needs to be justified, or the pitcher on the trading block. Because the minor league franchises must cater to the needs of their major league club, it "creates a bit of an artificial dynamic for what MLB's trying to accomplish."[22]

To increase the ability to make meaningful comparisons, the changes have mostly been A/B tested by splitting the season into two halves–one half with a rule change, one half without. In addition to the pace-of-play changes implemented in 2014, the Atlantic League has been experimenting over the past few years with ways to increase the amount of action in a game. Changes designed to boost baserunning have included banning the usual lefty pickoff move (pitcher must step off the rubber before making a move), limiting the number of pickoffs per at bat to two, increasing the width of the bases to 18 inches, and introducing the "steal of first base"—allowing a batter to run to first on any dropped strike, not just the third strike. The step-off-before-pickoff rule in particular "has led to Atlantic League games turning into track meets of sorts," according to *Baseball America*'s J.J. Cooper. "Since the rule was put into place, stolen bases have nearly doubled from 0.7 steals per team per game to 1.3."[23]

Defensive shifts work well—too well—so to encourage more success on balls in play, the Atlantic League has experimented with a rule that all infielders must be on the infield dirt when the ball is pitched. One rule tested to help batters at the plate looks small—you get two shots to bunt foul on the third strike instead of one—but one slated to be introduced in the latter half of 2021 looks huge: moving the pitching rubber back by a foot.

Originally the plan to move the rubber had been slated for the second half of 2019 and the move was slated to be two feet—to 62' 6"—but the plan was later scrapped. Instead, in 2021, the Atlantic League will try a 61' 6" distance. Some pitchers expressed worries the increase could lead to injuries.[24] But recent studies suggest that altering the distance between the mound and the plate doesn't change a pitcher's mechanics and won't lead to additional injury.[25] The change of one foot of distance is expected to be the equivalent of reducing pitch speed by 1.5 mph. Is one foot enough to make a difference? "If you look at the majority of hitters today, because they are trying to get an instant more time to see a pitched baseball, they methodically stand at the very back of the box," says White. "And if you really pay attention early in the game, most hitters at the big league level go in and start erasing the back line of the batters box."[26] With pitchers throwing 100 miles per hour with regularity now, hitters will take every inch they can get.

The Atlantic League has also experimented with a "consistent grip" baseball that "is tackier than the model used in both affiliated baseball and the Atlantic League," and would negate the need for pitchers to use something sticky merely to improve grip and control because the ball has already been pre-treated to be tacky.[27] The consistent-grip ball is also brighter white, and potentially easier to see, since it doesn't have to be rubbed with mud before each game the way the MLB ball is. (MLB has also experimented with the "consistent grip" baseball in the Arizona Fall League, but has been largely silent on the subject throughout the recent announcements about the sticky substance crackdown.)

But we haven't even talked yet about the Atlantic League experiment that seems the most futuristic, the so-called "robo umps." Automated Ball-Strike (ABS) uses the TrackMan radar system (the same system MLB used for PitchF/X before it was superseded by Hawk-Eye/Statcast) to judge balls and strikes and then relay the call to the home plate umpire via an earbud. To fans in the stands, ABS "runs so smoothly that most fans don't even know the home plate umpire isn't in charge of determining the strike zone."[28] To get into the nitty gritty of what using ABS is like, I spoke to the umpire whose earbud was sent to the National Baseball Hall of Fame and Museum after being the first to use the system in a game, Fred DeJesus.

"It's a blessing in my eyes," DeJesus said. "[With ABS] you don't have those Billy Martin/Earl Weaver style arguments anymore."[29] DeJesus was an umpire in the affiliated minor leagues for years before taking the gig with the Atlantic League (as well as a day job in public education). In DeJesus's view, ABS lets the home plate umpire concentrate on other aspects of the game—which, by the way, include maintaining the pace of play. "ABS helps all of us with slowing our timing down, being more patient, and letting the game come to us," he says. When asked whether a rules change can make the game more exciting, though, DeJesus is pragmatic: "It's players that make the game exciting, not the rules."[30]

Beta-testing systems like ABS and rules changes in the Atlantic League ultimately gives MLB what Rick White calls a "safety valve. They don't want to change their on-field product until they've fully parsed the results." MLB naturally wants to see if there are unintended consequences or bugs in the systems. Players don't always react to a rule as intended, as shown in MLB when attempted enforcement of rule 8.04 in 2009 merely led to pitchers shrugging and paying fines rather than speeding up their game.[31]

Among the lessons learned so far from the Atlantic League experiments is the realization that ABS was calling the high strike more than expected not just because the rulebook strike zone is higher than the one typically used in practice in MLB—but because it calculated the height based on each player's reported height. This meant that any player who had overstated his height (a common, if questionable, practice[32]) was penalized with a strike zone intended for a larger person. For the 2021 season, the ABS system is being

Hawk-Eye high speed cameras overlooking an athletic event in 2020.

tweaked to call a lower—and wider—strike zone, one that more closely resembles what major-league umpires call.[33]

The other big takeaway was that ABS revealed that everyone—catchers, hitters, umpires—reacts in-game as if the strike zone is a two-dimensional window at the front of the plate rather than the as-defined prism of three-dimensional space above home plate. No one I spoke to was sure why, but one guess is that this could be a consequence of what is now two decades of television "K-Zone"-style projections being subconsciously absorbed.[34] In theory, the strike zone is a column of air; in practice, it is a window, and to reflect that, the ABS system has been adjusted in 2021 to measure it like one. We'll see what effects that has in-game as the season goes along. Meanwhile, MLB has imported several successful experiments from the Atlantic League into one or more of its own affiliated minor leagues for the 2021 season:

- Triple A: 18-inch-square bases with a less-slippery surface
- Double A: Infielders must be on the infield dirt when the pitch is delivered
- High-A: Pitchers must step off the rubber to attempt a pickoff
- Low-A: A limit of two pickoff attempts per plate appearance
- Low-A (West) A 15-second pitch clock
- Low-A (Southeast) Automatic Ball-Strike system

THE FUTURE OF THE RULES

My first prediction is an easy one: Given the near-seamless success of ABS in the Atlantic League, it seems assured that in the short term—within five years—we will see some form of ABS adopted for use in Major League Baseball. In the bigs, it will likely utilize Hawk-Eye, which MLB claims is accurate down to 1/100th of an inch.[35] Although attendance figures are often quoted as the reason for taking action, there is little doubt that one of MLB's aims is to make the game more appealing, exciting, and engaging for the broadcast audience.[36] As such, it no longer makes any sense to have the viewers at home (or anyone in the stadium with the MLB At Bat App) better informed about the positions of balls and strikes than the home plate umpire. Umpires should be demanding this tool be put at their disposal as soon as possible so they can stop looking like fools every night on television. To make a small prediction based on previous reactions to change: MLB umpires won't do anything of the sort until it is imposed on them by the commissioner's office.

Future iterations of ABS could calculate the strike zone in real time based on the hitter's stance. Could we see some hitters adopting a boxer's crouch to reduce the target area? The big leagues changed the strike zone after the 1968 season to create a more hitter-friendly environment. With an ABS system, MLB could easily tweak the size and shape of the zone on a yearly basis, tipping the balance of power in either the pitcher's or hitter's favor, depending on which seemed to be gaining the upper hand.

Assuming ABS is a given, I asked DeJesus what's the one call he wishes umpires had technological help to make? "Checked swings," he said, without hesitation. Fred, I have good news: in the future, that'll be doable. By 2040, the cutting edge of technology won't merely be better cameras for Hawk-Eye or its successor, but more sophisticated software and data processing on what those cameras capture. These advances will allow "robo umps" to judge more than just the strike zone. Engineers at MLBAM are already working on using Hawk-Eye data to track not only the position of each player on the field, but biometric telemetry of their bodies' posture and joints.[37] Soon, processing the data will not only be able to recreate a VR simulation of actual play for entertainment purposes, it will be able to make safe/out calls that the human eye cannot: for example, plays that were obscured by a player's body.

You might think that my next prediction would be that by 2040 we won't have human umpires at all, but you'd be wrong. I don't believe it will be desirable to replace a human umpire entirely, and that technology should continue to be framed as a necessary tool to help umpires perform their jobs at the highest level. It is necessary to keep the umpires at least as well informed as the viewing public, and makes no sense to have the audience in the twenty-first century and umpires in the nineteenth. The earbud of 2021 could take the form of a wearable for umpires by 2040, maybe something akin to Google Glass (or a contact lens) with a visual heads-up display. Perhaps there will be an eye-in-the-sky—which could be an umpire in the press box, or in Secaucus like MLB's current video review crew—with access to all the tracking data, who automatically buzzes the on-field umps when their calls need to be amended.[38] In that vein, expect the current use of video replay—where each manager needs to issue a challenge to a call on the field—to be long gone by 2040. If MLB's goal is a faster-paced, more streamlined game, the manager challenge bringing the game to a halt needs to go. Incorporate technological feedback into all aspects of umpiring, and it will not only be seamless, the end result on the field will be a game that looks and feels more like "traditional" baseball than the manager challenge does.

By 2040, expect the baseball itself to have changed, as well as the rules governing the ball's specs. Another hallmark of the Manfred Era is MLB tinkering with the ball. Rawlings has been the official manufacturer of the baseballs used in the major leagues for over forty years. After the 2017 surge in both home runs and pitcher blisters may have been caused by a small change in ball manufacturing, MLB bought Rawlings in 2018 to solidify control over that process.[39] Prior to the 2021 season, MLB announced it had deliberately made changes to the ball intended to suppress the home run surge.[40] Whether the change worked as intended—and it doesn't appear that it did[41]—the new status quo appears to be MLB deliberately experimenting with the ball itself. Making the ball lighter, heavier, with denser or lighter wool, with seams higher or lower, perhaps with a "consistent grip" covering as previously mentioned, each will affect the ball's drag and Coefficient of Restitution (bounciness). With the same technology that is allowing pitchers to unlock the mechanics behind Seam-Shifted Wake, expect MLB to eventually master what each potential change to the ball itself will do.

The Atlantic League experiments presage that the distance from the plate to the pitching rubber will be increased in the future. But are we going to see field dimensions overall increase? The height of the average American has been growing for over 100 years. Why shouldn't the field dimensions adjust to reflect that? In 1918, the average American army soldier was 5-foot-6 (while Babe Ruth was 6-foot-2).[42] Nowadays, the average MLB hitter is over six feet tall, and pitchers are taller still. Increased player size alone accounted for an 11 percent jump in the annual home run rate from 1946 to 2005.[43] People and players continue to get bigger, and at the major league level they tend to be the biggest. We already have the concept that field size should be appropriate to player size: the Little League field has 60-foot basepaths and a 45-foot pitching distance, while Pony League (age 13–14) has 80-foot basepaths and a 54-foot pitching distance. The main reason I don't believe we'll see 100-foot basepaths and 450-foot outfield fences in MLB by 2040 is that it would be too expensive to retool stadiums to change the field size that drastically, plus there's the fact that if MLB is seeking a boost in baserunning and steals, increasing the distance between bases will hurt. (In fact, with the likelihood that larger bases will be adopted, the actual basepath will technically shrink by a few inches.) Rebuilding the entire field in major league ballparks isn't economically feasible, but moving the mound is.

When it comes to MLB in 2040, though, nearly everyone I mentioned my predictions to while writing this article wanted to know whether I thought there would eventually be a universal DH or if the DH would eventually be phased back out of the major leagues. If I am going to be logical about my predictions, I'm going to say that the players union will eventually get the DH approved in the National League. Of course, there's the possibility that the DH may take some other form, like the double hook rule being tested in—you guessed it—the Atlantic League in 2021. The double hook rule is intended to influence teams away from openers and extreme bullpenning because you lose the DH when you pull your starting pitcher from the game. My prediction if the double hook rule were to become standard in MLB is that the players union would only support it if it were accompanied by expanded active rosters. For those who are anti-DH, would that be better or worse than what we have now? The DH or no-DH question seems to inspire intense feelings in baseball fans. Trying to answer the question leads to existential questions about baseball itself.

WHAT IS BASEBALL, ANYWAY?

Perhaps it boils down to aesthetics. MLB would like the game to evolve in a direction that is more exciting, engaging, and appealing than the game as it is played today. (This is why I haven't predicted any rules against bat flips or home plate celebrations.) But batting average in 2021 is on pace to be as low as in 1968.[44] And balls in play are on pace to be even lower, having dropped from 133,000 balls in play in 2007 to 119,000 in 2019 and still decreasing.[45] MLB firmly believes that a game dominated by the "three true outcomes" is not the most engaging version of baseball. They believe more balls in play and traffic on the bases will equate to more excitement and more fans. A noble aim, but… would that mean we need more DHs or fewer?

It seems to me that if something looks and feels like "baseball" to die-hard fans, they'll accept it. If it feels like a gimmick or just plain weird—like the extra-innings tiebreaker rule feels to the Bleacher Creatures—then it's not "real baseball." And the danger is that if we have too many rules changes—or even one deal-breaker—such that the game no longer feels like the sport we love, that would drive fans away, too. What will fan reaction be to the Pioneer League's tiebreaker plan for the 2021 season: a home run derby?[46]

Perhaps the five-pitch swingoff will fly in the Pioneer League because the minor leagues have greater license to be unorthodox in the name of entertainment, whereas what the major leagues do, by definition, is the orthodoxy of the game. This is why to this day some opponents of the DH call it an abomination.[47] The way I see it, the schism over the DH reveals two opposing aesthetics of baseball. In the version of baseball where the DH is prized, the central conflict at the heart of the game is the confrontation between the pitcher and the batter. Everything else—including fielding and baserunning—is secondary to that one-on-one confrontation. By contrast, the aesthetic of pre-DH baseball comes in its purest form from the nineteenth century days of nine-versus-nine, when the game was not so far removed from when the "pitcher" was there to serve the ball to the batter *so that it could be put into play* and result in lots of running around. Looked at that way, if there's no one on base, it's not *base* ball.

By 1891 we already had the schism forming, though, between those who believed the aesthetics of the game centered around the ball in play, and those who believed it centered around the batter-pitcher confrontation. In 1890, the nine-versus-nine folks compromised to allow two additional players on the roster for substitutions, but in 1891 they stopped short of the pitcher being declared a non-batter despite the already obvious fact that most good pitchers can't hit.[48] Here we are, 130 years later—with rosters having grown to 26 players, and pitchers even worse at hitting than ever before[49]—still debating the same thing. The problem with aesthetic debates, of course, is that neither side can be proven right or wrong. Ultimately the "proof" will be measured by the number of fans in seats and eyeballs on screens. My prediction for 2040 is that baseball will retain its cultural relevance, no matter how much tinkering the powers that be may do. ∎

Acknowledgments
Thanks to Stew Thornley, J.J. Cooper, Rick White, and Fred DeJesus for speaking with me at length on this topic and to Cliff Blau for being the gold standard of fact-checking.

Notes

1. At Cactus League Media Day 2018, Manfred told the media, "Pace of game is a fan issue. Our research tells us that it's a fan issue. Our broadcast partners tell us it's a fan issue." (MLB's research on the subject has not been made public, however.) Richard Justice, "Manfred talks pace of play, rebuilding clubs," MLB.com, February 20, 2018. https:// www.mlb.com/news/commissioner-rob-manfred-talks-pace-of-play-c26681889.0; Tom Verducci, "Rob Manfred's stern message: MLB will modernize, no matter what players want," *Sports Illustrated*, February 21, 2017. https:// www.si.com/mlb/2017/02/22/rob-manfred-mlb-rules-changes-mlbpa-tony-clark.

2. Michael St. Clair, "Four stats show why the mound was lowered in 1968," MLB.com, December 3, 2015. https://www.mlb.com/cut4/why-was-the-mound-lowered-in-1968/c-158689966.

3. "Messrs. Temple and Spalding Agree That the Pitcher Should be Exempt From Batting," *Sporting Life*, December 19, 1891, 1. See also John Cronin, "The History of the Designated Hitter Rule," *Baseball Research Journal*, Vol 45, No. 2, Fall 2016, Society for American Baseball Research: 5–14.

4. If one needs more evidence of the traditionalist streak in baseball fandom, I'll note that nearly fifty years of the designated hitter in the American League still hasn't stopped a certain stripe of traditionalist from continuing to rail against it in the twenty-first century.

5. "Instant Replay," Baseball Reference Bullpen, Accessed June 20, 2021. https://www.baseball-reference.com/bullpen/Instant_replay.

6. Tyler Conway, "Rob Manfred: Fans Acted Like MLB Rule Changes Were 'Crime Against Humanity'" Bleacher Report, September 2, 2020. https://bleacherreport.com/articles/2907345-rob-manfred-fans-acted-like-mlb-rule-changes-were-crime-against-humanity.

7. "BASEBALL; Baseball Talks May Resume," *The New York Times*, July 9, 1995.

8. Steve Moyer, "In America's Pastime, Baseball Players Pass A Lot of Time," *Wall Street Journal*, July 16, 2013. https://www.wsj.com/articles/SB10001424127887323740804578597932341903720. From the article, "By WSJ calculations, a baseball fan will see 17 minutes and 58 seconds of action over the course of a three-hour game. This is roughly the equivalent of a TED Talk, a Broadway intermission or the missing section of the Watergate tapes. A similar *WSJ* study on NFL games in January 2010 found that the average action time for a football game was 11 minutes."

9. Bob Baum, "Manfred says pace of game rules crucial to luring young fans," AP News, February 23, 2015. Found in many places including https://www.usatoday.com/story/sports/mlb/2015/02/23/manfred-says-pace-of-game-rules-crucial-to-luring-young-fans/23911063.

10. Timothy Rapp, "MLB to Use Pitch Clock for Minor League Games," Bleacher Report, January 15, 2015. https:// bleacherreport.com/articles/2331469-mlb-to-use-pitch-clock-for-minor-league-games-latest-details-and-reation.

11. Paul Hagen, "New rules to speed up pace, replay," MLB.com, February 20, 2015. https://www.mlb.com/news/mlb-announces-new-pace-of-game-initiatives-changes-to-instant-replay/c-109822622.

12. Some notable examples included Mike Hargrove, who earned the nickname "The Human Rain Delay," and Chuck Knoblauch, whose 11-step between-pitches routine grew legendary as leadoff hitter for the turn-of-the-millennium Yankees. See Bob Sudyk, "Pokey Hargrove Streaks to Hot Start For Tribe," *The Sporting News*, May 31, 1980: 33; and Buster Olney, "BASEBALL; Between Pitches (Twist, Tap), a Game Within the Game," *The New York Times*, August 22, 1999. "Before every pitch, Knoblauch steps out of the batter's box to go through this elaborate preening, the pitcher waiting all the while." https://www.nytimes.com/1999/08/22/sports/baseball-between-pitches-twist-tap-a-game-within-the-game.html.

13. Jayson Stark, "MLB Commissioner Ron Manfred unhappy with length of games." ESPN.com, May 17, 2016. https://www.espn.com/mlb/story/_/id/15575004/mlb-commissioner-rob-manfred-unhappy-increased-length-games.

14. Mike Axisa, "Commissioner Rob Manfred confirms new pace of play rules coming to MLB in 2018," CBSSports.com, November, 16, 2017. https://www.cbssports.com/mlb/news/commissioner-rob-manfred-confirms-new-pace-of-play-rules-coming-to-mlb-in-2018.

15. "2019 MLB Rule Changes Unveiled," Ballpark Digest, March 14, 2019. https://ballparkdigest.com/2019/03/14/2019-mlb-rule-changes-unveiled.

16. Cliff Corcoran, "The new 3-batter minimum rule won't speed up games but will have negative unintended consequences," The Athletic, January 23, 2020. https://theathletic.com/1555626/2020/01/23/the-new-3-batter-minimum-rule-wont-speed-up-games-but-will-have-negative-unintended-consequences.

17. Alden Gonzalez and Jesse Rogers, "Sticky Stuff 101: Everything you need to know as MLB's foreign substance crackdown begins," ESPN.com, June 22, 2021. https://www.espn.com/mlb/story/_/id/31660574/sticky-stuff-101-everything-need-know-mlb-foreign-substance-crackdown-begins.

18. Teddy Cahill, "NCAA Committee Approves Pitch Clock for College Baseball in 2020," *Baseball America*, August 14, 2019. https://www.baseballamerica.com/stories/ncaa-committee-approves-pitch-clock-for-college-baseball-in-2020.

19. Craig Calcaterra, "Major League Baseball Creates a Pace of Game Committee," NBCSports.com, September 22, 2014. https://mlb.nbcsports.com/2014/09/22/major-league-baseball-creates-a-pace-of-game-committee.

20. Tom Verducci, "How MLB could learn from Atlantic League in speeding up the game," *Sports Illustrated*, August 5, 2014. https://www.si.com/mlb/2014/08/05/atlantic-league-pace-of-play-mlb.

21. Rick White, personal interview, May 17, 2021.

22. Rick White, personal interview, May 17, 2021.

23. J.J. Cooper, "Cooper: Atlantic League Rule Changes Aren't As Noticeable As You'd Expect," *Baseball America*, August 21, 2019. https://www.baseballamerica.com/stories/cooper-atlantic-league-rule-changes-aren-t-as-noticeable-as-you-d-expect.

24. J.J. Cooper, "New Mound Distance, Modified DH Among Atlantic League Rule Changes For 2021," *Baseball America*, April 14, 2021. https://www.baseballamerica.com/stories/new-mound-distance-modified-dh-among-atlantic-league-rule-changes-for-2021.

25. Alek Z. Diffendaffer, Jonathan S. Slowik, Karen Hart, James R. Andrews, Jeffrey R. Dugas, E. Lyle Cain Jr, Glenn S. Fleisig, "The influence of baseball pitching distance on pitching biomechanics, pitch velocity, and ball movement," *Journal of Science and Medicine in Sport*, February 8, 2020. https://pubmed.ncbi.nlm.nih.gov/32063509.

26. Rick White, personal interview, May 17, 2021.

27. Jacob Bogage, "National Baseball Hall of Fame accepts Atlantic League 'robo ump' items," *Washington Post*, July 25, 2019. https://www.washingtonpost.com/sports/2019/07/25/national-baseball-hall-fame-accepts-atlantic-league-robo-ump-items.

28. Cooper, "Atlantic League Rule Changes Aren't As Noticeable As You'd Expect."

29. Fred DeJesus, personal interview, May 20, 2021.

30. Fred DeJesus, personal interview, May 20, 2021.

31. Just one example: "Boston closer Papelbon again fined for slow play," Reuters, September 4, 2009. https:// www.reuters.com/article/us-baseball-redsox-papelbon/boston-closer-papelbon-again-fined-for-slow-play-idUSTRE58364W20090904.

32. David Fleming, "Tall tales: Getting an athlete's real measurements is rarely easy," *ESPN: The Magazine*, June 27, 2018. https://www.espn.com/nfl/story/_/id/23913544/the-body-issue-getting-athlete-real-measurements-rarely-easy.

33. Mike Gross, "The Atlantic League, the changeable strike zone, and the quest to revive baseball," Lancaster Online, May 29, 2021. https://lancasteronline.com/sports/local_sports/the-atlantic-league-the-changeable-strike-zone-and-the-quest-to-revive-baseball-column/article_1f1dbc74-c0c1-11eb-b8d1-07c763d7c466.html.

34. Andre Gueziec, "Tracking Pitches for Broadcast Television," *Computer*, March 2002. http://baseball.physics.illinois.edu/TrackingBaseballs.pdf.

35. Press Release, Sony Electronics, "Hawk-Eye Innovations and MLB Introduce Next-Gen Baseball Tracking and Analytics Platform," August 20, 2020. https://www.prnewswire.com/news-releases/hawk-eye-innovations-and-mlb-introduce-next-gen-baseball-tracking-and-analytics-platform-301115828.html.

36. Dayn Perry, "MLB seems to think its broadcast audience is more important than fans at the ballpark," CBSSports.com, February 21, 2018. https://www.cbssports.com/mlb/news/mlb-seems-to-think-its-broadcast-audience-is-more-important-than-fans-at-the-ballpark.

37. Graham Goldbeck, Marc Squire, Sid Sethupathi, "MLB Statcast Player Pose Tracking and Visualization," SABR Virtual Analytics Conference, March 14, 2021. https://www.youtube.com/watch?v=uLbzUkNi7oU.

38. When I mentioned this vision of the future to Atlantic League umpire Fred DeJesus, his comment was, "I agree: that signal should come out of Secaucus and you could have a buzzer at the plate guy's hip. But you'll have guys who say 'the buzzer didn't work' or 'we didn't get to it.' You think Joe West is going to say he felt the buzzer? Absolutely not. Angel

Hernandez is going to say he felt the buzzer? No way!" It'll take a new generation of umpires who have benefited from technological feedback to accept these changes. As it is, studies have shown that younger umpires—who came up in an era when they've always had some form of pitch tracking, be it QuesTec, Pitch F/x, or Statcast—call balls and strikes more accurately than older, more experienced ones, likely because of the beneficial effect of that feedback. See Mark T. Williams, "MLB Umpires Missed 34,294 Ball-Strike Calls in 2018. Bring on Robo-umps?" *BU Today*, April 8, 2019.

39. Dr. Meredith Wills, "How One Tiny Change to the Baseball May Have Led to Both the Home Run Surge and the Rise in Pitcher Blisters," The Athletic, June 6, 2018. https://theathletic.com/381544/2018/06/06/how-one-tiny-change-to-the-baseball-may-have-led-to-both-the-home-run-surge-and-the-rise-in-pitcher-blisters; Maria Armental, "MLB Buys Rawlings from Newell Brands for $395 Million," *Wall Street Journal*, June 5, 2018. https://www.wsj.com/articles/newell-brands-to-sell-rawlings-brands-for-395-million-1528203488.

40. Mark Feinsand, "MLB to Alter Baseballs for 2021," MLB.com, February 8, 2021. https://www.mlb.com/news/mlb-to-alter-baseballs-for-2021.

41. Thus far in 2021 homers are down slightly, from 1.39 per team game in 2019 to 1.17 now, but the season is not over yet and offense tends to heat up with the weather. As noted by J.J. Cooper, though, the trend of more homers, walks, and strikeouts and fewer balls in play and lower batting averages is not just being seen in MLB, but in college baseball, too, where the ball was not changed. J.J. Cooper, "Home Runs, Strikeouts and Low Averages Are Trending Throughout Baseball," *Baseball America*, May 26, 2021. https://www.baseballamerica.com/stories/home-runs-strikeouts-and-low-averages-are-trending-throughout-baseball.

42. Milicent L. Hathaway, "Trends in Heights and Weights," *Yearbook of Agriculture*, 1959, 181. https://naldc.nal.usda.gov/download/IND43861419/PDF.

43. Nate Silver, "Does Size Matter?" Baseball Prospectus, April 27, 2005. https://www.baseballprospectus.com/news/article/3979/lies-damned-lies-does-size-matter.

44. Chelsea Janes, "MLB's offensive woes are complicated, and they don't appear to be going away," *Washington Post*, May 17, 2021. https://www.washingtonpost.com/sports/2021/05/17/mlb-offense-complicated.

45. Stew Thornley, Personal Interview, May 17, 2021, follow-up email June 23.

46. Associated Press, "Home Run Derby, not extra innings will decide Pioneer League games this season," *Salt Lake Tribune*, April 27, 2021. https://www.sltrib.com/sports/2021/04/27/home-run-derby-not-extra.

47. Stew Thornley, the official scorer for the Minnesota Twins and longtime SABR member and rules historian, spoke to me for this article. His words: "Using terms like 'abomination' for the designated hitter is just overblown." But people do.

48. "Messrs. Temple and Spalding Agree That the Pitcher Should be Exempt From Batting," *Sporting Life*, December 19, 1891, 1.

49. Ryan Romano, "Pitchers are Hitting Even Worse," Beyond the Boxscore, April 20, 2015. https:// www.beyondtheboxscore.com/2015/4/20/8448085/pitchers-are-hitting-worse-mlb.

280 Park Ave.
New York, NY 10017
Office of the Commissioner
Contact: Dusty Baker / (212) 555-1876

For Immediate Release
June 18, 2031

LONDON ROUNDERS ACCUSED OF HACKING STADIUM ROBOT UMPIRE

(LONDON, U.K.)—In their second season as an organization, the London Rounders are being accused of cheating following allegations they employed an organizational technician to toy with the robot umpires at Wembley Stadium.

Commissioner Tony Reagins said, "This is a situation we've had knowledge of for a while. We will be launching a full investigation of this at this time as this is something that may compromise the game. We will not stand for cheating in a league that prides itself on tradition and winning in a fair manner."

Reagins also stated that Major League Baseball will have an innocent-until-proven-guilty mentality in dealing with London. He expects to get the facts and make a ruling as soon as possible on the situation.

The Rounders opened their first year as an organization with a 49–101 record.

A third of the way through the 2030 season, opposing teams became suspicious when virtually the same roster opened the season 47–22, including a 31–4 home record (16–18 on the road). League statistics show that the Rounders have had the fewest amount of balls called on their pitchers at home than any other team by 598 from the second closest team, the Mexico City Matadors.

Rounders star shortstop Wander Franco said, "This is ridiculous. We worked so hard over the offseason and now that the results are showing we are being told we're cheating. I can tell you right now I have no clue how one could hack a robot ump."

Manager Chris Jacobson said, "I don't understand how someone can assume we as a team planned to go out of our way and mess with the robot umpire technology we have in place. It's just absurd. We came here to play baseball and not play with the strike zone."

Robot umpires, which were fully integrated into MLB in 2031, have had their ups and downs, including some technological deficiencies and incorrect rulings despite video evidence.

Andrea, the robot umpire at Wembley, has also ejected the most road players in the league, including rival Philadelphia Phillies outfielder Bryce Harper twice in one series. Harper said, "That umpire is a complete joke. Trusting a robot to accurately handle an emotional task is absurd. Whatever they're doing in London has worked with Andrea."

- 30 -

INTERCONTINENTAL BASEBALL LEAGUE

ICBL Headquarters
Rue Charles Galland, 18
1206 Geneva, Switzerland
Contact: Gordon Gattie
ggattie@ICBLeague.com

For Immediate Release

INTERCONTINENTAL BASEBALL LEAGUE SCHEDULED TO START LEAGUE PLAY IN 2039

(GENEVA, Switzerland)—Several national baseball organizations throughout the world jointly announced today the creation of the Intercontinental Baseball League (ICBL), the world's first worldwide baseball league. Following earlier multinational competitions such as the World Baseball Classic, the Olympics, and numerous international exhibitions, the ICBL will feature eight divisions composed of eight teams from across the six populated continents.

The ICBL is slated to begin competition in 2039, the 200th anniversary of the mythical beginnings of American baseball in Cooperstown, New York. The world's largest countries and most populated cities have joined this unique endeavor. Most countries field a single ICBL team, but some have two (Canada, Japan) and the world's three most populous countries (China, India, and the United States of America) each having three teams.

The ICBL will differ from existing leagues in several ways: a worldwide presence, increased participation from countries more recently associated with baseball, mixed-sex rosters, player eligibility based on citizenship, timed nine-inning games, relocated umpires, and youth exhibition games preceding the ICBL ballgames.

Divisions

The eight divisions are named according to geographic location, with cities listed in alphabetical order:

1. **North America**: Chicago (United States), Guatemala City (Guatemala), Havana (Cuba), Los Angeles (United States), Mexico City (Mexico), New York City (United States), Toronto (Canada), Vancouver (Canada)

2. **South America**: Bogotá (Colombia), Buenos Aires (Argentina), Caracas (Venezuela), Lima (Peru), Quito (Ecuador), Rio de Janeiro (Brazil), Santiago (Chile), São Paulo (Brazil)

3. **Europe**: Ankara (Turkey), Berlin (Germany), Kyiv (Ukraine), London (United Kingdom), Madrid (Spain), Paris (France), Rome (Italy), Warsaw (Poland)

4. **Northern Africa**: Accra (Ghana), Addis Ababa (Ethiopia), Bamako (Mali), Cairo (Egypt), Casablanca (Morocco), Douala (Cameroon), Giza (Egypt), Riyadh (Saudi Arabia)

5. **Southern Africa**: Cape Town (South Africa), Dar es Salaam (Tanzania), Johannesburg (South Africa), Kampala (Uganda), Kinshasa (Democratic Republic of the Congo), Lagos (Nigeria), Luanda (Angola), Nairobi (Kenya)

6. **Western Asia**: Baghdad (Iraq), Delhi (India), Istanbul (Turkey), Jerusalem (Israel), Karachi (Pakistan), Kolkata (India), Mumbai (India), Tehran (Iran)

7. **Eastern Asia**: Beijing (People's Republic of China), Chongqing (People's Republic of China), Dhaka (Bangladesh), Moscow (Russia), Osaka (Japan), Seoul (South Korea), Shanghai (People's Republic of China), Tokyo (Japan)

8. **Southeastern Asia/Australia**: Bangkok (Thailand), Ho Chi Minh City (Vietnam), Jakarta (Indonesia), Kuala Lumpur (Malaysia), Manila (Philippines), Singapore (Singapore), Sydney (Australia), Yangon (Myanmar)

Division names have not yet been assigned; for the first season, the division names will reflect the division teams' geographic area. While team home cities have been finalized, team nicknames and logos will be announced at a later date.

Schedule

The ICBL's initial season will include a 120-game regular season and a 16-team, four-round post-season. During the regular season, teams will play two four-game series against each intradivisional opponent and two four-game series against all eight teams in a competing, geographically-adjacent division. Teams will play a single four-game series on a Monday–Thursday schedule, with Friday–Sunday reserved for travel, cultural, and religious events.

While this league will be travel-intensive, reducing time zone crossings will be considered whenever possible to minimize players' circadian rhythm interruptions when scheduling ballgames. The inter-divisional games matchups will consist of North America-South America, Europe-Western Asia, Northern Africa-Southern Africa, and Eastern Asia-Southeastern Asia/Australia.

Based on the 120-game season, the regular season will last 30 weeks, with a full week off between weeks 10–11 and 20–21.

The top two teams in each division are eligible for post-season play; with eight divisions, 16 of 64 teams will be eligible for post-season play. The first playoff round will feature the top two teams in each division squaring off for the division title in a best-of-three series. The eight division winners will be seeded #1 through #8 based on their regular season winning percentage.

In the event of a tie, face-to-face records will be the first tie-breaker, regular season run differentials for all regular season games will be the second tie-breaker, and face-to-face run differentials will be the third tie-breaker. The second playoff round will feature the #1 seed versus the #8 seed, #2 seed against the #7 seed, #3 seed versus the #6 seed, and #4 seed against the #5 seed. The second playoff round will feature a three-game series with locations yet to be determined. The third round will have the #1–#8 series winner play the #4–#5 series winner, with the winner advancing to the ICBL Championship. The other matchup will have the #2–#7 series winner face the #3–#6 series winner for the other spot in the ICBL Championship. The final two rounds will be decided using a best-of-five format.

Rosters and Player Eligibility

Each team will assemble a 50-player roster with a to-be-determined salary cap and individual contract limitations. Active rosters will consist of 40 players; transactions moving players with the active and 10-person non-active roster will occur on weekends between series.

The league will not restrict player eligibility based on race nor any other demographic characteristic. Players may identify as either male or female. The recent significant successes in women's baseball leagues worldwide and the mixed success of integrated mixed-sex leagues in certain countries and territories, has increased the sex diversity of the player talent pool greatly.

With the increase in prosthetics, artificial intelligence, elective surgeries, and robotics, the ongoing discussion of cyborg definition and eligibility will continue to be debated in the coming years. For the first three seasons of ICBL play, and in keeping with the standards of other international sporting governing bodies (e.g., International Olympic Committee, Fédération Internationale de Football Association (FIFA)), cyborgs will be ineligible as players. For ICBL purposes, cyborgs are defined as a combination of a living organism with robotic enhancements, and may be classified as either restorative or enhanced. While the eligibility of restored cyborgs will likely be established internationally within the next five years, we expect enhanced cyborgs to remain ineligible due to the outsized competitive advantage of robotic enhancements.

Countries will be free to assemble their rosters as customs and traditions allow; the only requirement will be similar to the precedent set by the World Baseball Classic from the early 2000s, where a player, or player's parent, is currently a citizen or permanent member of the country he or she will be representing. In cases where a player merits eligibility on his or her own citizenship, proof of citizenship such as a valid birth certificate, passport, or government-issued identification must be provided. In cases where a player's eligibility is based on a parent's citizenship, the player must provide their own birth certificate, with parents clearly identified, and a parent's birth certificate, passport, other government-issued identification, or death certificate.

In cases where a player is eligible to represent multiple countries' teams, the player may select one country as his or her team that season. One player cannot play for multiple countries during a single season, though they may play on different teams within a single country, and may switch countries between seasons. Players must provide eligibility at least 90 days prior to Opening Day.

Players including pitchers must appear in at least 50% of their team's games in a given season to participate in postseason play. Based on the current 120-game season with no cancelled games, at minimum, players need to make one plate appearance or play one inning in the field in at least 60 games. (See below: the ICBL will not allow the designated hitter.)

There are no restrictions on a player's professional status; current and past professional ballplayers are eligible to play, with ICBL teams making relevant agreements with a player's current professional organization.

Operations and Notable Rules

Based on perceived and real economic inequalities among the countries participating in the league, the ICBL will institute a league-wide revenue sharing approach; the sum total of broadcast rights sales, stadium naming sales, gate receipts, concessions, and souvenirs will be split equally among the teams. League officials are currently debating the percentage allocations given to host countries, players, and team management and staff.

Gameplay rules from established leagues in the United States (Major League Baseball), Australia (Australian Baseball League), China/Taiwan (Chinese Professional Baseball League), Cuba (Cuban National Series), Italy (Italian Baseball League), Japan (Nippon Professional Baseball), Korea (Unified Korean Baseball Association), Nigeria (Nigerian Baseball Organization), and Venezuela (Venezuelan Professional Baseball League) helped shape the ICBL rules, with some slight modifications.

Ballfield dimensions: Playing fields will feature the diamond-shaped, 90-foot basepaths, and will use the 60-feet six-inch distance from the pitcher's plate to home plate used internationally, as originally established in American baseball. The outfield dimensions will have a minimum-maximum range based on land availability and ballpark elevation, though notional distances between home plate and the outfield walls will range from at least 100 meters (328 feet) to no more than 125 meters (410 feet), with wall heights ranging from three meters (9.8 feet) to five meters (16.4 feet). The pitcher's plate will rise .25 meters (10 inches) above the playing surface, with a consistent slope of one inch per foot from six inches in front of the pitcher's plate to the playing surface.

Time Limit: Teams will play nine-inning games, though no full inning may start two hours and 30 minutes after the first pitch is thrown. The so-called curfew rule has been adopted from Major League Baseball, which instituted it to staunch shrinking attendance correlated with shrinking attention spans. This approach mirrors the rules of worldwide Formula One racing, where races are completed after a certain number of laps or a two-hour time limit. League members are exploring additional options for ensuring timely pace of game; there will be fewer in-game promotions and television commercial breaks compared with other professional leagues.

Fourth-Inning Feast: One unique feature of ICBL ballgames will be the "Fourth-Inning Feast." Analogous to the tradition practiced in the US and Japan of the seventh-inning stretch when fans stand and sing a song, the Fourth-Inning Feast will feature a sampling of the host nation or city's notable cuisine, with a lucky section or row receiving the food delivered directly to their seats. Informal competitions among prominent chefs to showcase their dishes has already occurred in several countries.

No Designated Hitter: After significant debate, league founders decided against allowing designated hitters. Based on the notable proliferation and success of star two-way players following in Shohei Ohtani's footsteps, the ICBL decided against allowing specialized pitching or batting roles in the league.

Assisted Umpiring: Rather than crouching behind the catcher as usually seen in most professional leagues, or standing behind the pitcher as seen in many youth leagues, the umpire will be located in an undisclosed location near the playing field, but not directly on the field. The umpire will have access to audio, video, and biometric telemetry feeds in real-time. League officials are also exploring the use of augmented reality to assist with play calling.

Equipment: While most foundational decisions have been made, issues related to game equipment (e.g., catchers' gear), uniform requirements, rules, and official statistics will be finalized in the coming months.

Future Developments

One major concern permeating the worldwide sports industry is the potential ability of androids and cyborgs to completely dominate living ballplayers. Technological advancements in prosthetics, artificial intelligence, and robotics have made possible the development of baseball teams consisting entirely of "robot ballplayers." Androids—completely robotic entities resembling a human—will be ineligible to play in ICBL. They and other forms of robots with silicon-based cognition will be allowed to participate in limited roles, such as batting practice pitcher, pitching practice catcher, or retrieving balls hit during batting practice.

Cyborgs with carbon-based cognition are expected to have well-developed cognitive and physical capabilities for full participation during games. Restored cyborgs have played in exhibition games against minor league players in Japan, China, and the United States. While differences in cognitive and physical abilities occur naturally, ICBL wants to focus on human versus human competition, as opposed to human-enhanced cyborg versus human-enhanced cyborg competition. League members are currently debating where to draw the line between necessary medical treatment and robotic enhancements that would provide an unfair advantage.

ICBL founders have initiated discussions with participating nations and teams regarding minor leagues to serve as a developmental opportunity for future ICBL players. ICBL founders are currently debating minor league size, location, and playing time during the calendar year; founders have been split between playing ICBL major and minor league seasons concurrently and starting the minor league season after the major league season has started. The second issue related to establishing minor leagues is game locations. Since the major and minor leagues will overlap, and may run concurrently, minor league games may be placed in other cities for scheduling and financial reasons.

Recognizing that many professional ballplayers may make more money playing for a team in their own national organization instead of an international organization, ICBL is exploring options for providing incentives to professional national baseball organizations, allowing their players to participate in ICBL during the individual national organization's off-season or on a limited basis during their regular season. However, players will still be required to participate in at least half of their team's games to be eligible for postseason games.

Mission
Encouraging youth worldwide to play baseball is a foundational value for the ICBL. Before every ICBL game, two local youth baseball teams will compete in a three-inning exhibition game using the same field that the major league ICBL players use. During the ICBL game, youth players from the exhibition game will accompany ICBL players to their positions during the top and bottom of the first inning.

The ICBL is excited to start league play for the 2039 season! As the largest league to date, with a worldwide presence spanning six continents, the ICBL seeks to quickly become a global phenomenon. Participation from countries not ordinarily associated with baseball will not only introduce baseball to a new generation of fans, the league will potentially contribute to global stability. ICBL standards such as mixed-sex rosters, time-limited games, telemetry-assisted umpires, and youth exhibition partnerships will provide an example for individual nationally-based baseball organizations to follow during the coming years.

-30-

The Future of Baseball Cards

Steven M. Glassman

Statcast will be 25 years old in 2040. The oldest Millennials will be 59 and the oldest Generation Z's will be 43. These generations were raised on technology and, according to the Pew Research Center, over 81% of them actively use and engage in social media in 2021.[1] Their shopping and media consumption habits skew heavily digital.[2] Baseball card companies need to engage and involve these generations to stay relevant. This article details how the leading card companies are trying to do that, laying the groundwork for an increasingly digital future.

The mindset of the industry leaders is illustrated by two quotations from a 2018 *Chicago Tribune* article. Said Jason Horwath, Vice President of Marketing for Panini, the parent company of Donruss and the card company that produces the official card sets for the NBA, FIFA World Cup, and others: "Nothing can be taken away from the grass-roots opportunities of getting the product into the kids' hands. [But] there's ways to engage kids in the [digital] trenches." Topps Vice President of Marketing and Sales Dan Kinton added, "[We] continue to look for unique…ways to bring the fan and collector closer to the game, closer to their heroes."[3]

The pace of change in the collectibles business has accelerated in recent years, and between now and 2040, three key elements of the baseball card business will continue to evolve. One is the methods of engagement with fans, now that the primary way that consumers learn about new products is through the Internet/social media and via direct-to-consumer relations instead of on the shelves of local brick-and-mortar retailers. Another is the statistics included on the card backs. And expect a change in the digital product offerings: The future of baseball cards is in the digital space, whether via blockchain, digital apps, or on-demand and online exclusives.

UPDATING STATISTICAL CARD BACKS

One of the most iconic and salient features of a baseball card is the stats on the back. Although sabermetrics has long since revolutionized which stats matter most to teams and players, card backs have been slower to change. The sabermetric era in baseball card stats began in 1995 when Score added "OB%" (on-base percentage) to their card backs. Topps would add OPS (on-base plus slugging) in 2004, and in 2013 the Topps Finest cards began to include WAR (wins above replacement).[4] In 2014, Topps partnered with Bloomberg Sports to add a raft of advanced metrics to the Bowman Chrome card backs (see Figure 1.) Wrote SportTechie.com's Jesus Salas of the 2014 set, "Six different analytical templates will be showcased on the cards including spray charts that document veteran power hitters' home run locations and strikeout pitchers' pitch selection."[5] Prospect cards included "statistics that include organizational rankings and comparisons rankings and comparisons to minor league averages."[6]

"Every year we strive to find new ways to engage both the casual fan and the ardent collector, and we feel that the partnership with Bloomberg Sports accomplishes that. These revolutionized card backs has given us another unique point of engagement that is

Figure 1. Bowman Chrome Card Back Statistics in 2014

Hitters	Pitchers
WAR	WAR
OPS+	Innings Pitches
Plate Appearances	Quality Start Percentage
Total Bases	Runs Support per Games Started
Walk Percentage	Home Runs per Nine Innings
Strikeout Percentage	Strikeout-to-Walk Ratio
Batting Average of Balls Put Into Play (BABIP)	Left on Base Percentage
Isolated Slugging Percentage (ISO)	Ground Ball Percentage
Weighted Runs Created Plus (wRC+)	Walks plus Hits divided by Innings Pitched
Win Probability Added (WPA)	ERA+
Stolen Base Percentage	Fielding Independent Pitching
Total Zone Rating	Win Probability Added (WPA)

both eye-catching and educational and fun for all," said Zvee Geffen, Topps MLS and Bowman Brand Manager, in a press release. "Analytics are an essential part of today's conversations in every sport and this new content will document that emerging trend, and the new data we are providing will help enhance the experience for all."[7] Topps Vice President of Product Development Clay Luraschi added, "As a company that's been making baseball cards since 1951, we always want to be in line with the evolution of the game."[8] He also said: "We want to be in a position as a company to chronicle all sides of the game, including stats. In addition, we want to help usher in new concepts and expose fans as well." The designs for the 2014 card sets included such ideas as putting a hitter's home run spray chart on the back. (See Figure 2.)

But not everyone felt the implementation of the new stats was done well. (See Figure 3 for Mike Trout's 2014 Series 1 and Series 2 cards.)

The advanced stats were listed by their abbreviations, without any explanation of what they meant. Jay Jaffe of *Sports Illustrated* concluded: "To bring in new audiences and keep pace with existing ones, it makes sense to integrate sabermetrics onto the backs of the cards, but as with on broadcasts and in print/electronic media, restraint—ideally with explanation and context—is far preferable to overkill. I certainly don't think Topps should abandon the endeavor of expanding statistical horizons on its product, but hard-won experience tells me that a measured approach would be more fruitful."[9]

In 2019, Topps base and update sets printed Advanced Stat parallel cards for every individual player card in each set, using Statcast data, in runs limited to 300 copies. These parallels also existed in 2020 and 2021. Figure 3, below, is a Mike Trout 2021 "regular" stats card.

Although Trout's WAR is there, you'd need to pick up the parallel card in the 2021 Topps Series 1 Baseball Advanced Stat Parallels set to see BABIP or wOBA. Since the Advanced Stat sets are limited to 300 numbered copies, if you just bought a pack of cards down at the corner store, you'd see the "traditional" stats. Now that we're in the Statcast era, will we see launch angle, exit velocity, or some other stat derived from Statcast data introduced soon? Now that pitcher usage is changing in the big leagues, with bullpenning, openers and "bulk" innings eaters becoming more prevalent, pitching stats as a whole are surely due for an overhaul. Perhaps 20 more years of Statcast data and Hawk-Eye tracking will yield a new metric for fielding ability. By 2040, perhaps wOBA will be considered an "old school" stat, and some other newfangled metric will be trying to break through. Figure 4 (next page) imagines what Washington Nationals outfielder Juan Soto's 2040 card back could look like:[10]

CONSUMER ENGAGEMENT

For the past two decades, Topps has been building its digital footprint and expanding its online presence. You can look back to 2000, when Topps launched the eTopps line in which cards were treated and traded almost like stocks. The collector would purchase the card for a low initial price (like an IPO) and then trade/sell them on a stock market while Topps held the physical cards until the collector decided to take possession. "[eTopps] seemed like the future of card collecting," according to Cardboard Connection. The eTopps system also had "features that allowed you to seek or sell specific cards to other collectors on the eTopps site, sell them directly on eBay, or track the actual values on eBay. There was also a rewards program that was based around player production for the cards you owned, as well as other criteria, like fantasy

Figure 2. Bryce Harper's 2014 Card (back)

Figure 3. Mike Trout 2021 Card (back)

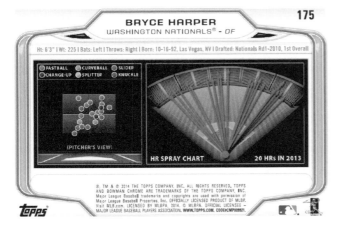

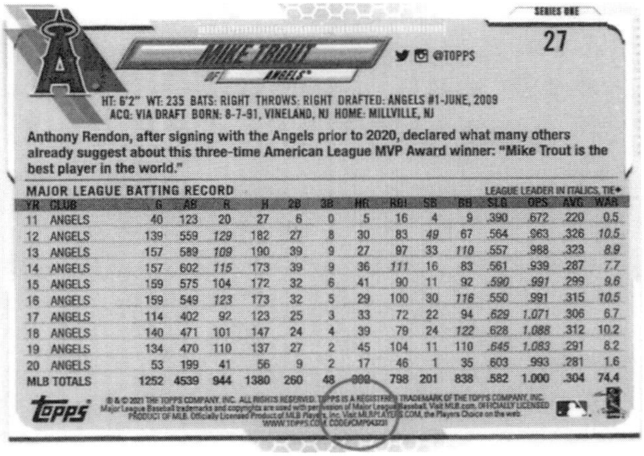

Figure 4. Juan Soto 2040 Career Commemorative Card (back)

Year	BA	OBP	SLG	AB	R	H	HR	RBI	BB	xOOA	SB	OPS+	FD+	WAR
2021	.305	.420	.595	528	122	161	37	141	105	3	19	160	1.43	6.3
2022	.312	.435	.628	516	127	161	40	148	112	2.5	16	172	1.59	7.0
2023	.311	.441	.647	515	131	160	43	153	120	-2	17	178	1.70	7.5
2024	.307	.441	.638	511	131	157	42	151	123	2	17	176	1.68	7.4
2025	.306	.446	.645	504	132	154	43	152	128	4	17	179	1.70	7.5
2026	.304	.446	.650	500	132	152	44	153	128	3.5	16	180	1.70	7.5
2027	.300	.443	.648	486	128	146	43	148	125	3	16	179	1.61	7.1
2028	.297	.440	.625	472	122	140	39	137	121	2	16	173	1.48	6.5
2029	.297	.439	.620	455	116	135	37	131	115	2	14	172	1.38	6.1
2030	.294	.434	.606	439	108	129	34	122	108	1.5	13	167	1.25	5.5
2031	.294	.425	.568	405	84	119	26	92	93	0	12	156	1.04	4.6
2032	.290	.417	.543	372	74	108	22	80	81	-1	9	148	0.82	3.6
2033	.286	.406	.507	343	64	98	18	67	69	-2	7	136	0.57	2.5
2034	.281	.393	.473	317	54	89	14	57	58	-1	5	125	0.36	1.6
2035	.274	.378	.442	292	46	80	11	47	48	-4	4	113	0.16	0.7
Ages 22–36	.299	.430	.600	6655	1571	1989	493	1779	1534	13.5	198	165	18.48	81.4
Thru Age 21	.295	.415	.557	1110	226	328	69	217	228	-1	23	151	2.20	9.7
Total Thru 36	.298	.428	.593	7765	1797	2317	562	1996	1762	12.5	221	163	20.68	91.1

We assume by 2040 we may have some new stats measuring fielding and defensive contributions, hence xOOA and FD+.

games."[11] The eTopps line was plagued by various problems, but the trend of digital marketplace speculation was established, leading to businesses like COMC ("Check out My Cards"). COMC advertises itself as not only a marketplace to sell one's cards, but as a place for "Easy & Fun Sports Card Flipping. Filter by team, player, set & more. Purchase, instantly relist, & flip for profit."[12] And eTopps clearly presaged the NFT collectibles market that would arise some twenty years later.

In 2011, Topps acquired GMG Entertainment. GMG was founded in 2002 to capitalize on the opportunity to link the digital and retail worlds, and in 2007 pioneered the business of developing digital currency products and services for digital entertainment companies attempting to monetize their businesses via offline channels.[13] By the next year, 2012, Topps had stopped production of eTopps cards and launched a digital division with Topps-branded baseball and football apps. These apps have since evolved to include additional sports, as well as entertainment and pop culture properties. Topps Digital and some of the apps under their umbrella maintain fan engagement through dedicated Twitter accounts.[14]

On Opening Day 2012, Topps launched two new apps, Topps Bunt and Topps Pennant. Pennant cost $2.99–$3.99 to download and was described by the company as a "modern box score."[15] The app would update each day with the previous day's game information

and also included play-by-play information for games dating back to 1952. Topps Bunt was free to download, and while one aspect of the app was the ability to build a digital collection of baseball cards, the app also presented "a game that incorporates fantasy baseball type of strategies. Users pick nine players regardless of position and can trade with other users. You rack up points and see how you do against other players in the game. The baseball players are depicted on baseball cards."[16] Topps continued to make significant investments in app development throughout the 2010s.[17]

One of Topps's challenges was sustaining interest in the app. Topps Director of Digital Content Chris Vaccaro spoke of the legitimacy of digital baseball cards by relating them to the popularity of other digital media: "It is a picture on your phone. But books are read on phones. Movies are viewed on phones. Bank accounts are accessed on phones. Music is listened to through apps. The world is connected and functions through mobile devices, so to extend our deeply historic and physical brand into the digital world is where we need to be as a company." Bunt had the advantage that the game component helped maintain interest. "These cards also score in a game-play mode through the fantasy contests, so this extends the notion of it just being a picture, rather, it's a commodity that scores in our custom platform,"[18] Vaccaro said.

By 2018, Topps Bunt was still growing in popularity. "A majority of our fans participate in the daily contests," said Vaccaro. "It provides a way for almost every card in the app to be more valuable."[19] Beckett.com's Ryan Cracknell wrote of the 2018 update of the app: "The cards themselves are also more dynamic. Traditional cards are a printed medium. While that has its advantages, they're static. When it comes to card backs, they're more like historical artifacts. With BUNT, those backs are always updating in real-time with each new game. So for those who might not be using the game side of the app, there's still value in using them to see how a player is doing at any given moment."[20]

By 2019, Topps competitor Panini was also in the digital game, offering not only a fantasy-baseball-like app and digital collecting, but print-on-demand offerings and building online connections with fans. As Panini Vice President of Marketing Jason Howarth said about Panini's philosophy in an August 2019 interview with SportTechie.com writer Andrew Cohen: "We are authentic to the players more than anything else. We do a lot of storytelling on social media, a lot of show and tell. We have over 2,000 contracts across all sports, where guys are signing our trading cards. When we're with them, we're always trying to capture that content and then share that on our social platforms. Getting that energy of being around the players—and showing off the product—is really what drives our fan engagement."[21] In their digital collecting apps like NFL Blitz and NBA Dunk, Panini offered collectors not only the ability to have a digital version of cards they physically owned, they offered some digital-only exclusives.

But what does it mean to "own" a digital card? Isn't it just an image that can be infinitely copied and shared? Not if blockchain gets involved.

BLOCKCHAIN TECHNOLOGY

Player Tokens, Inc., a Seattle, Washington, startup backed by Madrona Venture Group, announced in 2018 that they had "signed a deal with the Major League Baseball Players Association to sell digital 'tokens' featuring real MLB players." Furthermore, Player Tokens said theirs was the "first crypto-collectible that doesn't require a cryptocurrency wallet."[22] A pack of tokens was priced $5.99–$8.49 and could be purchased with a credit card. The idea behind tokens— now largely referred to as "non-fungible tokens" or NFTs—was to use blockchain technology to ensure there would be a finite number of tokens sold, and "each [token has] unique IDs based on the Ethereum blockchain that confirms authenticity, which creates digital scarcity. Token owners will be able to use tokens in various ways,

including in-stadium experiences and engagement with MLB players. The tokens are non-interchangeable and can't be used as a digital currency, but can be transferred to other owners."[23]

MLBPA Director of Licensing and Business Development Evan Kaplan stated at the time, "We believe Player Tokens is taking a great step forward, modernizing the fan and collector experience while paying homage to the rich history of baseball collectibles."[24] Player Tokens CEO Kush Parikh added: "Our goal is to create a modern platform that ultimately connects fans and players through digital."[25] Madrona Managing Director Scott Jacobson wrote in the company's blog: "[This] is an opportunity to bring together the digital and physical worlds (something my partner Matt lovingly describes as DiPhy) to create an entirely new and compelling collectible experience, powered by blockchain. Second, this intersection of worlds is particularly powerful in professional sports, where fans have the opportunity to encounter and interact with their favorite athletes, at games, on television, and through social media."[26] Parikh described the Player Token product as "New economy baseball cards for the modern age…across all sports! The collectibles we create will always change and continue to evolve over time—something that any static, tangible asset will never be able to do (except age)."[27] One of Player Tokens' stated goals: "Making crypto understandable and easy to use for the common fan. There is no requirement to own cryptocurrency, or even understand it. All you need to know is that the player tokens you buy from us are yours and cannot be faked. From there, you will be able to join the journey with us as the collecting and engagement experience evolves with players."[28]

It wouldn't take long for other sports to jump on board. In 2019, Dapper Labs started creating NFT collectibles for the NBA called Top Shots. Top Shots are official video highlights from NBA games, authenticated by blockchain, that collectors can buy and trade. Although the initial cost for a pack of tokens is only $9, the tokens sell out fast, and the bidding and trading of a Top Shot can quickly drive up the price. A single highlight of LeBron James has sold for $200,000, and as of February 2021, over $230 million had been spent on Top Shots, with the NBA raking in a percentage on every sale.[29] "The bet for traders is that in 2051, a LeBron James NFT could be worth what a 1952 Topps Mickey Mantle card is worth today—one of those rare cards recently sold for $5.2 million," reported CNBC. Dapper Labs feels the same way: "We think it could be a 100-year product," said Caty Tedman, head of marketing and team partnerships. "Everyone who is participating now is really getting in on the ground floor."[30]

A little over a year later, in December 2019, Panini became the first of the traditional card companies to introduce blockchain technology, utilizing its National Treasures design for 100 athletes in January 2020. Some of the baseball players in the multi-sports release included Aaron Judge, Mickey Mantle, Shohei Ohtani, Mariano Rivera, and Honus Wagner. These digital trading cards were to "be sold in an auction format in US dollars as opposed to a digital currency. The blockchain asset will live on a closed Panini platform where sports fans and collectors can buy, sell and store their blockchain trading card assets. Each card is a unique one-of-one card that not only includes a blockchain digital asset—but will be accompanied by a physical version of the card that includes an autograph of the respective player. In some cases, the physical card also will include a piece of memorabilia. The blockchain asset will be an exact representation of the physical version of the card."[31]

By March 2020, the hunger for NFTs had grown. Dapper Labs signed up the UFC (mixed martial arts) and said that other sports leagues had been talking to them about using NFTs.[32] Meanwhile Topps got into the NFT game to commemorate the 35th anniversary of the Garbage Pail Kids, a parody of the Cabbage Patch Kids. The foray into blockchain cards came in a partnership with NFT creation and trading platform Worldwide Asset Exchange (WAX).[33]

In a November 2020 piece entitled "Why Would Anyone Bother Collecting Digital Baseball Cards?" *Slate*'s Michael Waters laid out the challenges facing creators of digital collectibles: "What made physical cards work is that collectors could put faith in their longevity. They stay yours until you decide to sell them or, if they become sentimentally precious enough, pass them on to family or friends. But the digital economy has done little to recreate that trust. It's a problem that extends well beyond the world of card collecting into all digital 'purchases.'"[34] Waters pointed out that some problems with selling digital products are not unique to collectible cards, Books, songs, and other digital media are "tenuous" and the way we buy, store, use, and retrieve them is at the whim of current technologies and the companies that may or may not still be going concerns in the future.

So-called "crypto collectibles" use of blockchain should have at least solved the question of authenticity and recreated via digital medium the experience of owning "the original" of a collectible, not a "copy." Waters continued: "If [crypto collectibles] spread far

enough, they might make us rethink ownership on the internet writ large."[35] Indeed, the rules of ownership had already been upended by the time of his article, and are likely to continue to change as crypto-currencies and NFTs continue to be a rapidly changing and volatile market.

For the 2021 season, Topps began issuing baseball NFTs in its Topps Series 1 NFT Collection. As of May 2021, the Topps website featured card images with animated elements and enthused about the collection thus: "The first ever Topps MLB NFT collection celebrates 70 years of Topps Baseball, showcasing modern-day stars in new and classic Topps card designs. Collectors can find their favorite players reimagined as digitally enhanced, officially licensed Topps MLB NFT collectibles—ushering in a new age of baseball card collecting." These NFT cards include animation effects not recreatable on cardboard. New startups also continue to move into the NFT space. As this article was going to press, MLB announced it was partnering with Candy Digital in a "long-term deal" to produce NFTs. The first was slated to be a Lou Gehrig one-of-one featuring "Gehrig's iconic 'Luckiest Man' speech that the Yankees legend delivered on July 4, 1939, at Yankee Stadium, after being diagnosed with ALS. The Gehrig NFT will be released July 4th weekend, and proceeds from the sale will support ALS charities."[36]

Sports commerce has many other ways to incorporate blockchain besides collectibles, of course: SeatGeek just hired a new VP of Engineering from a blockchain company with an eye toward making digital ticket resale ironclad, and pro teams are excited about the fact this could give them a piece of each ticket's resale.[37] NFTs could be used to authenticate not just ticket licenses, but other forms of exclusive fan engagement such as VIP experiences, meet-and-greets with players, and the like.

But are NFT collectibles truly here to stay? In mid-May a lawsuit filed in New York State challenged Dapper Labs over Top Shots, alleging that the NFTs are essentially unregistered securities and should be regulated by the Securities and Exchange Commission.[38] In spring 2021 signs began to point to the bursting of the blockchain speculation bubble with NFT collectibles taking a major dive at the end of May.[39] Another major issue is that blockchain is not ecologically sustainable. Maintaining the technology and driving the value of most cryptocurrencies and NFTs requires an endlessly increasing need for computing power and electricity. (The negative environmental impact was cited as one reason auto manufacturing company Tesla no longer accepts Bitcoin.[40]) And skepticism from previous failed forays into high tech collecting is justified. "The largest reason people are skeptical of digital cards is that every single one of us knows how computer programs go obsolete within a year," said Nick Vossbrink, co-chair of SABR's Baseball Cards research committee. He points to some previous examples: In 1998, Pacific Online printed a unique URL on each card that supposedly went to a website about the player, but the domains are now long gone, and in 1999 the Upper Deck Powerdeck set consisted of baseball-card-sized CD-ROMs with movies on them, but CD-ROM drives are no longer ubiquitous and going the way of the VHS tape. Will a company like Topps keep the digital-asset servers running if at some point those servers cost them more than the profit the assets bring in?[41]

But whether the NFT collectibles bubble bursts in 2021, recovers to become a longlasting standard, or is superseded by some other technology, one has to expect that some form of digital authentication is going to be in place in the future.

Imagine in 2040, as part of Juan Soto's career retrospective, Topps reissues NFTs from 2021–36 and retroactively creates Soto NFTs for the 2019 and 2020 sets. By then they also have MLB equivalents of Top Shots, creating the digital equivalent of game-used memorabilia: perhaps Launch Angle for hitting, Velocity for pitching, and Web Gems for fielding. Soto's majestic home runs featured prominently in Launch Angle. Instead of autographed cards or a game-worn jersey of Soto's being cut into slivers and included in selected lucky packs of cards, each limited-edition Soto NFT also provides access to a virtual reality meet-and-greet with the player.

VIRTUAL EVENTS

Speaking of virtual reality, during the COVID-19 pandemic, we saw the rise of many kinds of online events, including both in virtual replacements for in-person card-trading and selling conventions and the rise in popularity of new forms of interaction, for example "box breaks" and card pack opening livestreamed via Twitch.[42] Although it's expected that once the pandemic ends, in-person events will resume, the benefits and unique opportunities afforded by online interactions are likely here to stay.

On August 24–27, 2020, Topps Digital held its first online convention, Topps DigiCon2020 via its Digicast Twitch Channel. The convention included live and pre-recorded question and answer sessions, app activations, and watch parties. "Collector conventions are traditionally a great way for us to interact directly with our fans," said Tobin Lent, VP & Global General Manager of Digital at The Topps Company. "But the impossibility of meeting in-person this year created an opportunity for our portfolio of apps to shine, and for us to engage digitally with our fans in this unique way for the first time." The convention made the Topps Digital apps accessible to all attendees, and tried to "replicate the exciting experience of visiting show-floor booths."[43]

While many virtual conventions in 2020 used streaming video platforms such as Zoom and Gather.town supplemented with text-based chat fora such as Discord or Slack, as virtual reality technology becomes ubiquitous through entertainment devices like the Facebook-owned Oculus Rift, can VR events be far behind?[44] Imagine an online collector event to unveil the latest card set that would award each attendee a "door prize" NFT of some exclusive digital collectible. Expect Topps Digital to continue to host DigiCons, adding virtual reality for a more realistic attendee experience. By 2040, it's possible the digital baseball card won't be a mere "picture in your phone" but an interactive VR representation of the player. Software that is currently in use for analyzing the biomechanics of professional players and animating the players in video games like MLB: The Show could be used to create a virtual version of the 2040 Cy Young Award winner—or even Juan Soto, or Babe Ruth.

This could lead to a whole new meaning for the term "fantasy baseball." Collectible card games like Magic: The Gathering already pit one player's card collection against another. In 2009 Sega introduced an arcade cabinet game, Sega Card-Gen MLB 2009 that used real cards to populate a team.[45] Imagine if you could create a fantasy team based on cards you owned, and then play that team against a friend's lineup in a realistically simulated game? You could stack your lineup with Juan Soto as cleanup hitter against the friend who built a collection of the 1927 Murderers Row Yankees. Now imagine if you could insert yourself through VR as a player in that game. The value of owning digital cards would only be increased by such capabilities.

Another way Topps has already leveraged their online presence is through Topps Now. In 2016 they launched a program that would produce cards commemorating daily moments in sports and culture with varying print runs and prices. They issued base, autographed, relic cards, and sets. These cards are only available for 24 hours. Along with Topps Now, they instituted "Moment of the Week" cards. Fans would vote online in a weekly ballot of potential cards by ordering one of the cards featured, and the cards would only be available for a limited time. "That creates a certain level of engagement and competition among fans to have their favorites chosen, which is an excellent strategy Topps uses it to effectively generate excitement," wrote John Collins at FrontOfficeSports.com.[46]

In the future we could see Topps Now or its successor commemorate not just current events, but daily or weekly anniversaries of milestones by great players. Topps Now issued a career retrospective for Derek Jeter before he was to be inducted to the National Baseball Hall of Fame in 2021. We could eventually see Soto's accomplishments highlighted through Topps Now: his 2000th hit, 1,500th run, 400th home run, 1500th RBI, and so on. Perhaps we'll see a Topps Now card when he becomes eligible for the 2041 BBWAA Hall of Fame Ballot.

Topps has also leveraged their deep back catalog with online exclusives. In 2017 they added Throwback Thursday, a weekly set, with various themes, set sizes, and print runs. These sets utilized Topps's vast baseball, basketball, football, hockey, and non-sport card design library. With weekly turnaround, such offerings are made possible by the fast pace of e-commerce. Another online item is Topps On Demand sets with various themes, print runs, and set sizes.

In 2018, Topps added the Living Set, a set without a final card. These cards are in the 1953 Topps design and feature active and retired players, with varying print runs and prices. The Living Set is available in single cards and fine art prints. In 2018 they also introduced another online-exclusive product, Topps 3D, a 100-card set 3-D version of its base and update sets.[47] Then in 2019, continuing to leverage nostalgia, Topps issued 1955 Bowman Baseball-designed rookies and prospects cards. Some other examples of Topps online exclusives include the 2018 Topps Chrome Baseball Sapphire Edition and the return of Topps Total in 2019. Topps also issued 2019 Bowman Chrome X as a StockX Initial Public Offering (IPO) for three days in October 2019.

In 2020, Topps launched Project 2020 Baseball, with 20 different artists interpreting and redesigning 20 cards, for 400 total cards. These are also available in Silver Frame Artist Proofs, Gold Frames, and Fine Art Prints. Each weekday Topps would release 2–3 cards via their website, and the cards would only be available to buy for 48 hours. In a similar vein, to celebrate its 70th anniversary of producing baseball cards, Topps launched another series of art cards, Project70. These cards were created by a group of 51 artists utilizing 70 years of Topps baseball card designs, with each artist creating

20 cards. New cards launched daily on Topps.com and were only available for 70 hours. These cards were also available in various premium formats, including Rainbow Foil, Gold Frame, and Artist Proofs, and if a collector bought all 20 individual cards from a specific artist, they would receive a print with all 20 cards on it. Print runs for each card were posted after the sales window ended.[48] In 2021, Topps is continuing to offer "fine art" style offerings, with the set of art cards entitled Game Within the Game. These art cards are available individually, with varying print runs and 10" x 14" fine art prints, serial numbered from one to 99. Topps also launched another online product, *Sports Illustrated* Trading Cards.

Given the success of these exclusive sets and high quality, premium printing options, we can expect that trend to continue. Topps will continue to create limited print run and varying print run sets through online exclusives. Major League Baseball creates new moments for nostalgia every season, providing a never-ending vein to be mined. In addition to the 2040 Juan Soto career-commemorative set, imagine that every year as more cards are added to it, the Living Set breaks its own Guinness World Record as the largest baseball card set. I'm going to predict that by 2040, Topps will have opened its own museum—with both physical and virtual exhibits—featuring works from the Fine Art Prints, Living Set, Project 70 and its successors, and original pictures from the Topps Vault.

As Front Office Sports' John Collins concludes, "Topps has managed to bring tradition and nostalgia into the future by evolving with consumer purchasing habits and behaviors. Who would've thought we'd be talking about on-demand baseball cards one day? Yet, initiatives like that have enabled Topps to continue solidifying its place at the top of the baseball card industry."[49] We can expect Panini and other collectibles producers to follow suit as well as digital upstarts with new "disruptive" technologies. Collectibles companies will keep adapting to the changes in media, technology, and consumption habits, and collecting will remain a vital form of engagement for fans with their favorite sports and culture far into the future. ■

Acknowledgments
Thanks to Nick Vossbrink and Jason Schwartz of SABR's Baseball Cards committee for sharing their expertise.

Sources
In addition to the sources cited in the Notes, the author also used the following online sources for this article: Newspapers.com and Trading-CardDatabase.com.

Notes

1. Pew poll results show 84% of the age 18-29 and 81% of the age 30-49 cohorts are active social media users. "Social Media Fact Sheet," Pew Research Center, April 7, 2021. https://www.pewresearch.org/internet/fact-sheet/social-media.

2. Aaron Smith and Monica Anderson, "Online Shopping and E-Commerce," Pew Research Center, December 19, 2016. https://www.pewresearch.org/internet/2016/12/19/online-shopping-and-ecommerce.

3. Alex Parker, "From wax packs to mobile apps: Baseball card collecting goes digital to reconnect with kids," *Chicago Tribune*, March 26, 2018. https://www.chicagotribune.com/business/ct-biz-baseball-card-collecting-industry-20180326-story.html.

4. The card backs indicate whether it is either Baseball-Reference.com or Fangraphs WAR.

5. Jesus Salas, "Topps and Bloomberg Sports Partner to Add Analytics to Baseball Trading Cards," SportTechie.com, September 24, 2014. https://www.sporttechie.com/topps-and-bloomberg-sports-partner-to-add-analytics-to-baseball-trading-cards.

6. Salas.

7. Press release, September 23, 2014, Stats LLC, http://www.stats.com/pr_092314.asp.

8. Fred Goodall, "Evolving Topps going to WAR on card stats," *Dayton Daily News*, June 3, 2014, C2.

9. Jay Jaffe "Topps baseball cards go to WAR. Here's how they could be even better," *Sports Illustrated*, June 13, 2014. https://www.si.com/mlb/2014/06/13/topps-baseball-cards-go-to-war-heres-how-they-could-be-even-better.

10. Based on the projections of Jay, Jaffe, "Extending Juan Soto... All the Way to Cooperstown," https://blogs.fangraphs.com/extending-juan-soto-all-the-way-to-cooperstown, but extended with two invented stats for illustrative purposes, "xOAA" Extended Outs Above Average under the assumption that by 2040 we'll have advanced OAA, and FD+.

11. Trey Treutal, "Top eTopps Cards of All Time," CardboardConnection.com, May 3, 2018. https://www.cardboardconnection.com/top-etopps-cards-of-all-time.

12. COMC home page, accessed June 2, 2021. https://www.comc.com.

13. Cision PR Newswire, "Topps Announces Acquisition of Leading Digital Currency Card Company, GMG Entertainment," https://www.prnewswire.com/news-releases/topps-announces-acquisition-of-leading-digital-currency-card-company-gmg-entertainment-126163153.html.

14. Topps joined Twitter in July 2009. Topps Digital joined in December 2014.

15. Amy Chozick, "Apps Take Positions in the Topps Baseball Lineup," *The New York Times*, April 8, 2021. https://www.nytimes.com/2012/04/09/business/media/apps-take-positions-in-the-topps-baseball-lineup.html.

16. Susan Lulgjuraj, "Topps Creates Baseball-Centric IPhone, IPad Apps," Beckett Collectibles website, undated 2012 article. https://www.beckett.com/news/topps-adds-baseball-centric-apps-to-the-apple-store.

17. Lulgjuraj, "Topps Creates Baseball-Centric Apps."

18. Cracknell.

19. Cracknell.

20. Cracknell.

21. Andrew Cohen, "Nostalgia Never Dies: Panini Gives Fans What They Crave With Digital Collectibles, On-Demand Printing," https://www.sporttechie.com/panini-america-trading-cards-digital-collectibles-fan-engagement-sports-technology.

22. Taylor Soper, "Future of sports collectibles? Player Tokens brings together blockchain and baseball cards," GeekWire, September 2, 2018. https://www.geekwire.com/2018/player-tokens.

23. Soper.

24. Soper.

25. Soper.

26. Soper.

27. Soper.

28. Soper.

29. Jabari Young, "People have spent more than $230 million buying and trading digital collectibles of NBA highlights," February 28, 2021, CNBC. https://www.cnbc.com/2021/02/28/230-million-dollars-spent-on-nba-top-shot.html.

30. Tedman presumably did not predict the May 2021 turn of events in which Dapper Labs is being sued by users who allege that the NFTs are essentially unregistered securities. "The documents claim that NBA Top Shot moments are securities because their value increases with the success of the project. The plaintiff says Dapper should therefore be registered with the U.S. Securities and Exchanges Commission, which Dapper Labs has allegedly failed to do. The company is also said to have used its control of NBA Top Shot to prevent investors from withdrawing funds for "months on end," ensuring the money stays on the platform "propping up" its value." Jamie Crawley, "Dapper Labs Sued on Allegations NBA Top Shot Moments Are Unregistered Securities," Coindesk, May 14, 2021. https://www.coindesk.com/dapper-labs-sued-on-allegations-nba-top-shot-moments-are-unregistered-securities.

31. Panini America, "Panini America Becomes First to Launch Officially Licensed Trading Cards Featuring Blockchain Technology," https://blog.paniniamerica.net/panini-america-becomes-first-to-launch-officially-licensed-trading-cards-featuring-blockchain-technology.

32. Tim Copeland, "UFC to put fighters like Conor McGregor on the blockchain," Decrypt, February 25, 2020. https://decrypt.co/20479/ufc-to-put-fighters-like-conor-mcgregor-on-the-blockchain.

33. T. Skevington and M. Bacina, "Trash to treasure: Garbage Pail Kids NFTs sell out in 28 hours," Bits of Blocks, June 11, 2020. https://www.bitsofblocks.io/post/trash-to-treasure-garbagepail-kids-nfts-sellout-in-28-hours.

34. Michael Waters, "Why Would Anyone Bother Collecting Digital Baseball Cards?," Slate, November 12, 2020. https://slate.com/technology/2020/11/digital-baseball-cards-collectibles-blockchain-cryptocurrency-investment.html.

35. Waters wrote about blockchains: "You can think of blockchain as an open-source ledger. It records each transaction and pegs it to a location, represented by a number string that allows a digital good to exist independently of the company that sold it. A blockchain-based trading card, for instance, can be moved between online platforms in the same way that collectors can sell physical baseball cards wherever they want."

36. David Adler, "MLB Strikes Long Term Deal as First NFT Partner of Candy Digital,"MLB.com, June 1, 2021. https://www.mlb.com/news/mlb-strikes-long-term-deal-as-first-nft-partner-of-candy-digital.

37. Andrew Cohen, "SeatGeek Hires Blockchain Executive As VP of Engineering," SportTechie, May 21, 2021. https://sporrtechie.com/seatgeek-hires-blockchain-executive-as-vp-of-engineering. From the article: "SeatGeek chief product officer Eric Waller told SportTechie that his company is talking with NBA and NFL teams about creating tickets as NFTs, with hopes to launch a marketplace for blockchain-backed tickets by the end of this year. 'I think what a lot of teams are most excited about is, if we put our tickets on the blockchain, can we collect a royalty on every resale and can we always know who's in every seat?' Waller told SportTechie in April. 'I think that's something we hope to get to eventually.'"

38. Jamie Crawley, "Dapper Labs Sued on Allegations NBA Top Shot Moments Are Unregistered Securities," Coindesk, May 14, 2021. https://www.coindesk.com/dapper-labs-sued-on-allegations-nba-top-shot-moments-are-unregistered-securities.

39. "The NFT market bubble has popped and we've got the charts to prove it," Protos.com, June 2, 2021. https://protos.com/nk-market-bubble-popped-crypto-collectibles-are-over.

40. As of June 2021, Bitcoin, Etherium, and even Dogecoin are falling in value as some speculators have begun to suspect that cryptocurrency may ultimately be more of a Ponzi scheme than initially believed, as revealed in the New York state attorney general's case against Tether, a "stablecoin" exchange supposedly backed by real dollars, but exposed as holding only the equivalent of 3 cents per dollar. See Stephen

Diehl, Twitter thread, May 15, 2021. https://twitter.com/smdiehl/status/1393669812220465162; and Jemima Kelly, "Tether says its reserves are backed by cash to the tune of…2.9%," May 14, 2021, *Financial Times*. https://www.ft.com/content/529eb4e6-796a-4e81-8064-5967bbe3b4d9. Re: the environmental impact, see Elizabeth Kolbert, "Why Bitcoin is Bad for the Environment," *The New Yorker*, April 21, 2021. https://www.newyorker.com/news/daily-comment/why-bitcoin-is-bad-for-the-environment.

41. Nick Vossbrink, private email correspondence, May 23, 2021.

42. Rick West, "Watching People Opening Trading Cards Online is Actually Big Business," *Chicago Daily Herald*, September 4, 2020. https://www.dailyherald.com/business/20200904/watching-people-opening-trading-cards-online-is-actually-big-business.

43. Topps, "Topps' DigiCon 2020 to Celebrate Collector Fandom Across Sports and Entertainment with First Virtual Convention," https://www.topps.com/blog/topps-digicon-2020-to-celebrate-collector-fandom-across-sports-and-entertainment-with-first-virtual-convention.html.

44. Over 1 million Oculus Rift headsets were sold in the fourth quarter of 2020 according to Statista. Thomas Alsop, "Virtual reality (VR) headset unit sales worldwide in 4th quarter 2019 and 4th quarter 2020, by device," February 25, 2021. https://www.statista.com/statistics/987701/vr-unit-sales-brand.

45. "Sega Card-Gen reportedly failed in its location tests in North America, but succeeded in Japan (despite the use of American teams), where it gained sequels," according to SegaRetro.com. "You stick the cards on top of the cabinet to simulate eleven position (*sic*) of a real baseball field. The game is played with just the touchscreen and one button that is shaped like a baseball. The cards have stats in Power, Contact, Speed, Throwing and Fielding. The game has both pitching and batting, with the former being simply played with the button, while the former has some more touchscreen elements." From "Sega Card-Gen MLB 2009," Segaretro.com, accessed June 2, 2021. https://segaretro.org/Sega_Card-Gen_MLB_2009. To see an example of the game in action, see "Let's Play Sega Card Gen," Uploaded by DJDriveus, January 23, 2013, YouTube.com. https://www.youtube.com/watch?v=c919Q0ypHZk.

46. John Collins, "Topps Keeps Tradition and Nostalgia Alive by Innovating the Trading Card Industry," https://frontofficesports.com/topps-trading-card-industry.

47. Topps also produced 3-D versions of its 2019 base and update and 2020 base sets.

48. https://www.topps.com/project70.

49. Collins.

BASEBALL HALL OF FAME

For Immediate Release
July 9, 2069

Contact: Audrey Reinert
1-888-HALL-OF-FAME

STEVENS NOMINATION TO HALL OF FAME TO PROCEED

(COOPERSTOWN, New York)—Simon Ng, President of the Baseball Writers' Association of America (BBWAA), announced today that the BBWAA will reconsider their previous stance on inducting Jared Stevens and other "enhanced individuals" into the National Baseball Hall of Fame in Cooperstown, New York. "In light of recent developments, the BBWAA has decided to reexamine the eligibility criteria for augmented individuals," Ng told reporters via streamcast.

Jared Stevens, former pitcher for the St. Louis Cardinals, was first nominated for induction into the Hall of Fame in 2063, but his nomination faced stiff resistance from the electors. Those who voted in his favor cited his performance in Games Two and Four of the 2055 World Series against the Milwaukee Brewers, in which he pitched perfect games, in addition to his advocacy work with the Special Olympics, as grounds for induction. Those who voted against his induction noted that Mr. Stevens's bionic pitching arm provided him a distinctly unfair material advantage compared to other pitchers.

Meredith Cartwright, president of the BBWAA from 2060 to 2065, had likened the decision to classify Mr. Stevens's bionics as an unfair advantage to the BBWAA's attitude on performance-enhancing drugs. During Cartwright's tenure, the BBWAA modified their induction criteria to include the Cartwright Rule. The Cartwright Rule stated that enhanced individuals were ineligible for induction into the Hall of Fame.

The rule originally defined an enhanced individual "*as a person who has received one or more significant augmentations **including bionics, prosthetics, and other non-biological implants** that provide them palpably unfair advantage during gameplay*." Contemporaneous BBWAA members noted that the definition of "enhanced individuals" in the rule was sufficiently broad that it could include anyone who had any reconstructive surgery, such as "Tommy John" UCL replacement, and objected to the definition on the grounds that it was too vague to be enforceable. The rule was subsequently revised after disability advocates noted that individuals who relied on assistive devices or reconstructive surgeries would be unfairly disqualified from consideration.

Once revised, the Cartwright Rule included a controversial test to determine if an augmentation or enhancement provided a player with a "palpably unfair advantage." First, the augmented individual had to provide clear documentation that their augmentations were medically necessary. Second, the enhancements—including bionics and cyber physical augmentations—could not be further modified or altered beyond regularly scheduled maintenance and updates. Records of these updates were to be made available to opposing teams and MLB officials upon demand. Finally, an enhanced individual's performance had to be within the 95% percentile of all active players.

Michael Stuber, an early advocate of Mr. Stevens's nomination, noted that Jared had lost the arm at an early age and had been using commercially available bionics for most of his life. "Jared never concealed the fact that he was pitching using a bionic arm during his storied career," Stuber wrote in 2063. "He was transparent about the specific make and model he used and allowed the members of the National Baseball Association to examine his arm prior to each pitching appearance. There were no substantiated complaints regarding his performance during his career from fellow players. It seems odd that we should object to his inclusion in the Hall of Fame when the sport's governing body and the players' union found no credible evidence of misconduct."

Cartwright defended the rule stating that Stevens's bionic enhancements increased the average speed of his pitch beyond that of an average unmodified pitcher. But numerous statistical analyses of Mr. Stevens's pitching career failed to find sufficient evidence that his bionics meaningfully improved his performance.

The most damning condemnation of the rule came from Edgar Rojas, former pitcher for the Brewers between 2053 and 2060. Despite a chilly onfield relationship between Rojas and Stevens during their careers, the two men would later found a charity together, dedicated to increasing involvement in youth sports. "If anyone had grounds to complain about Jared's enhancements presenting an unfair advantage, it was the 2055 Brewers. I remember the attitude in the locker room after Game Four being grim and a few guys were upset. Can you blame them though?" Rojas said in a 2043 interview. "Players should be judged by what happened on the field, and what Jared did on the mound was unbeatable."

-30-

Cooperstown 2040

Where the Baseball Hall of Fame Might Be in Roughly 20 Years

Graham Womack

For an 82-year-old organization, the National Baseball Hall of Fame has remained surprisingly static in some respects. Baseball Writers Association of America members vote on recently-retired players, as the writers have done since the first Hall of Fame election in 1936. A small group of veteran voters meets privately to discuss older candidates, as has happened, at least more or less, since the beginning. The Hall of Fame also announced in 2016 that it would once more consider Negro League contributors, as either special committees or veteran voters had done for decades.

Through the different avenues, the Hall of Fame has enshrined 332 men and one woman, a pace of roughly four honorees per year. Cooperstown voters hit this pace in 2020, selecting a class of Derek Jeter, Marvin Miller, Ted Simmons, and Larry Walker that will be honored this fall, though it helps obscure the fact that no one was selected for 2021.

One would, of course, be foolish to chart the next 20 years for the Hall of Fame based on a quick look at its history. Particularly in the veteran voting department, ever-shifting historical changes promise a far-from-certain future, even in the near term.

But history also suggests that by 2040, the Hall of Fame shouldn't have anything major to worry about. From the dozens of worthy contemporary players likely to come before the BBWAA and veteran voters in the next two decades to recent developments with the Negro Leagues that could bring new Hall of Famers to the fore, Cooperstown's long-term future is promising.

BBWAA: POSSIBLE SLOWING IN STORE FOLLOWING A BIG SPIKE

It's safe to say the pace of BBWAA inductions for the Hall of Fame has picked up in the past decade. From 1936 through 2013, the writers held Hall of Fame elections a total of 69 years, voting in 107 players through their normal process, three players through run-off votes, and two through special elections, according to data culled from Baseball-Reference.com. That averages out to 1.62 Hall of Famers courtesy of the BBWAA each year in that span.

Through good times and bad for baseball and the world, the writers have remained the driving force for most of the greatest contemporary National and American League players selected to the Hall of Fame.

Occasionally, an outstanding player the BBWAA seemingly should have inducted, such as Arky Vaughan, has slipped to veteran voters. Generally, though, the BBWAA has enshrined the best of the best, even if it sometimes has come close to the wire, such as 2011 when Bert Blyleven made it on his 14th try.

In 2013, however, the writers failed to vote anyone in. For whatever reason—and there are a number of potential reasons we'll consider shortly—the BBWAA followed its blank slate in 2013 by voting in a startling 22 players over the next seven elections from 2014 through 2020, a pace of 3.14 annually, before declining to vote in anyone in 2021.

It's definitely reasonable to look at 2013 for a possible explanation for the spike in BBWAA honorees for Cooperstown, as historically, goose eggs by the writers have seemed to spur immediate, trackable changes at the Hall of Fame. (It remains to be seen if the blank slate from 2021 will do this.)

In 1960, an empty induction class led to the Veterans Committee being allowed to resume voting annually after a few years of voting biannually. Then in 1971, the committee was allowed on a special, one-time basis to vote in seven members, a notoriously poor class that included Chick Hafey and Rube Marquard, weeks after the BBWAA voted no one in.

Certainly, a lack of honorees isn't great for the village of Cooperstown, which counts on Hall of Fame Weekends for tourism dollars. All the same, that's not the only factor that's increased the pace of BBWAA inductees.

In July 2014, the Hall of Fame announced it would reduce the years players could remain on the BBWAA ballot for Cooperstown from 15 to 10. Since then, candidates like Walker, Edgar Martinez, and Tim Raines, who in years past might have slowly accumulated votes toward a Year 14 or 15 induction, instead saw their vote totals rapidly increase.

Walker, Martinez, and Raines also likely owe some of their rises to Ryan Thibodaux, who began tracking Hall of Fame votes in 2014. Thibodaux has done this by aggregating votes in a public spreadsheet, typically when a BBWAA member either published them in an article, tweeted them out, or emailed them directly to him.

Thibodaux's work has arguably done a few things. For one thing, it's allowed BBWAA voters to optimize their Hall of Fame ballots before sending them in, reminding them to vote for a candidate gathering momentum. This used to happen annually, though thanks to Thibodaux, it's been occurring in real-time the past several years.

Thibodaux's work has also coincided with some rough treatment of writers that occurs on Twitter when he shares questionable ballots and people who see the posts react. Far from being allowed to make their own decisions, Hall of Fame voters now face pressure to vote however people on social media want.

Some of this is not on Thibodaux, with yours truly even having participated in some Twitter rumbles over crappy Hall of Fame ballots long before Thibodaux's tracker became ubiquitous. Still, the current climate for writers has led some to quit voting, with *The New York Times* offering a January 2021 piece headlined, "Hall of Fame Voting, Once an Honor, Is Now Seen as a Hassle." The Hall of Fame has also culled voting ranks considerably in recent years, no longer taking votes from writers no longer actively covering the game. The most recent election had 401 voters, as opposed to 549 in 2015.

Those writers who've stuck around have been more willing to vote with the tribe. Between 1936 and 2013, the 107 players the BBWAA voted in through its normal process, not counting run-offs or special elections, received 85.1 percent of the vote in the years they were inducted and needed an average of 4.38 years on the ballot to get in. From 2014 through 2021, this shifted to 88.3 percent and 3.09 years respectively. Mariano Rivera also became the first-ever unanimous selection in 2019, with Jeter and Ken Griffey Jr. each falling just short in other years.

Speaking of Rivera, one would also be remiss to discuss the run of BBWAA selections for Cooperstown from 2014 through 2020 without discussing all the stellar candidates who hit the ballot in those years.

Of the 22 players the writers voted in, 13 were first-ballot selections: Tom Glavine, Griffey, Roy Halladay,

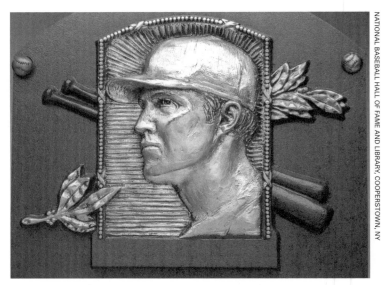

Mike Mussina's induction was a clear sign that Hall of Fame voters had entered the twenty-first century.

Jeter, Randy Johnson, Chipper Jones, Greg Maddux, Pedro Martinez, Rivera, Ivan Rodriguez, John Smoltz, Frank Thomas, and Jim Thome. It's arguably as superb a run of selections as Cooperstown has had since the late 1970s and early '80s, when greats like Willie Mays, Hank Aaron, and Frank Robinson were going in.

A possible slowing might be in store, though, with 2021's goose egg a possible early signal. While some shoo-in candidates such as Adrian Beltre are due to soon become eligible, many of the big names, from Alex Rodriguez to Carlos Beltran, have at least one significant issue clouding their candidacy.

There's also always the chance that work might wrap up for Thibodaux, who now has two children and three interns according to his Twitter bio. Whenever he decides to step away, it's unclear who might succeed him. While Thibodaux's not the first to track votes, he's been by far the most diligent.

Whatever happens, the total of 134 BBWAA selections for the Hall of Fame over 77 elections suggests the writers will enshrine at least 33 players from their 2022 through 2040 elections. The 22 selections in the eight years Thibodaux has been active suggests the number of honorees over the next 19 BBWAA elections might be as high as 52 if he keeps up his work.

In either scenario, who the honorees might be remains to be seen. In his seminal 1994 book, *The Politics of Glory*, Bill James attempted to predict 20 years of inductees and included Ruben Sierra. My own predictions of this sort on my blog in 2014 included Jose Reyes.

Still, while these predictions look foolish now, it's clear a good road lies ahead for BBWAA selections for

Cooperstown. Too many fine players will hit the ballot between now and 2040, from Mike Trout to Clayton Kershaw, for there to be too much cause for concern.

VETERAN VOTING: AN EVER-CHANGING PROCESS

About the only thing that's stayed consistent about the veteran voting process for the Hall of Fame over the years is that voters have had anonymity.

Seemingly from the time of the first one-off Veterans Committee election of 1936 to the ongoing process that began in 1953 to the different-name, similar-thing Era Committee setup in place since 2010, the Hall of Fame has allowed small groups of generally middle-aged or elderly men to gather and debate for however long it's taken each time to choose honorees.

While it'd be fascinating to know these conversations, the Hall of Fame swears members to secrecy and doesn't publish full committee voting results, ostensibly to protect candidates who receive the fewest votes. Since 2015, I've aggregated the names of more than 2,000 veteran candidates since 1953 by going through news archives, though the Hall of Fame doesn't keep this info handy for the public either.

It can be hard to know what goes on with the veteran voting groups at the Hall of Fame and harder to predict what they might do. That said, some general observable trends that have gone on long-term can help plot a course.

The first thing to know is that veteran groups at the Hall of Fame often consider the same candidates in different years, and occasionally these candidates get in. For instance, when the Veterans Committee voted in Deadball Era pitcher Vic Willis in 1995, it was at least the 23rd time going back to 1957 he'd been up for consideration.

Repeat candidates have continued to come before veteran voters in recent years. When Bill Dahlen received eight of 16 votes from what was then known as the Pre-Integration Era Committee in 2016, it was at least his 15th time up for consideration as a veteran candidate going back to 1953. Miller got in on no less than his 12th try as a veteran candidate, dating to 2001.

Following Bill Mazeroski's selection in 2001, the Hall of Fame stopped holding veteran voting annually. While it resumed this in 2008, the same era of veteran players hasn't been considered in consecutive years since Mazeroski. Not surprisingly, the veterans went 17 years without inducting a living player before enshrining Alan Trammell and Jack Morris in 2018. Harold Baines and Lee Smith followed in 2019 and Simmons in 2020.

Clearly, the Hall has been making an effort to finally enshrine living veteran candidates and it's good

news for former stars like Dwight Evans and Dave Parker, who drew eight votes and seven votes out of a possible 16 respectively with the Modern Baseball Era Committee in 2020 and could look to build momentum to the dozen votes they need for enshrinement. It will be interesting as well to see what the committee does with Steroid Era candidates like Barry Bonds and Roger Clemens if they can't make it to 75 percent with the BBWAA.

Still, there have been limits to the uptick in inductions of living veteran players.

Hall of Fame expert Jay Jaffe alluded to one limit in a Baseball By the Book podcast with former *Sporting News* editor Justin McGuire and myself last year. Jaffe said that due to not wanting to meet via video conference during the COVID-19 pandemic, the Hall of Fame postponed the votes for the Golden Days and Early Baseball era committees that would have occurred last December.

This postponement had a quick consequence, with Dick Allen dying December 7. It was one day after veteran panelists would have voted on Allen for the first time since he missed induction by one vote with the then-Golden Era Committee in its 2015 election.

As of now, the Golden Days and Early Baseball votes, covering contributors who made their greatest contributions prior to 1950, or between 1950 and 1960, are slated to take place this fall. The Today's Game Era Committee, covering 1988 to 2006, will next meet in the fall of 2022, while the Modern Baseball Era Committee, covering 1970 to 1987, next meets the year after that.

Given the Hall's history of continually tinkering with the veteran voting process, it will more than likely do so again before 2040, though when this might occur is anyone's guess.

Historically, the Veterans or Era Committee have enshrined roughly 25 percent more candidates than the BBWAA, with veteran voters putting in a total of 136 candidates in 62 elections since 1953, a pace of 2.19 annually compared to the writers' average of 1.74 the years it votes.

These averages would suggest another 41 Era Committee candidates, approximately, could be going in the Hall of Fame over the next 19 years. That said, in the last 19 times the Veterans or Era Committee has met dating to 1999, it has enshrined a total of 33 candidates, not counting 17 Negro League contributors enshrined by a special committee in 2006.

The Hall of Fame had sought to close the book on Negro League inductions following the 2006 mass induction. However, after public outcry, they decided in

2016 to make Negro Leaguers eligible once every 10 years with the Early Baseball Era Committee.

Then last December, Major League Baseball announced Negro Leaguers from 1920 to 1948 would be given MLB status. This was followed by Baseball-Reference.com's announcement June 15 that it had started to incorporate Negro League stats from those years into MLB numbers. While Negro League stats are still being found, the shift that's occurring has momentous implications for Cooperstown's future.

INDUCTION DAY 2040

One criticism people will sometimes level at the Hall of Fame is that it has become irrelevant because a selection they don't agree with occurred. Someone once said this to me because of the enshrinement of Barry Larkin, a solid Hall of Famer by sabermetrics.

The truth, though, is that the Hall of Fame has survived every questionable induction from mediocrities like Tommy McCarthy to racists like Cap Anson.

And on a hypothetical induction day in 2040, Cooperstown is looking vibrant as ever. Four new selections stand on the dais, a recently-retired MLB star, two candidates in their 50s or 60s, and the relative of a long-dead Negro Leaguer selected due to research that has helped them be rediscovered.

On the dais with them, dozens of new Hall of Famers sit, tens of thousands of fans before them who've trekked to Cooperstown, a brutal pandemic and other domestic troubles long forgotten. It's paradise if we can just get there. ∎

References

Associated Press, "'Hall' Voting Annual Now," *Oneonta Star* (Oneonta, NY), 8, June 28, 1960.

Bloom, Barry. "Hall reduces eligibility from 15 years to 10," MLB.com, July 27, 2014

Daley, Arthur. "Sports of the Times." New York Times News Service. *El Paso Times* (El Paso, Texas), 15, February 2, 1971.

Darowski, Adam. "Hall of Fame Announces Changes to Era Committees," HallofStats.com, July 23, 2016.

Draper, Kevin. "Hall of Fame Voting, Once an Honor, Is Now Seen as a Hassle," *The New York Times*, January 24, 2021.

"Hall of Famers," BaseballHall.org

James, Bill. *The Politics of Glory*. Macmillan: 1994.

Vote results for BBWAA for Hall of Fame accessed via Baseball-Reference.com

The Game Is Afoot

James Breaux, MSF

Emma Hasford cycles through the civic dome at a leisurely pace. She keeps an eye on the crowded lanes, an ear on her comm, and her hands on the bars. The bike's autopilot and gyros keep her upright and dodging the unconcerned pedestrians.

This evening she will be meeting her partner Daan Markus and can't help but wonder if this is a real stakeout of the fence Milo Cardoza, or if Daan is taking advantage of the police department expense accounts to have a night of dinner and baseball. She grins to herself, but her mien turns severe as her sound implant crackles to life. "All telemetry for surveillance operation #6157558 is being recorded following regulations under the authority of Sargeant Ujarak Jansen, Police, New Amsterdam."[1] *Well, that answers that question*, she thinks.

Daan Markus is on a public shuttle in a tunnel below the dome when he receives the same recorded warning. Daan speaks softly, "Lewis, are you online?"

Lewis coos, "In your ear, Constable!"

Daan rolls his eyes and pulls up from his usual slouch, involuntarily trying to look more masculine. "Roger that."

Daan has done all the prep work for the stakeout: processed all of the orders and forms for surveillance approval, as well as requisition forms for the tickets, drinks, and dinner for himself and Emma. When Daan had first arrived in the colony as an investigator after the 2030 dome collapse, he had found that taking part in team sports provided relief from the stressful work. Enterprising colonists had imported football (soccer) from Earth, though the game had to be modified greatly to be played in Mars gravity. He naturally migrated to the batting cages in 2040 when they opened.

The first small shop had opened up with four batting cages. To create a realistic experience, batters faced a virtual pitcher with the ball feeder under randomized control. The cage shop owners soon found that they were making more money from the VR feeds out of the cages than on the cage rentals themselves. VR is used for so many things in the colony—education, training, communications with family, friends, and corporate liaisons back on Luna and Earth—and, of course, entertainment. And watching the local heroes smash the ball is great fun.

Daan shifts in his seat as he waits for his stop. As the long-term constable, he habitually sizes up the other riders, sorting and categorizing them. The shuttle lurches to a halt, and Daan hefts his bulk off the bench and pushes into the exiting crowd.

Emma is already at the door of the sports bar as Daan saunters up. Attending the game's public viewing at the local watering hole is Daan's idea. It's a big game, and Milo will be there. Daan shows the door the tickets, and the bar drops, allowing them entry. Emma pokes Daan and says, "I almost didn't recognize you without your headgear. You do have hair after all."

Daan shrugs and tugs at his stubbled chin. "We're over there, I think," he says, ignoring her comment. It is well known that Daan has a perfect record of one demerit at every monthly readiness and presentation inspection for his unshaven chin—twenty years of consistency.

They move through the loud crowd to find their assigned table. The multi-screens scream various sports, from cards to team sports to individual endurance contests. But tonight, the big screen is all about the two local teams battling to avoid elimination. As always, the hype is high for this early October game. One team will be eliminated, and one will compete in the semi-finals.

The two undercover constables are there to continue their surveillance of Milo Cardoza, whom they suspect is fencing stolen bicycles. They don't know who is stealing the bikes or buying them, but most iffy goods seemed to be in Milo's orbit, so he is a good one to watch.

What they do know is that organized gangs have followed humans into space seeking easy profits and weak prey. The strongest gang in New Amsterdam is the Infinity Soldiers (IS). This high-tech group of modern-day pirates has roots back in Curaçao. They play in the hijacking of technology and command an enormous bankroll of grey market currency, while keeping up their mainstays of blackmail, racketeering, and loan sharking. The IS are the "usual suspects" whenever something comes up smelling rotten in the colony. A veil of secrecy covers the IS, bolstered by the occasional accidental fatal airlock malfunction. The constables suspect Milo is a member, or perhaps just a tool of the IS.

After ordering some food and the weak beer allowed to officers on surveillance, Emma keeps pumping Daan for conversation like the manual air pump on a broken airlock—it works, but it is work. At least until she hits upon one of his favorite subjects. "I did not expect to find baseball on Mars, Daan. How'd it start here?"

Daan straightens up and starts talking. Really talking, not like his listless reports and observations, but with feeling and a few uncharacteristic gestures. He tells her how it all began with the batting cages and the unexpected popularity of the VR feeds of the hitters. "My friend Hiroshi Hirokawa, a baseball fanatic and communications technician who spent hours at the cages, began to organize tournaments between the batters. Eventually he organized into competitive batting teams under a league."

"So it's just batting?"

"It was at first, but Hiroshi doodled up a plan using the available technologies to create a game that added pitching and fielding, too. It didn't take too much hacking to allow the opposing team to control the Shugs Autofeed BP 3 Mark 16 pitching machine." Daan describes how the amped-up three-wheeled machines can throw nine standard pitches with near-infinite adjustments. "A human pitcher is projected holographically behind the machine to give the batter somewhat normalized pitching cues. Instead of a ball, the pitcher holds a release switch which controls the ball's ejection and the pitch. A catcher still squats behind the batter signaling the pitcher."

The food and drink arrive, but Daan ignores the food and instead opens an app on his comm and begins finger typing furiously, referring to the posted game lineup on one of the screens.

Emma, though not usually curious about Daan's communications, has to ask, "What are you doing?"

He does not look up. "I'm preparing a sheet to score the game."

"Doesn't all that come across the screen?" Emma makes a q with her mouth.

"Oh, yes." Daan smiles and looks up. "The announcers will tell it all, we will see it all, and there will be a record of the game available for download immediately afterward. But I like to hand score. It keeps

my head in the game; I can see the strategy, and it's fun to look back on sometimes."

"Crazy!" she mouths. The bar is getting louder. She can't understand why a tech-head like Daan would need a more tactile, personal experience of the game, but there it is. Emma learns more about Daan all the time.

"Not everything about the game is super-duper high technology, you know," Daan says.

"No?"

"The ball, for example." The Rawlings ball in the pitching machine is still "dumb" and made in the same manner as the 2030 MLB rule 3.01 calls for. "It's a sphere of yarn wound around a synthetic core, covered with two strips of tightly stitched together synthetic leather. They import them from Earth."

"That is what we call an anachronism, Daan." Emma loves to tease the older constable about his age and the past he holds onto. It makes him squirm, and she considers getting any reaction from the normally staid policeman to be a victory. "Are you betting on the game?"

"No, I never bet on baseball. But Milo is a long-time member of the New Amsterdam City gambling cooperative." The cooperative is a special committee of the City council which seems to operate under the motto *If you're going to have organized crime, it should be organized.* He gets to vote on licensing all of the participants and organizations involved and setting the gamblers' rules and houses, and there will surely be heavy betting on tonight's game.

Daan sets his comm to generate a privacy bubble around the table, to keep their conversation private from all but the most sophisticated AI snooping. "Tonight is a historic first, you know," Daan volunteers.

Emma leans in to hear him, curious because he started the conversation this time.

"The Highlanders have added a late-season pitcher to their roster, and she is on Earth." As Dan speaks, the pitcher, Kathy (child of Budi and Natalen), is shown comfortably warming up on Earth in a pitching cabin set up in South Tangerang, Indonesia. The text scroll reads that she is a college ballplayer in an Indonesian city that is now shockingly coastal due to rising water. Her family relocated from Jakarta following the terrible storms and floods of 2034.

"They can do that?" Emma asks.

"The league rules allow late-season additions," Dan explains.

"No, no, I mean, have a player on Earth while the rest of the team is on Mars? What about the time delay?"

Daan explains that the expensive telemetry which allows her to participate with imperceptible lag is via the new quantum comm link satellites. The cost is being underwritten (in exchange for advertising rights) by the communications giant HNC (Hefei National Communications).[2] Yes, Mars's little pastime is growing into big business.

The game starts with a patriotic recital of the New Amsterdam jingle and the ceremonial recognition of some dignitaries, including the current Earth-based MLB commissioner, seated at a special remote field box. The presence of the MLB commissioner seems to give credence to the fan mags reporting that the New Amsterdam leagues might be under scrutiny to join the global MLB conferences.

The first pitch is thrown out by a local religious and charitable figure, Johana van Galen. Emma leans toward Daan. "Isn't that…?"

Daan nods. He knows Johana is popular with the baseball organizations, but didn't expect to see her recognized so publicly. Her slim, sturdy figure is hard to miss. Her self-sewn flowy robe exaggerates her motions as she overhand pitches the ball to the catcher, who seems surprised when the changeup drops obediently into his waiting glove. The catcher gives her a nod of approval, and the AI umpire declares, "Play ball!"

The game is between the home team Valles Mariners—named with a nod to the US Seattle team and the largest canyon on the red planet—and the Columbia Hills Highlanders Baseball Club, named with a nod to the old nickname of the Yankees and the Mars rover Spirit's landing site.[3]

The media color team announces the team lineups to great fanfare in the bar, and after a few warm-up pitches between Kathy on Earth and the Highlanders catcher on Mars, the first Valles batter steps up to the plate. Emma sees he is Center Fielder #7, and he and the catcher are in the same physical space. "Where are the rest of the players?"

"The defense is in separate fielding cabins," Daan explains. "They can see the catcher virtually, and vice versa. One of Hiroshi's best ideas." Not only that, sensors routed to an AI judge replace field umpires, while the Master Umpire is a human with expertise in the rules.

Number 7 crouches into his stance and is hit by the first pitch. The Highlanders fans in the bar sigh and groan as he takes his base. Next, Valles Short Stop #8 steps up, makes her adjustment, swings on the first pitch, and drives

it straight to the Highlanders Right Fielder. The Highlander fans breathe a sigh of relief. The Valles Right Fielder #21 steps in but quickly backs out, signaling time. After a long look at the bat and his shoes, #21 steps in and cocks the bat behind his shoulder. Kathy throws a ball, then a strike, then a ball, and another strike, painting the corners and tempting the batter with off-speed junk. Her final pitch to #21 catches him looking, and Daan scores a backward K with a smug grin. With two outs on the board, #18, the Valles Left Fielder, steps into the batter's box, and at a 3–2 count, Kathy slyly picks off the Center Fielder #7 at first, and the side is retired.

Around the second inning, Milo comes in and takes his regular table. A drink and some appetizers appear, which Milo ignores, busy with his comm. Later a slight person—built like a teenager—sidles up to his table, drops a small package without a word, and leaves. Emma gets a good video of the transaction using the optic recorder, but the small person's glasses and hoodie will make facial recognition difficult if not wholly inconclusive.

"How's the game going?" the mysterious Lewis again.

"Terrific," Emma replies, pleased with their ability to surveil Milo, at the same time Daan says, "Terrible," because the Valles Mariners have two on and their best hitter at the plate.

Hoping to ID Milo's messenger, Lewis immediately starts pushing the video through NALANI.[4] To avoid looking directly at Milo, Emma returns her attention to the game. "If the fielders are in separate cabins, how can the batters run the bases?"

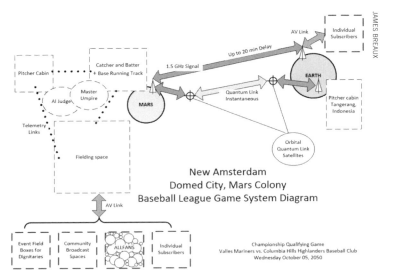

New Amsterdam
Domed City, Mars Colony
Baseball League Game System Diagram

Championship Qualifying Game
Valles Mariners vs. Columbia Hills Highlanders Baseball Club
Wednesday October 05, 2050

"The unused batting cages are converted into running lanes," Daan says, eyeing the simulation on the screen anxiously. "The batter runs between two bases only, with their VR hood showing the correct bases' view. The batter can see the defenders but can't physically contact them in a slide because they are in the other fielding space. Besides, sliding on Mars is terrible because the runner rarely comes back down in time to touch the base."

At the bottom of the fourth, a pair of well-dressed businessmen greet Milo, sit down, and begin eating his appetizers and ordering drinks. It appears to be a convivial meeting, the men ignoring the game except for the peak plays when they stop chatting to watch the replays.

One of Milo's guests speaks with a soft accent, asking, "This game. It is so much inaction and then… well, I don't know what? What do you see in it?"

Milo leans forward with a grin and says, "Opportunity. Casual viewers watch the games from a standard subscription feed; those proceeds are shared with the teams, players, and the physical site owner. But that isn't the only way players earn money. The ALLFANS app allows fans to support specific players and participate in the games from the player's visual perspective. ALLFANS supporters have access to a simultaneously curated AV feed of the player and special pre- and post-game experiences."

"And you are a big fan?" the other guest asks.

Milo's grin widens. "I own the app. Combined with my position in the gambling cooperative; it is a great opportunity. Besides, what can you do for fun on a hole in the vacuum like this one?"

The men have a chuckle and go back to discussing their other business and, after reaching an agreement, slip away from the table, pick up their bodyguards and exit the club.

As the game moves into the late innings, the Valles Mariners are clearly in the hunt, scoring despite the best efforts of the Highlanders. The Highlanders bring in a relief pitcher, then another and another, but can't catch the Mariners. The final score is Valles Mariners 6 runs to the Highlander Baseball Club's 4. The Valles Mariners are advancing in the playoffs! The Highlanders are sent packing.

Milo finishes up and leaves as well. Once he goes, Emma and Daan climb down from their stools and direct Lewis to end the surveillance recording. Emma is happy to get a few more players onto the case board back at her workstation. The loss by his dear Highlanders let Daan down, but all seasons come to an end, and there is always next year. ∎

Notes

1. Refer to Appendix 1, "Formation of Mars Colony New Amsterdam."
2. See Appendix 2, "Quantum communications network."
3. Team names suggested by Matt Glose, avid baseball fan and supportive friend, via text 2/22/2021
4. NALANI – New Amsterdam Local and National Intelligence (Hawaiian for "silence of the heavens")—Acronym for the AI that watches the cameras and integrates all of the criminal data bases and detective queries for local and national Martian colonies.

Appendix 1. "Formation of Mars Colony New Amsterdam"

From an early commercial settlement with company hierarchy interspersed with UN military oversight to a city-state member of the UN, the New Amsterdam political evolution has been straightforward. In the mid-2020s, the UN commissions the Cooperative Mars Initiative (CMI) to join the global efforts of the five permanent members of the UN Security Council and the other aligned countries. The CMI spends billions of dollars to spur large-scale commercial interplanetary development. The CMI had begun as a subcommittee of the Security Council—a peer to the Climate Change Refugee task force. The latter begins to demand action in the face of weather disasters on a previously unknown scale. In 2034 Earth's food supply becomes more precarious as arable land declines. The political chaos of food insecurity leads to a willingness to loosen the apron strings, allowing the Mars colony to organize as a city-state, incorporating governance documents, form, and spirit similar to modern Singapore. By 2037, most government decisions and citizen interactions are ceded to an AI (Artificial Intelligence) modeled on the UN governance algorithms. Elected mayoral, parliamentarian council, and a minimal professional bureaucracy and police agency serve as the human face.

Appendix 2. "Quantum communications network"

The new Mars satellite system linked to Luna and Earth orbital relays improves the early 20-minute radio wave communications delay between Earth and Mars. The best light-speed comms required just over three minutes but were extremely temperamental and consumed an uncomfortable amount of power. Quantum communications introduced in 2045 cover the gap with instantaneous manipulation of transmitter and receiver elements. But it is expensive. The quantum comm units require cryogenic temperatures and exotic calibration. They are best disposed to be in orbit, where they can be reached for the occasionally required maintenance, maintain near-constant temperatures, and receive and retransmit to line-of-sight stations on the ground.

The Future of Baseball Gaming Simulations

Gordon Gattie

The magnificent September sunset offered the perfect backdrop for the final game of a four-game series between the Pittsburgh Pirates and Washington Nationals. A cool northerly wind blew. Autumn had arrived, and the postseason was rapidly approaching. Although that breeze provided a momentary chill, the battle on the diamond—along with the sold-out ballpark and deafening noise—provided more than enough heat to stay warm. Looking overhead, beyond the reach of the stadium's light towers, the brightest stars in the sky were shining, just like the brightest stars in the ballpark below.

The Pirates and Nationals exchanged runs during the fourth inning of a classic pitchers' duel. Both Satchel Paige and Walter Johnson pitched brilliantly; each starting pitcher limited his opponent to one run on five hits while allowing only three other runners to even reach scoring position. In the top of the ninth, Pittsburgh jumped ahead on a solo home run by Willie Stargell. The Nationals were now down, 2–1 with two outs and facing elimination from the pennant race with a loss. Joe Judge, Washington's underrated first baseman, reached on a right-field double to start the inning. Hank Aaron, who earlier that afternoon had tied the game with a fourth-inning run-scoring single, walked on five pitches. With the tying run on second base and the winning run at first, Pittsburgh manager John McGraw walked to the mound to talk with his ace. "Throw it low and outside," demanded McGraw. "You know he can't hit anything outside the strike zone, not even if it's water and he just fell out of a boat." Paige barely acknowledged McGraw's comments, though he chuckled and suggested he throw his famous "whipsy-dipsy-do" instead.

As the noise levels at Nationals Park increased, Paige's smile widened. He heard the cheers coming from his own dugout, and the jeers coming from the crowd. The scoreboard was playing some walk-up music he had never heard before, though he thought he recognized the artist. He watched Lou Gehrig, his first baseman, and Judy Johnson, his third baseman, inch closer to their respective foul lines to cut off any potential extra-base hits down the line. He heard center fielder Larry Doby suggest the next batter receive Paige's "Midnight Express" since nobody could hit that pitch. Everyone in the dugout was standing on the top step. The crowd was waving rally towels, yet Paige was cool as a cucumber on the mound. As McGraw reached the visitor's dugout, he glanced at the batter standing in the on-deck circle.

That batter is you.

Aaron encourages you from first base as he walks off the bag. Opposing catcher Mickey Cochrane wakes you from your trance, shakes his head as you dig in, and mutters, "Yeah…good luck, kid. You haven't exactly hit ol' Satch too well tonight." Staring at you 60 feet and six inches away is Satchel Paige, with his determined yet calm demeanor. So far today, you've struck out twice and grounded out to third base against the legendary hurler. The season rests on your shoulders. Feet now planted and bat gripped loosely, you watch Paige's unusual wind-up, determine he's throwing you his famous hesitation pitch, and manage to make decent contact. Your eyes follow the ball's trajectory into center field, but you lose sight of the sphere as you sprint toward first base…

* * *

Since baseball stars first emerged, fans have dreamt about exciting potential pitcher-batter matchups and asked, "What if this batter faced this pitcher in this situation?" As baseball continues building its long and storied history, the question isn't just about contemporary matchups. Baseball fans wonder about the outcome of batter-pitcher matchups when the players are from different eras, geographical locations, and leagues. Those matchups aren't limited to pitcher-batter matchups, but include team-versus-team contests such as playing a single game—or even World Series—between the 1927 New York Yankees and the 1975 Cincinnati Reds. What about dynasty-versus-dynasty, like the 1930s Pittsburgh Crawfords facing the 1970s Oakland Athletics if they'd been in the same league over multiple seasons?

During the early years of baseball history, matchups like these mostly existed as thought experiments. Before widespread communication through radio and television, only those fans lucky enough to catch a barnstorming team of stars during the offseason or an exhibition game could have seen such unorthodox matchups. Those thought experiments eventually gave rise to games fans could play at home. In the mid-twentieth century, combining baseball statistics with tabletop gaming brought us some of the earliest simulation games, as Strat-O-Matic baseball and APBA arrived on the scene. In the 1980s, we saw the rise of "rotisserie league" fantasy baseball and variations. Putting baseball on video game platforms soon followed, and in today's world, baseball fans have several ways to create simulated historical pitcher-batter confrontations such as Walter Johnson versus Josh Gibson or Sandy Koufax versus Babe Ruth. Those simulations aren't limited to a specific matchup or a single game; fantasy baseball simulation enthusiasts will create an entire season, and even entire careers, for their fantasy teams and players.

Some fans immerse themselves in the role of a general manager, playing from a strategic level, building one's own team through drafting and trading, using either historical, present-day, or fictitious players depending on the league/playing system. Some gameplay allows fans to manage their simulated baseball teams as a field manager, setting lineups and pitching rotations, and making numerous in-game decisions such as player substitutions, stolen base attempts, or fielding shifts. Other fans play first-person games at a tactical level, where they become the pitcher or batter, and playing the game as a ballplayer is the focus.

Now imagine a game that combined the best of all worlds by using technology. The ideal baseball game would combine all three approaches, allowing you to play an entire season starting with using qualitative and quantitative player assessments to build a roster before the season begins, setting your team's starting lineup during the season based on the roster you've built, and then inserting yourself playing shortstop and hitting third in the lineup. The stats you generate by playing the game will be part of the daily box score and contribute to the overall season statistics. And to play the games, you'll immerse yourself in an environment using virtual reality (VR) or augmented reality (AR), pitting yourself and your team against simulated historical, present-day, or fictious players.

VR creates an artificial environment with a computer where a user's actions may influence events in that environment. In 2021 to enter a virtual reality, users wear headgear and control an input device (e.g., joystick), and the action is contained entirely within a computer. The artificial model is only as realistic as the physics equations underlying the simulation and the field of view provided to the user. For example, depending on computer processing power, environmental details in one's periphery may be sharply detailed or relatively fuzzy, or certain lesser details may not be added in an artificial environment (e.g., uniform details, subtle differences in the color of infield dirt on the basepaths).

AR, by contrast, creates an enhanced version of reality that uses technology to project additional information onto a natural or artificial environment. An example of mixed reality, AR falls between the real word and the virtual world. With AR, users view

In the future of baseball gaming simulations, you'll be able to insert yourself into the lineup of the Big Red Machine.

VOLODYMYR MELNYK / DREAMSTIME.COM

both the natural and artificial environment through a phone/mobile device, computer display, or headgear similar to virtual reality applications, and can use real physical objects. AR projects images in a fixed and limited area in front of one's field of view. So your baseball opponents, instead of being represented as baseball cards or static images on a desktop or laptop computer screen,would appear more life-like, looking and behaving similar to their real-life counterparts. From this perspective, you could play a virtual game while interacting in the physical world. Envision a real pitching machine overlaid with an image of Bullet Rogan; the pitching machine and ball would be physical, and Rogan's delivery would be displayed virtually, so the hitter "sees" a simulated Rogan windup delivering an actual physical pitch. The day is coming when you'll be able to swing a real bat at a real ball and hit a double down the line of your virtual stadium. But that's not all.

Immersive realism will come through improved physics models—capturing ball bounces through an infield or light changes as a fly ball travels into the outfield, background noises such as spikes pawing the dirt or uniform ruffling caused by slight movements, and other ballpark details. As processing power continues to expand, why not use the ability to create immersive spaces to expand what aspects of the game are included? Most baseball simulation games, whether of the tabletop or first-person player variety, focus naturally on the pitcher-batter confrontation. However, there are additional, often overlooked aspects of the game that would benefit from realistic simulation: fielding, baserunning, and umpiring.

For many years, fielding was an underemphasized part of baseball simulations, but as our understanding of fielding effectiveness grows, so should our ability to simulate it. Baseball analysts now rely on much more than counting stats (e.g., putouts, assists, and errors), generating metrics such as Defensive Runs Saved, Zone Ratings, and catch probabilities. The enthusiasm for measuring fielding greatness has not yet translated into simulations of baseball's greatest fielders, but it will. MLB and other sports are building 3D modeling of player movement that can be extrapolated from 2D video input. How long will it be before MLB's three million historical videos in the MLB Film Room archive are processed into the data for simulations? When that happens, for those who want to play alongside the 1980s Detroit Tigers Lou Whitaker or Alan Trammell, or the 1950s Brooklyn Dodgers Jackie Robinson or Pee Wee Reese, virtual simulations will offer an opportunity to turn double plays with some

of the best infields in baseball history. One could compare the footwork around second base between Joe Morgan and Willie Randolph, or evaluate if one could effectively play as part of the 1970s Los Angeles Dodgers infield of Steve Garvey, Davey Lopes, Bill Russell, and Ron Cey. (And for those players we don't have footage of, like many of the Negro Leagues greats or players from before the film era, for gameplay purposes we will use statistical modeling to approximate as best we can.)

A virtual simulation could also recreate a given game scenario, so one doesn't need to wait for the rare opportunity in a game to make a highlight-reel catch or turn a 6–4–3 double play. One could attempt to make over-the-fence acrobatic catches to rob home runs, like Willie Mays, Doris Sams, and Ken Griffey Jr., did throughout their storied careers.

Picture taking infield practice using AR with the 1970s Dodgers infield. With the appropriate technology and some space in the physical world, watch and listen to a virtual Tommy Lasorda hitting ground balls and creating game situations during practice sessions. Put on your real baseball mitt and step into virtual Davey Lopes's cleats at second base, with a virtual Garvey on your left, Russell to your immediate right, and Cey in your periphery at third. The virtual Lasorda calls out the game situation: bottom of the seventh, one out, runners on the corners. "He" hits a grounder to you, and a sharply hit ball comes straight at you; do you field the grounder and turn right to attempt a double play, or turn left and ensure at least one out?

Next, take outfield practice using AR from famed fungo hitter Jimmie Reese in the deep part of center field in the Polo Grounds. One could notably improve catching skills when the ball is hit consistently, but the surrounding environmental conditions (e.g., light source and shadows, wind velocity, wind direction) change. VR/AR can simulate weather conditions. Whether the sun is shining brightly in Florida, or a cool wind is blowing across Wrigley Field from Lake Michigan, or a steady New England rain is falling in Fenway, given atmospheric characteristics (e.g., temperature, air density, cloud coverage) will cause a batted ball to fly differently or challenge a catcher to successfully catch a relay from center field and apply a tag to an incoming runner. Playing as an outfielder, one could learn how to quickly judge the ball's trajectory in different conditions and adjust accordingly without having to get rained on in real life.

Baserunning is another oversimplified aspect of baseball simulations that has yet to be effectively translated into simulations using AR. Tabletop games and computer simulations may assign a specific player a speed rating, stolen base attempt success probability, or ability to reach third from first on a single to right field, but having the ability to attempt stealing against great pitchers and catchers hasn't happened yet. Suppose you're taking a lead off first base against Steve Carlton, who is throwing to Dottie Green behind the plate. You're looking for an opening to steal second base off this historic pair. How far is your lead off first? Can you successfully anticipate when Carlton will throw home instead of attempting to pick you off first base? If you read Carlton right and get a good jump off first, do you have the quickness and speed to beat Green's throw to second base?

Using either VR or AR, that entire steal attempt can be completed virtually. As a virtual Carlton starts his windup, you take off for second, with your virtual representation (your "avatar") running down the basepath. Here comes the throw: You need to decide if you'll slide feet-first, head-first, or attempt to elude the virtual second baseman's tag with a hook slide. In a video game you'd just hit a button to make the choice and wait to see the outcome, but in an AR scenario, biomechanical markers and sensors could determine your speed and your sliding position. Whether the ball is real or virtual would depend on the game's setup. In multi-player mode, maybe a real second baseman could even attempt to catch the throw and apply the tag.

Video games today often try to incorporate real world differences between ballparks right down to the billboards in the outfield. Ballpark differences will be captured in future baseball simulations as well. A similarly-hit ball in Miami, Philadelphia, and Denver could play differently depending on the field dimensions, weather, and park factor. How does the size of the foul territory at Dodger Stadium compare with Guaranteed Rate Field and impact one's ability to catch a foul ball? Certain local weather conditions notably impact ballgames. You could attempt to catch fly balls in the swirling winds of Wrigley Field, field groundballs on Three Rivers Stadium's artificial turf, or roam the Polo Grounds vast center field on a warm July afternoon.

Umpires have been chronically underappreciated throughout baseball's history, and now movements are afoot to replace human umpires with robotic umpires—or at least to provide them with technological assistance—based on the perceived ability of current technology to provide more accurate calls compared with human umpires. Another potential AR/VR application could put you in the role of home plate ump to see how accurately you can call balls and strikes, and make the correct calls on the field. Perhaps these virtual simulations could build empathy for the roles umpires play in the game, as well as provide a tool for umpires to gain extensive experience in evaluating whether a ball has crossed the three-dimensional strike zone—not just the plane at the front of home plate—from different angles and under different lighting conditions. In addition to fielders and baserunners creating specific game situations, umpires could recreate game scenarios to determine if different calls should have been made or different rules invoked. Because of course any sophisticated AR game simulation will have applications in training and practice as well as entertainment.

*   *   *

… As you cross first base and look toward the warning track in center field, you watch your fly ball land softly in Oscar Charleston's glove. Charleston runs toward the infield with hands raised high above his head to excitedly celebrate with his winning teammates. You watch Cochrane race toward Paige and congratulate him on another fine performance. Among the deafening silence of the stunned Nationals Park fans, you begrudgingly turn toward the dugout, knowing the game, and your season, just ended. Your teammates stare blankly ahead, and nobody utters a word as you toss your helmet aside. There's no music blasting from the scoreboard. The sky even seems to grow darker when you look up.

As you review your season, where will you make changes so you're on the winning side next time? From a general manager's perspective, will you draft different players or make trades you hadn't considered before? From a field manager's perspective, will you change your lineup, perhaps dropping yourself down in the lineup? From a player's perspective, will you take more batting practice against a simulated Satchel Paige to improve your timing?

Future simulations will allow everyone from fantasy owners to aspiring general managers to fans the ability to play against or watch their favorite historical, present, or even fictitious players and experience different aspects of baseball more than ever. ∎

280 Park Ave.
New York, NY 10017
Office of the Commissioner
Contact: Dusty Baker / (212) 555-1876

For Immediate Release
February 8, 2032

FAN EXPERIENCE TO INCLUDE VIRTUAL REALITY BETTING IN REAL TIME

Baseball fans are about to enter a new level of the in-game fan experience. With Opening Day two months away, Major League Baseball announced it will implement stations dedicated to augmented reality (AR) gambling in all 32 big league parks.

It is the first major advance in real-time fan interaction since 2028 when augmented reality pitch sensors were installed at Dodger Stadium and Yankee Stadium. Four years later, fans in the stands will be able to not only view the game from the perspective of a hitter or a pitcher, they can now bet on where a pitch will be located, whether a hitter will swing, and where the ball will go if contact is made.

SIE Worldwide Studios President Hermen Hulst said, "After consulting with augmented reality professionals, we decided to partner with MLB to bring a similar experience into the ballpark to the one our own game, 'MLB: The Show,' brings to fans at home every day. The pitch tracking mechanism we established years ago as a way for the game-player to make better contact based on guessing the correct pitch is now being implemented in a real life version of the game with augmented reality."

MLB Commissioner Scarlett Anderson said, "We've been working to find ways of bringing fans closer to the action each year. Giving them a chance to view the game from the lens of a player in 2028 was a huge step in the right direction. Now, they can place bets based on a real time educated guess on what they see. Hitters take educated guesses on pitches thrown their way; now fans can do the same and the savvy ones may benefit financially."

Following the legalization of sports betting in all 50 states in 2027, the MLB has looked for ways to give fans more opportunities to place bets at the ballpark and at home.

The technology for this "real life betting video game," as Anderson calls it, will be free for all ticket-holders to access at all 32 MLB ballparks via multiple kiosks stationed around the parks. For fans at home, the technology can be accessed on their smartphones and head-mounted displays with an upgrade of $39.99 per month to their MLB.TV subscription.

While the popular virtual reality application "Life in Color" offers a similar experience of the ability for a user to witness a location in 360 degrees, MLB has chosen not to partner with LIC and instead will exclusively use the SIE Worldwide Studios sensors for realtime VR and AR access to games. Familiarity with the video game "MLB: The Show" should ensure many users a smooth transition to adopting the new in-game wagering features.

- 30 -

Future of Baseball Training Starts with VR but Leads to the Metaverse

Cathy Hackl and Nate Nelson

A NEW KIND OF BATTING PRACTICE

Mariano Rivera wasn't always destined to be the greatest closer of all time. He entered the majors as an old rookie at age 25 and took a season to adjust. Soon after settling into the big leagues, though, it happened. Rivera gripped the ball the same way as always, but now the ball dipped and darted. "The wicked movement just…happened."[1]

It was the pitch handed down by God.[2]

Today's baseball players don't need to wait for miracles handed down from above. They have technology. Devices like Rapsodo use "machine-learning algorithms to track pitchers' velocity, spin rate, spin efficiency, pitch break and spin axis" among other information.[3] Players wear devices like the K-Vest to capture details about their swing efficiency. There's the Swingtracker, which attaches to the end of the bat and "transmits data about angles, planes, and velocity to produce a 3D model of a player's swing."[4]

All the data collected during games and practices are put into virtual reality, where players immerse themselves to improve their technique and even to face their upcoming opponents to prepare for a game. Players all over the globe can step up to the virtual plate. The future of baseball is in the metaverse.

THE MERITS AND PROMISES OF VR TRAINING

Baseball VR developers use data-driven, artificial intelligence-powered virtual reality to offer training exercises for players from amateur to the pros. These developers include WIN Reality, EON Reality, TrinityVR, and Monsterful.[5] Among the merits of using VR technology for player skills development are the following:

1. It's easy to jump in on your own.

We already have pitching machines for people who practice solo, but they're severely limited by pitch type, location, and predictability. As WIN CEO, Chris O'Dowd, points out: "Every player likes to face some type of actual pitcher, seeing the ball come out of a hand. Pitching machines can't provide that type of experience and a coach can't throw all day."[6]

Virtual reality usually requires no partners (some platforms may require a person controlling the simulation from a nearby laptop). Software can simulate any kind of pitch imaginable. And, unlike a machine, you don't have to pick up balls every three minutes to refill the machine.

2. Rote practice can be "gamified" to be more enjoyable.

Baseball is fun, but repetitive daily practice (the kind necessary to gaining significant improvement) can be boring. One of the easiest things to do with software is to gamify ordinary or repetitive tasks. As EON Sports VR CEO, Brendan Reilly, told *Fortune*: "Is there a way we can provide a value-add where we can take non-fun things in the game, like strike-zone awareness, and make that fun? [W]e gamify the learning process, and help hitters identify whether it's a strike or ball in a fun way."[7]

Experience points, progress bars, bright colors, and sound cues make daily practice exciting for everyone. Gamification is especially useful for getting kids to stick with their practice routines.

3. Players can build confidence in a solitary, low-pressure setting.

The most direct study of VR training in baseball wasn't actually focused on performance, at least not directly. Dr. Lindsay Ross-Stewart, a professor at Southern Illinois University Edwardsville, is a sports psychologist whose focus is imagery.[8] She studies whether positive imagery improves thinking and performance, as well as if picturing hitting the game-winning home run really helps a player to do it in real life.

In 2017, Ross-Stewart enlisted her home university's Division I baseball team to study "a preliminary applied Imagery Assisted Virtual Reality protocol that focused on increasing psychological skill development (e.g., confidence, motivation) and psychological strategy use (e.g., imagery, relaxation)."[9] In simpler terms: would players who practiced with VR develop real-life confidence? If they saw themselves hitting homers in VR might they be better-prepared to do it in an actual game?

Confidence and relaxation are difficult metrics to quantify but, anecdotally at least, some players reported positive experiences. SIUE's most improved player of the season stated, "For myself, it was really mainly just about: relax and confident…were the two key terms for me."[10] One of his freshman teammates, eager to impress, often practiced in his dorm room away from the other guys. He found that the VR "helped me to relax and be calm in the box. The program also gave me some confidence because I watched myself succeed so many times."

4. Artificial intelligence can accommodate a player's unique weaknesses.

Hitters who struggle against a particular pitch or a particular zone can program their VR software to target focus more in that area. But software can do more than just that.

We've mentioned already how these programs source large quantities of MLB data in order to simulate the characteristics of real pitchers. But this data-gathering capability goes two ways: they also record real-time data on the performance of users.[11] A hitter might not even be aware that they swing over curveballs more often than average, but the program will deduce it after a while. The program can then be throttled to throw more curves, until the hitter learns to adjust.

5. Software can be tailored to introduce handicaps.

Players can practice pitch recognition training in virtual reality. VR exercises shorten the distance from mound to plate, forcing hitters to read and react more quickly.

GameSense Sports offers a pitch-recognition exercise based on what they call "occlusion training."[12] In

Lucas Giolito trying out VR during spring training in 2016.

occlusion training, a batter watches a pitch come at them on-screen, but the screen blacks out just after the ball is released. Based on the release angle, arm velocity and ball spin, the batter is tasked with identifying the kind of pitch coming their way. They're forced to distinguish the subtle cues that separate fastballs and sliders early in the process, without the luxury of waiting for the break. GameSense's occlusion training occurs in 2-D, on a television or laptop screen, and similar tech isn't yet part of any major VR platform.

6. You can play even when you can't play.

Paul Goldschmidt of the St. Louis Cardinals was already in a bit of a slump. From 2013 to 2018 he'd made the top three in NL MVP voting three times, top 12 five times, and made the All-Star team every season. In 2019 his power remained, but his walks dropped and his batting average plummeted 30 points, signs of worsening plate discipline.[13]

Then 2020 brought the COVID-19 lockdowns. Being stuck at home was a bummer, and social distancing ruled out normal practices. Not wanting to just sit around and let his skills deteriorate further, Goldschmidt ventured to try out WIN Reality (which, whether he consciously realized it or not, was expressly designed to train his most receded attribute: plate discipline[14]).

Goldschmidt wasn't the only one to have the thought. His teammate, utility infielder Matt Carpenter, joined him, as did San Francisco Giants outfielder Mike Yastrzemski. According to WIN Reality, New York's two biggest sluggers, Pete Alonso and Aaron Judge, used the system, too.[15]

BUT DOES IT WORK?

Leading up to the 2019 season, Todd Frazier was 0-for-8 in his career against Washington Nationals pitcher Max Scherzer. So Frazier loaded Scherzer up in VR. "I'm just trying to see how his slider moves or how his fastball moves…I actually think that's helped me out a lot along the way this year, for sure."[16] That May, Frazier laced a double off the Cy Young Award winner. By season's end, his batting average was 38 points higher than his previous season's total, and his highest mark since 2015.[17]

Brock Weimer, starting center fielder for the Southern Illinois University-Edwardsville (SIUE) Cougars, was a solid-enough player before he ever put on a headset. But after spending just a few minutes per day wearing one over the course of five months, he credited VR training with helping him to his best season ever: 15 homers, 50 RBIs, .329 BA.[18,19]

The Cougars' coach analyzed all the players across the team. He noted, "After using the VR program I noticed several improvements in our players. Players were better able to visualize mechanical adjustments to their swing. Before the use of the program, players would be told how to make a mechanical adjustment but would often have trouble visualizing what the adjustment entailed. After use of the program, players were better able to understand what adjustment needed to be made because they had practiced with the VR goggles."[20]

According to the developers of these platforms, there are actual, measurable data demonstrating the efficacy of VR in improving hitting. Chris O'Dowd of WIN Reality touts a third-party study which "found improvement in plate discipline" among MLB hitters using his platform, and that "MLB clients exhibited in-game improvements of at least 12 percent in batting average, on-base percentage, slugging percentage, and on-base plus slugging following optimized WIN Reality Game prep usage."[21]

Rahat Ahmed, Strategy Chief at TrinityVR, told Sport Techie about one major league club's "Latin American academy, where its predominantly teenage prospects reside, set up a drill in which the batters are prompted to identify each type of pitch they saw. In two months of use, those players improved their pitch recognition skills, on average, from 53 percent to 66 percent."[22]

In 2017, the Tampa Bay Rays became the first MLB team to invest in a VR cage: the 10x10-foot "iCube" from EON Sports VR. In just the few years since then, nearly every major league team has installed their own VR cages.[23]

YOU CAN LEARN TO HIT MARIANO

Fully digitized training has its drawbacks. There are aspects to the real thing that simply cannot be put in ones and zeros, like the satisfying crack of bat-against-ball. But according to the limited data we have, virtual reality is most promising when it comes to training one of the most important qualities of any hitter: visual perception. Batters can train their visual centers to potentially perceive a Kershaw curve just as it exits his hand, or a Rivera cutter before it's too late to react.

If virtual reality simulations can continue to improve on their visual fidelity, data crunching and artificial intelligence capabilities, hitters will no longer face so much trouble from future Mariano Riveras, and they won't have to work quite as hard as Edgar Martinez once did. By facing the same pitchers dozens or hundreds of times over before ever getting into a game situation, they'll have developed their most important mental attribute: preparation. And their most vital physical skill: their reaction time.

BASEBALL IN THE METAVERSE

Virtual reality training in baseball is just the beginning. Not too far off is the day when players will be able to compete against a virtual version of themselves, or, after their retirement, hire a famed eSports gamer to

A WIN Reality training program challenges the player/batter to recognize and identify the pitch as early as possible.

play as their avatar in order to make more money in the virtual space. VR is the stepping stone to an immersive world where players, trainers, and fans come together. In virtual reality, teams will be able to play against each other on a whole new level. In a live VR baseball game, machine learning algorithms and players' data will update in real time to create a game the likes of which we've never seen. Virtual reality can create new dynamics and exciting challenges for players to overcome, including bringing great players of the past back onto the field. People will be able to watch baseball matchups between teams today and teams from 50 years ago. Virtual reality starts out as a training tool, but it will end up revolutionizing the game by bringing it into the metaverse. ■

Notes

1. Tom Verducci, "Mariano Saves," *Sports Illustrated*, October 5, 2009. https://vault.si.com/vault/2009/10/05/mariano-saves.

2. John Harper, "Mariano Rivera says it was divine intervention, but for hitters, his cutter has been pure Hell" *New York Daily News*, September 21, 2011. https://www.nydailynews.com/sports/baseball/yankees/mo-gift-god-pure-hell-hitters-article-1.956109.

3. James Sayles, "How Baseball Teams Are Using Technology to Change the Game," *Forbes*, June 24, 2019. https://www.forbes.com/sites/jamesayles/2019/06/24/how-baseball-teams-are-using-technology-to-change-the-game.

4. Jay Woodruff, "5 Technologies That Are Changing Baseball," *Fast Company*, August 22, 2019. https://www.fastcompany.com/90378232/5-technologies-that-are-changing-baseball.

5. Company websites: https://winreality.com/, https://eonreality.com/eon-sports-vr-provides-state-art-baseball-training-system-yokohama-dena-baystars/, https://www.trinityvr.com, https://gomonsterful.com.

6. Lisa Rabasca Roepe, "Virtual Reality Hits a Home Run With MLB Sluggers," Dell Technologies website, September 21, 2020. https://www.delltechnologies.com/en-us/perspectives/virtual-reality-hits-a-home-run-with-mlb-slugger.

7. Jonathan Chew, "Why Major League Baseball Teams Are Turning to Virtual Reality," *Fortune*, April 29, 2016. https://fortune.com/2016/04/29/mlb-eon-sports-vr.

8. Dr. Lindsay Ross-Stewart, SIUE Faculty profile page, https://www.siue.edu/education/applied-health/faculty-staff/ross-stewartbio.shtml.

9. Dr. Lindsay Ross-Stewart, Jeffrey Price, Daniel Jackson, Christopher Hawkins, "A Preliminary Investigation into the Use of an Imagery Assisted Virtual Reality Intervention in Sport," *Journal of Sports Science* 6 (2018), 20–30. https://www.researchgate.net/publication/323425692_A_Preliminary_Investigation_into_the_Use_of_an_Imagery_Assisted_Virtual_Reality_Intervention_in_Sport_httpwwwdavidpublisherorgindexphpHomeJournaldetailjournalid1jxJSScontallissues.

10. "Virtual Reality Strategy for Sports Training Proven to Enhance Baseball, Softball and Soccer Skills," HEC Science and Technology Youtube Channel, October 11, 2020, https://www.youtube.com/watch?v=IY9qQyDJoJM.

11. Jason Bristol, "Future of baseball training now here with Monsterful virtual reality," KHOU, February 19, 2018. https://www.khou.com/article/sports/sports-extra/future-of-baseball-training-now-here-with-monsterful-virtual-reality/285-520553794.

12. "Occlusion vs Full View Pitch Recognition Training For Ballplayers," gameSense Youtube Channel, June 15, 2019. https://www.youtube.com/watch?v=u5X_3N4PwPI.

13. Paul Goldschmidt, player profile page, Baseball-Reference.com. https://www.baseball-reference.com/players/g/goldspa01.shtml.

14. Roepe, "Virtual Reality Hits a Home Run With MLB Sluggers."

15. WIN Reality website, https://winreality.com/baseball; John Griffin, "How the Yankees can benefit from virtual reality training," April 5, 2019, Pinstripe Alley, SBNation.com. https://www.pinstripealley.com/2019/4/5/18286137/yankees-aaron-judge-virtual-reality-training-impact-villanova-jupina-mulvey; Lemire, "Tech Makes Baseball a Simple Game."

16. Joe Lemire, "Tech Makes Baseball a Simple Game: You See the Ball, You Hit the Ball, You Got It?" SportTechie, July 23, 2019. https://www.sporttechie.com/mlb-baseball-hitters-swings-visual-cues-mental-approach.

17. Todd Frazier, player profile page, Baseball-Reference.com. https://www.baseball-reference.com/players/f/frazito01.shtml.

18. HEC Science and Technology, "Virtual Reality Strategy for Sports Training."

19. Brock Weimer Player Card, The Baseball Cube. http://www.thebaseballcube.com/players/profile.asp?ID=201507.

20. Ross-Stewart, Price, Jackson, Hawkins, "A Preliminary Investigation…" The name of the coach is not given in the published study.

21. Roepe, "Virtual Reality Hits a Home Run With MLB Sluggers."

22. Joe Lemire, "TrinityVR's DiamondFX Hitting Simulation Now In Use By Two MLB Clubs," SportTechie, December 5, 2017. https://www.sporttechie.com/trinityvr-diamondfx-hitting-simulation-virtual-reality-mlb.

23. David Leffler, "This Local Virtual Reality Company is Shaping the Future of Major League Baseball" *Austin Monthly*, May 2020. https://www.austinmonthly.com/this-local-virtual-reality-company-is-shaping-the-future-of-major-league-baseball.

Contributors

DUSTY BAKER was born to love the game of baseball after being named after the player and manager. Baker began his journey in the sports world as an Athletic Ambassador for the TCU Football program while he was a student at the university. After his graduation, Baker took over as a Sports Anchor and Reporter for KTAB and KRBC in Abilene, Texas, for three years where he covered the Texas Rangers and the 2020 MLB Postseason. Baker is currently a Sports Anchor and Reporter in San Luis Obispo for KSBY.

JAMES BREAUX is an engineer, futurist, and sci-fi writer working in Houston, Texas. He teaches part-time at the University of Houston, College of Technology, and works in the Oil and Gas industry. Follow him on Twitter @bagelx. This story is a chapter from a novel that James is working on, set in 2050 at the New Amsterdam Colony domes on Mars. The book is expected to be published in the first quarter of 2022 — currently under the working title, *Bicycle Police of New Amsterdam*.

ALAN COHEN has been a SABR member since 2010. He chairs the BioProject factchecking committee and serves as Vice President-Treasurer of the Connecticut Smoky Joe Wood Chapter. He is MiLB First Pitch stringer for the Hartford Yard Goats, Double-A affiliate of the Rockies. His biographies, game stories and essays have appeared in more than 50 SABR publications. His major area of research is the Hearst Sandlot Classic (1946-1965) from which 88 players advanced to the majors. He has four children and eight grandchildren and resides in Connecticut with wife Frances, their cats Morty, Ava, and Zoe, and their dog Buddy.

HARRIE KEVILL-DAVIES is a doctoral candidate in Rhetoric and Public Culture at Northwestern University. Her dissertation focuses on early Cold War non-sports trading cards, especially how they depict history, science, and war. She is also interested in how non-sports cards overlap with sports, and always enjoys seeing baseball in non-sports cards. Although originally from London, she has lived in Chicago for almost 10 years, and has enjoyed the return to post-pandemic Wrigley Field to root for the Cubbies!

GORDON J. GATTIE is a lifelong baseball fan and SABR member since 1998. A civilian US Navy engineer, his baseball research interests include ballparks, historical trends, and statistical analysis. Gordon earned his PhD from SUNY Buffalo, where he used baseball to investigate judgment performance in complex dynamic environments. Ever the optimist, he dreams of a Cleveland Indians World Series championship. Lisa, his wonderful wife who roots for the New York Yankees, and Morrigan, their beloved Labrador Retriever, enjoy traveling across the country visiting ballparks and other baseball-related sites. Gordon has contributed to several SABR publications, including multiple issues of *The National Pastime* and the Games Project.

STEVEN M. GLASSMAN's article, The Future of Baseball Cards, will be his seventh for *The National Pastime*. He previously wrote for the Philadelphia, Chicago, New York, San Diego, Miami, and Baltimore editions of the journal. Steven has been a SABR member since 1994. He graduated with a Bachelor of Science Degree in Sport and Recreation Management from Temple University. Originally born in Philadelphia, Steven currently lives in Warminster, Pennsylvania.

CATHY HACKL is a globally recognized tech futurist. She's a business executive, keynote speaker, and strategist that specializes in AR, VR, spatial computing & the Metaverse. One of the most influential women in tech, Hackl is considered a leading management thinker and a top voice on LinkedIn. She founded the Futures Intelligence Group and has worked for Amazon Web Services, Magic Leap, and HTC VIVE.

BRIAN HALL recently joined the NYU Tisch Institute for Global Sport, where his work focuses on AI, machine learning, and their application to the sports world. At NYU, he teaches "Artificial Intelligence and Machine Learning," an on-demand course that is open to both professionals and sports fans alike. Prior to joining the NYU faculty, Brian served as Vice-President at Two Sigma Investments, a New York City-based hedge fund primarily known for its use of artificial intelligence, machine learning, and distributed computing trading strategies.

STEPHEN KEENEY is a lifelong Reds fan. He graduated from Miami University in 2010 and from Northern Kentucky University's Chase College of Law in 2013. He lives in Dayton, Ohio, as a union staff representative with his wife and two children. He has contributed to several SABR publications, and his article "The Roster Depreciation Allowance: How Major League Baseball Teams Turn Profits into Losses" was selected for *SABR 50 at 50: The Society for American Baseball Research's Fifty Most Essential Contributions to the Game*.

KATIE KRALL is in her second season as a Baseball Operations Analyst for the Cincinnati Reds. In her role she develops tools to improve decision-making processes for roster construction, game planning and R & D in addition to providing pro scouting coverage. Krall previously worked for 18 months at the Office of the Commissioner of Major League Baseball. In 2016, she planned the World Series Trophy Tour for the Chicago Cubs. The following summer, she was an Assistant General Manager in the Cape Cod Baseball League. She graduated from Northwestern University and is pursuing her MBA from the University of Chicago.

DAVID KRELL is the author of *1962: Baseball and America in the Time of JFK* and *Our Bums: The Brooklyn Dodgers in History, Memory and Popular Culture*. He is the editor of the anthologies *The New York Yankees in Popular Culture* and *The New York Mets in Popular Culture*. David is the chair of SABR's Elysian Fields Chapter (Northern New Jersey). He has twice been awarded Honorable Mention in SABR's Ron Gabriel Award.

ALLISON R. LEVIN is a Professor of Sports Communication at Webster University in St. Louis, Missouri, a member of the SABR Board of Directors, and the chair of the Educational Resources Committee. Her research builds upon an eclectic background in political science, economics, women's studies, communications, and law. In recent years she has focused on the effects of social media on pop culture, communications, and sports, primarily baseball. Born and raised in St. Louis, Allison is an unapologetic Cardinals fan, even if her favorite player is Clayton Kershaw.

NATE NELSON is a freelance writer for some of the world's largest technology companies—Wix.com, Check Point Software and more, as well as organizations in finance and government—from Dash Core Group to The World Holocaust Remembrance Center. His podcast, "Malicious Life," recently received honors from the European Cybersecurity Blogger Awards and the Webby Awards. You can find his work on *Forbes*, Medium, and publications around the web.

AUDREY REINERT is a Postdoctoral Researcher at the University of Oklahoma's Data Science Institute for Societal Challenges (DISC Center). She holds a PhD in Industrial Engineering from Purdue University (2019), a Masters in Human Computer Interaction from the Georgia Institute of technology (2015), and a Bachelors in Cognitive Neuropsychology from the University of California, San Diego (2012). Her research interests lie at the intersection of human centered computing, data visualization, and human machine interaction. She is a member of IEEE, HFES, and the AGU and can be reached at areinert@ou.edu

MARTY RESNICK is an avid, lifelong Dodgers fan living in Braves Country. He is an expert in future studies, continuous foresight, and combinatorial innovation. Marty's background in strategy, innovation, emerging technologies, trendspotting and human augmentation gives him a strong perspective for understanding the potential impacts of disruptions on the future. He is best described as a futurist but is a storyteller at heart. Marty specifically enjoys telling stories visually through photography and envisaging the future through writing science fiction.

DR. LAWRENCE ROCKS has had a research career that has spanned from analytical chemistry to sports biochemistry to novel antiviral research. His 1972 book, *The Energy Crisis*, published just prior to the 1973 oil crisis, was widely acclaimed by both national television and print media, and influenced the creation of the US Department of Energy during the Carter Administration. He has been featured as an energy expert in *The New York Times*, *Time Magazine*, and *National Review*, and he has addressed the United Nations, and appeared on shows spanning many decades from the *Today* show to MLB Network. Dr. Rocks has been honored multiple times with commemorative baseball cards, including the 2019 official Lawrence Rocks Topps Allen and Ginter card, a 2020 Topps of the Class card, a 2021 Topps Now WeatherStationMoon card, and an Upper Deck WeatherStationMoon hockey card. On Earth Day 2021, the New York Islanders honored Dr. Rocks with a special commemorative silver hockey puck. Dr. Rocks, Professor Emeritus at Long Island University, received an MS in chemistry from Purdue University and his DSc (Doctor of Science) from Technische Hochschule Vienna. He and his wife Marlene are supporters of Ronald McDonald House Charities and have one son, Burton.

GARY A. SARNOFF has been an active SABR member since 1994. A member of SABR's Bob Davids chapter, he has contributed to SABR's Bio and games projects, and to the annual publication of *The National Pastime*. He is also member of the SABR Negro Leagues committee and serves as chairman of the Ron Gabriel Committee. In addition, he has authored two baseball books: *The Wrecking Crew of '33* and *The First Yankees Dynasty*. He currently resides in Alexandria, Virginia.

CECILIA M. TAN was a professional science fiction writer and editor for two decades before she became SABR's Publications Director in 2011. Her short stories have previously appeared in *Asimov's Science Fiction Magazine*, *Absolute Magnitude*, *Strange Horizons*, and *Ms. Magazine*, among many other places. In addition to comma-jockeying for SABR, she has exhibited her baseball editing prowess for various sites and publications, including *Baseball Prospectus*, the *Yankees Annual*, and Baseball-Reference.com. This issue of *The National Pastime* has given her a rare chance to combine her favorite subjects.

HARRY TURTLEDOVE has been a baseball fan since 1956, when dinosaurs like the PCL Los Angeles Angels and Hollywood Stars roamed the earth. He's been a stats-crazed baseball fan since he started collecting baseball cards a couple of years later. A 50-plus year addiction to APBA baseball sure doesn't help. This shows up in his writing in the current story, in earlier ones like "Batboy," "Designated Hitter," "The House That George Built," and "The Star and the Rockets," and in the Depression-era semipro-baseball fantasy novel, *The House of Daniel*.

RICK WILBER's new science-fiction novel, *Alien Day* (Tor, 2021), features a near-future journalist who uses a Sweep media system for his reporting, where his audience becomes one with the journalist as he works. Wilber has published a half-dozen novels and short-story collections and some sixty short stories in major markets, including the award-winning "Something Real," in 2012, that features a fictional version of famous ballplayer and spy, Moe Berg. He is a visiting professor in the low-residency MFA in Creative Writing at Western Colorado University and he lives in St. Petersburg, Florida. His website is www.rickwilber.net.

GRAHAM WOMACK has written about baseball history for various publications, including *The Sporting News*, *Sports Illustrated*, and the *San Francisco Chronicle*. A Hall of Fame enthusiast, Womack has run a project several times at his website—baseballpastandpresent.com—asking people to vote on the 50 best players not in Cooperstown. Having been a SABR member since 2010, Womack lives with his wife Kate Johnson and their animals in Sacramento.

Society for American Baseball Research

Cronkite School at ASU
555 N. Central Ave. #416, Phoenix, AZ 85004
602.496.1460 (phone)
SABR.org

Become a SABR member today!

If you're interested in baseball — writing about it, reading about it, talking about it — there's a place for you in the Society for American Baseball Research.

SABR memberships are available on annual, multi-year, or monthly subscription basis. Annual and monthly subscription memberships auto-renew for your convenience. Young Professional memberships are for ages 30 and under. Senior memberships are for ages 65 and older. Student memberships are available to currently enrolled middle/high school or full-time college/university students. Monthly subscription members receive SABR publications electronically and are eligible for SABR event discounts after 12 months.

Here's a list of some of the key benefits you'll receive as a SABR member:

- Receive two editions (spring and fall) of the *Baseball Research Journal*, our flagship publication
- Receive expanded e-book edition of *The National Pastime*, our annual convention journal
- 8-10 new e-books published by the SABR Digital Library, all FREE to members
- "This Week in SABR" e-newsletter, sent to members every Friday
- Join dozens of research committees, from Statistical Analysis to Women in Baseball.
- Join one of 70+ regional chapters in the U.S., Canada, Latin America, and abroad
- Participate in online discussion groups
- Ask and answer baseball research questions on the SABR-L e-mail listserv
- Complete archives of *The Sporting News* dating back to 1886 and other research resources
- Promote your research in "This Week in SABR"
- Diamond Dollars Case Competition
- Yoseloff Scholarships

- Discounts on SABR national conferences, including the SABR National Convention, the SABR Analytics Conference, Jerry Malloy Negro League Conference, Frederick Ivor-Campbell 19th Century Conference, and the Arizona Fall League Experience
- Publish your research in peer-reviewed SABR journals
- Collaborate with SABR researchers and experts
- Contribute to Baseball Biography Project or the SABR Games Project
- List your new book in the SABR Bookshelf
- Lead a SABR research committee or chapter
- Networking opportunities at SABR Analytics Conference
- Meet baseball authors and historians at SABR events and chapter meetings
- 50% discounts on paperback versions of SABR e-books
- Discounts with other partners in the baseball community
- SABR research awards

We hope you'll join the most passionate international community of baseball fans at SABR! Check us out online at SABR.org/join.

- -

SABR MEMBERSHIP FORM

	Standard	Senior	Young Pro.	Student
Annual:	☐ $65	☐ $45	☐ $45	☐ $25
3 Year:	☐ $175	☐ $129	☐ $129	
5 Year:	☐ $249			
Monthly:	☐ $6.95	☐ $4.95	☐ $4.95	

(International members wishing to be mailed the Baseball Research Journal should add $10/yr for Canada/Mexico or $19/yr for overseas locations.)

Participate in Our Donor Program!

Support the preservation of baseball research. Designate your gift toward:

☐ General Fund   ☐ Endowment Fund   ☐ Research Resources   ☐_____
☐ I want to maximize the impact of my gift; do not send any donor premiums
☐ I would like this gift to remain anonymous.

Note: Any donation not designated will be placed in the General Fund.
SABR is a 501 (c) (3) not-for-profit organization & donations are tax-deductible to the extent allowed by law.

Name _____

E-mail* _____

Address _____

City _____ ST_____ ZIP_____

Phone _____ Birthday _____

* **Your e-mail address on file ensures you will receive the most recent SABR news.**

Dues $_____

Donation $_____

Amount Enclosed $_____

Do you work for a matching grant corporation? Call (602) 496-1460 for details.

If you wish to pay by credit card, please contact the SABR office at (602) 496-1460 or sign up securely online at SABR.org/join. We accept Visa, Mastercard & Discover.

Do you wish to receive the *Baseball Research Journal* electronically? ☐ Yes   ☐ No
Our e-books are available in PDF, Kindle, or EPUB (iBooks, iPad, Nook) formats.

Mail to: SABR, Cronkite School at ASU, 555 N. Central Ave. #416, Phoenix, AZ 85004

10/19